THE CIVIL COSTS ASSESSMENT HANDBOOK

How to maximise costs recovery

Peter Burdge LLB

Maritza Legal Services Ltd
2004

Copyright

(a) The book

(b) The specimen documents

(c) Statutory material

Disclaimer

Published by Word4Word Design & Publishing, 107 High Street, Evesham WR11 4EB

Distributed by Maritza Legal Services Ltd, The Limes, Tickenham Hill, Tickenham, Clevedon, North Somerset BS21 6SW (Tel: 01275 857845 Fax: 01275 856094)

Printed and bound in Great Britain

ISBN 0-9541209-4-9

The aim of this book

This book is written for solicitors, their staff and costs draftsmen who have to deal with the negotiation and assessment of costs awarded to the successful party in civil proceedings.

The rules dealing with the assessment of costs are sometimes said to be the least successful part of the Woolf reforms. However, most of the practical difficulties seem to arise not because the rules are inadequate or are badly devised, but because they are so extensive and detailed that the choices they offer and how to benefit from them are not immediately apparent. As in substantive litigation, the usual problem is not knowing what to do next.

This book provides the solution, by guiding the reader step by step through the entire detailed assessment process, from the point at which the bill is received from the costs draftsman to its completion after the assessment hearing. By working chronologically through each stage, the logic behind the rules is revealed and each alternative is explained at the point at which it arises.

- Part I explains the system of the costs rules and where to find the law, the forms and official guidance.

- Part II takes the reader through the procedure for detailed assessment of a bill claiming costs between the parties (with or without a claim for costs against the CLS Fund).

- Part III goes through the procedure for detailed assessment by the court of a bill claiming costs only against the CLS Fund ('LSC only' detailed assessment).

- Part IV deals with the summary assessment of costs, 'costs only' proceedings and fixed recoverable costs in minor road traffic accident cases. It also looks at the similarities between the procedure for the assessment of costs in family cases and that for civil costs generally.

A key feature of the book is the immediate cross-referencing to the relevant rules, practice directions and forms. The accompanying CD-ROM contains the relevant statutory materials as well as a full set of easily adapted precedent forms, letters and work-sheets.

However, this book is not a mere paraphrase of the costs rules. It presents effective systems and techniques that are not to be found in the rules, including how to keep track of the figures, to reply to points of dispute and to negotiate costs successfully. The emphasis throughout is on maximising and speeding up the recovery of costs, by encouraging early settlement through the use of pre-emptive offers, by maintaining momentum while negotiating effectively, by using the costs rules to obtain default or interim costs certificates, by making the best use of the entitlement to interest and by claiming realistic amounts for the costs of the detailed assessment proceedings.

It is only fair to point out what topics are not covered by this book. Because its primary concern is the process by which a bill is assessed, it does not deal with those parts of the costs rules that govern matters before the bill is prepared (such as the way in which the court should exercise its discretion as to the award of costs in the substantive proceedings, or the wasted costs jurisdiction), nor does it cover the preparation of the bill. The assessment of costs as between solicitor and client is a topic too large to include here. Finally, while the assessment by the court of costs payable by the LSC is covered, this book does not deal with assessments carried out by the LSC itself.

The text of the book is based on the costs rules (by which I mean Parts 43–48 of the Civil Procedure Rules and the Costs Practice Direction) as they were after the publication of the 33rd update to the CPR on 24 September 2003. The general law is stated as at 22 December 2003.

The CD-ROM was completed on 9 January 2004 and the costs rules included in it incorporate the changes made by the 33rd update. In file 00.00 on the CD-ROM you will find details of some changes made to the costs rules since the 33rd update, including changes to the fixed costs regime for use in minor road traffic accident cases and a pilot scheme for the detailed assessment by the Supreme Court Costs Office of the costs of civil proceedings in London county courts. I suggest that you look at that file first. The 34th update was not due to be released before the end of January 2004 and I advise you to check the DCA website (see 2.2) periodically for this update and to download and/or print for future reference any of the costs rules which are amended by it.

Peter Burdge

Conventions and references used in the main text (pages 1–284)

Numerical references in the main text are, unless otherwise stated, references to other paragraphs in the main text. References appearing in the right-hand column are as follows:

- **CPR** – the Civil Procedure Rules

- **PDP** – a practice direction made under a particular part of the CPR

- *CPD* – the Costs Practice Direction

- **Table** – One of the tables that appear in the main text 9 (Table 1 is on page 7, Table 2 on page 11, Table 3 on page 19, Table 4 on pages 96-97 and Table 5 on page 225).

- **Worksheet** – one of the worksheets in Appendix I

- **Precedent** – one of the costs precedents in Appendix II

- **Form** – one of the forms prescribed by the costs rules

- **CD-ROM** refers to a file on the CD-ROM supplied with this book

For brevity, the conventions of the Interpretation Act 1978 are followed so that, where appropiate, words importing the male gender may equally import the female or neuter genders and words importing the singular may equally import the plural, and vice versa.

The assumption throughout is that you are acting for a receiving party and/or a legally aided/LSC funded client.

Contents

PART I
UNDERSTANDING THE COSTS RULES ABOUT ASSESSMENT AND KNOWING WHERE TO FIND THEM

PART II
THE PROCEDURE FOR DETAILED ASSESSMENT BY THE COURT OF A BILL CLAIMING COSTS BETWEEN THE PARTIES (WITH OR WITHOUT A CLAIM FOR COSTS AGAINST THE CLS FUND)

PART III
THE PROCEDURE FOR THE DETAILED ASSESSMENT BY THE COURT OF A BILL CLAIMING COSTS ONLY AGAINST THE CLS FUND ('LSC ONLY' DETAILED ASSESSMENT)

PART IV
OTHER FORMS OF ASSESSMENT AND 'COSTS ONLY' PROCEEDINGS

Appendix I Specimen worksheets

Appendix II Costs precedents

Appendix III Prescribed forms

List of files on the CD-ROM

References are to paragraph numbers in the text.

Skeleton arguments

Table of cases and judicial practice directions

References are to paragraph numbers in the text.

Table of statutes

References are to paragraph numbers in the text.

Table of statutory instruments

References are to paragraph numbers in the text.

Table of references to the Civil Procedure Rules 1998

References are to paragraph numbers in the text.

Part 43 Practice Direction – see table of references to the Costs Practice Direction

Part 44 – General rules about costs

Part 44 Practice Direction – see table of references to the Costs Practice Direction

Part 45 – Fixed costs

45.10(1) 52.4
45.10(2)(b) .... 52.4(b)
45.10(2)(c) .... 52.4(c)
45.10(2)(d) .... 52.4(d)
45.11 .... 51.7(a)
45.11(1) .... 52.5(a)
45.11(2) .... 52.5(b)
45.12(1) .... 52.6(a)
45.12(2) .... 52.6(b)
45.12(2)(a) .... 52.6(b)
45.12(2)(b) .... 52.6(b)
45.12(3) .... 52.6(c)
45.13 .... 52.6(d)
45.14 .... 52.9

Part 45 Practice Direction – see table of references to the Costs Practice Direction

Part 46 – Fast track trial costs .... 2.1, 49.1(b), 50.12(a)

Part 46 Practice Direction – see table of references to the Costs Practice Direction

Part 47 – Procedure for detailed assessment of costs and default provisions

47 .... 2.1
47.1 .... 3.2(a)
47.2 .... 3.2(a)
47.4 .... 23.3(a)
47.4(1) 4.2
47.4(2) .... 23.3(b)
47.4(3) .... 23.3(b)
47.4(4) .... 23.3(b)
47.6(1) 1.10, 3.4, 8,
47.6(2) 8.7
47.7 .... 3.1, 3.2(a), 3.2(b)
47.8(1) .... 3.7(b)

Part 47 Practice Direction – see table of references to the Costs Practice Direction

Part 48 – Costs – special cases

Part 48 Practice Direction – see table of references to the Costs Practice Direction

Part 52 – Appeals

Part 52 Practice Direction

Table of references to the Costs Practice Direction ('the Practice Direction About Costs Supplementing Parts 43–48 of the Civil Procedure Rules')

References are to paragraph numbers in the text.

Directions relating to Part 43

Directions relating to Part 44 – general rules about costs

Directions relating to Part 45 – fixed costs

Directions relating to Part 46 – fast track trial costs

No references

Directions relating to Part 47 – procedure for detailed assessment of costs and default provisions

Directions relating to Part 48 – costs – special cases

Schedule of costs precedents

Glossary of terms and abbreviations

This glossary gives concise explanations of some of the terms and abbreviations used in this book. Not all the terms are 'official' and the explanations should not necessarily be treated as definitive. Where the term is defined in the costs rules or elsewhere in the CPR, the reference is given.

Additional liability

The percentage increase (ie the 'success fee'), the insurance premium, or the additional amount in respect of provision made by a membership organisation, as the case may be.

CPR 43.2(1)(o)

After the event insurance

See 'insurance premium' below.

Application notice

A document in which the applicant states his intention to seek a court order.

CPR 23.1

Appropriate office

The court or office at which all applications or requests in detailed assessment proceedings must be made or filed.

CPR 47.4
CPD 31.1

Assisted person

A person with the benefit of a Legal Aid certificate issued under the Legal Aid Act 1988

CPR 43.2(1)(h)

Authorised court officer

Any officer of a county court, a district registry, the Principal Registry of the Family Division or the Supreme Court Costs Office, whom the Lord Chancellor has authorised to assess costs. Their powers are set out at CPR 47.3.

CPR 43.2(1)(d)
CPR 47.3
CPD 30.1

Base costs

The fees payable to a solicitor (see below) under a CFA (see below) before the addition of any success fee (see below).

CFA

A conditional fee agreement (see below).

CLS Fund

The Community Legal Service Fund

CPD

The Costs Practice Direction (see below).

CPR

The Civil Procedure Rules 1998.

Child

A person under 18.

CPR 21.1(2)(a)

Claim form

The form in which the claimant sets out certain details of his claim which, when issued by the court, starts the proceedings

Commencement of detailed assessment

When the receiving party serves on the paying party a notice of commencement (see below) and a copy of the bill of costs.

CPR 47.6

Conditional fee agreement

An agreement with a person providing advocacy or litigation services which provides for his fees and expenses, or part of them, to be payable only in specified circumstances, whether or not it provides for a success fee (see below). To be valid it must satisfy all the conditions applicable to it by virtue of section 58 of the Courts and Legal Services Act 1990.

CPR 43.2(4)
CPD 2.2

Consent order

An order in agreed terms expressed as being 'by consent'.

CPR 40.6

Contentious business

Business done, whether as solicitor or advocate, in or for the purpose of proceedings begun before a court or before an arbitrator appointed under the Arbitration Act 1996, not being business which falls within the definition of non-contentious or common form probate business contained in s128 of the Supreme Court Act 1981.

Costs

Sums payable for legal services. They include fees, charges, disbursements, expenses, remuneration. See 1.1.

CPR 43.2(1)(a)

Costs judge

A taxing master of the Supreme Court

CPR 43.2(1)(b)

Costs officer

A costs judge, a district judge or an authorised court officer

CPR 43.2(1)(c)

'Costs only' proceedings

A way of obtaining an order for the detailed assessment of the costs of a claim that was settled without substantive proceedings (see below) being issued. See chapter 51.

Costs Practice Direction

The 'Practice Direction About Costs Supplementing Parts 43 to 48 of the Civil Procedure Rules'.

CPD 1.1

Costs rules

CPR 43–48 and the CPD. See 1.3.

Counsel

A barrister or other person with a right of audience in relation to proceedings in the High Court or county court in which he is instructed to act.

CPD 1.4

Default costs certificate

An order addressed to the paying party to pay the costs at the amount claimed in the bill, plus fixed costs and interest. See 11.1.

CPR 47.11
CPD 37.3

Detailed assessment

The procedure by which the amount of costs is decided by a costs officer in accordance with CPR 47.

CPR 43.4

Disbursements

The payments which a solicitor makes on behalf of his client. See 1.1(b).

CPD 5.11–12

Fast track

The case management track for most claims between £5,000 and £15,000.

CPR 26.6(1)

Fee-earner

A solicitor or member of his staff who carries out work for which a charge can properly be made (as opposed to secretarial and support staff, the cost of whose time is normally included in the solicitor's overheads).

Filing

In relation to a document, delivering it by post or otherwise to the court office

Final costs certificate

A certificate issued by the court declaring the amount of costs assessed or agreed. See chapter 31.

CPD 42.7

Fixed costs

The amounts to be allowed in respect of solicitors' charges in the circumstances set out in Section I of CPR 45. See 1.8(a).

Fixed recoverable costs

The fixed costs recoverable where 'costs only' proceedings are issued in cases where the dispute arises from a minor road traffic accident. See chapter 52.

Fund

Any estate or property held for the benefit of any person or class of person and any fund to which a trustee or personal representative is entitled in his capacity as such

CPR 43.2(1)(e)

Funding arrangement

An arrangement where a person has (i) entered into a conditional fee agreement or a collective conditional fee agreement which provides for a success fee within the meaning of section 58(2) of the Courts and Legal Services Act 1990; (ii) taken out an insurance policy to which section 29 of the Access to Justice Act 1999 (recovery of insurance premiums by way of costs) applies; or (iii) made an arrangement with a membership organisation to meet his legal costs.

CPR 43.2(1)(k)

Indemnity basis

A more generous basis of assessment than the standard basis (see below), under which the court will allow costs which have been reasonably incurred and are reasonable in amount (any doubt being resolved in favour of the receiving party). Proportionality is not a factor which the court is required to take into account.

CPR 44.4

Indemnity principle

The principle that a successful party cannot recover from an unsuccessful party more by way of costs than the successful party is liable to pay his legal representatives.

Insurance premium

A sum of money paid or payable for insurance against the risk of incurring a costs liability in the proceedings, taken out after the event that is the subject matter of the claim.

CPR 43.2(1)(m)

Inter partes

Latin for 'between the parties'.

Interim costs certificate

A certificate ordering the paying party to pay a sum on account of the costs claimed in the bill. See chapter 29.

LSC

The Legal Services Commission.

CPD 1.4

LSC-funded client

An individual who receives services funded by the Legal Services

CPR 43.2(1)(i)

Commission as part of the Community Legal Service within the meaning of Part I of the Access to Justice Act 1999.

LSC funding certificate

A certificate issued by the LSC setting out the scope of a person's public funding and any conditions and limitations applied to it.

'LSC only' detailed assessment

A case where costs are to be assessed only against the CLS Fund (see above). See chapters 41–47.

LSC schedule

A kind of 'shadow bill' in which the costs claimed between the parties in the main bill are recalculated at prescribed rates (see below) for assessment against the CLS Fund (see above). See 24.15.

Legal Aid

The system administered by the Legal Aid Board under which public funding was made available in certain circumstances to enable persons to bring or defend claims. It has now been replaced, in part, by LSC funding (see below).

Legal Aid certificate

A certificate issued by the Legal Aid Board setting out the scope of a person's Legal Aid and any conditions and limitations applied to it.

Legal Aid/LSC Assessment Certificate

A form (EX80A) sealed by the court certifying the amount of costs payable by the CLS Fund. See chapter 40.

Legal representative

A barrister or a solicitor, solicitor's employee or other authorised litigator (as defined in the Courts and Legal Services Act 1990) who has been instructed to act for a party in relation to a claim.

Membership organisation

A body prescribed for the purposes of section 30 of the Access to Justice Act 1999 (recovery where body undertakes to meet costs liabilities).

CPR 43.2(1)(n)

Multi-track

The case management track for cases which are suitable neither for the small claims track nor for the fast track.

CPR 26.6(1)

Non-contentious business

Any business done as a solicitor which is not contentious business (see above).

Notice of commencement

The document (form N252) that enables the receiving party (see below) to start the detailed assessment proceedings.

CPR 47.6(1)
CPD 32.8

Part 36 offer/payment

An offer or payment made in accordance with CPR 36, in an attempt to settle substantive proceedings, acceptance or rejection of which may have certain costs consequences.

CPR 36

Part 47.19 offer

An offer to settle the costs of the substantive proceedings. See chapter 17.

CPR 47.19

Patient

A person who, by reason of mental disorder within the meaning of the Mental Health Act 1983, is incapable of managing and administering his own affairs.

CPR 21.1(2)(b)

Paying party

A party liable to pay costs.

CPR 43.2(1)(g)

Payment on account

A payment made by the paying party on account of the costs claimed by the receiving party. It may be made either voluntarily (see chapter 15) or as a result of a court order (see chapter 16).

Percentage increase

The percentage by which the amount of a legal representative's fee can

CPR 43.2(1)(l)

be increased in accordance with a conditional fee agreement which provides for a success fee.

Points of dispute

The paying party's objections to the receiving party's bill. See chapter 20.

CPD 35

Practice direction

Published statement indicating the procedure to be followed in particular matters.

Practice form

Form to be used for a particular purpose in proceedings, the form and purpose being specified by a practice direction.

Pre-emptive offer of settlement

An offer in settlement of costs put to the paying party at the same time as the notice of commencement is served on them. See chapter 7.

Prescribed rates

In civil cases, the rates prescribed by the Legal Aid in Civil Proceedings (Remuneration) Regulations 1994, as amended, at which costs payable by the LSC are to be assessed. See 24.15. In family cases, the rates are prescribed by the Legal Aid in Family Proceedings (Remuneration) Regulations 1991.

Privilege

The right of a party to refuse to disclose a document or produce a document or to refuse to answer questions on the ground of some special interest recognised by law.

Proceedings

Generally, this means 'court proceedings', ie the process which follows the issue by the court of a claim or application. However, it can in some circumstances mean steps taken which do not necessarily involve the court (eg detailed assessment proceedings).

Profit costs

The fees which a solicitor charges to his client for his work.

Provisional assessment

A postal detailed assessment, the result of which the receiving party may either accept or reject. See chapter 44.

Public funding

The same as LSC funding (see above).

Receiving party

A party entitled to be paid costs.

CPR 43.2(1)(f)

Retainer

The contract under which a solicitor is engaged to act for a client.

SAR

The Solicitors Accounts Rules 1998.

SCCO

The Supreme Court Costs Office (see below).

Schedule of Costs Precedents

The list of 'model' forms of bill, points of dispute etc published with the CPD, the use of which is encouraged although not compulsory.

Seal

A mark put on a document by the court to indicate that it has been issued by the court.

Semi-detached 'LSC only' detailed assessment

A detailed assessment of the 'LSC only' costs made after the costs between the parties have been agreed. See chapter 37.

Service

Steps required by rules of court to bring documents used in court proceedings to a person's attention.

Set aside

Cancelling a judgment or order or a step taken by a party in proceedings.

Skeleton argument

A written outline of the argument a party intends to use at a hearing.

Small claims track

The case management track for most claims with a value of not more than £5,000.

CPR 26.6(1)

Solicitor

A solicitor of the Supreme Court or other person with a right of audience in relation to proceedings, who is conducting the claim or defence (as the case may be) on behalf of a party to the proceedings.

CPD 1.4

Standard basis

The usual basis of assessment, under which the court will allow costs which have been reasonably incurred, are reasonable in amount and are proportionate to the matters in issue (any doubt being resolved in favour of the paying party).

CPR 44.4

Statement of costs

A concise statement of the costs a party intends to claim at a hearing at which there might be a summary assessment of the costs. It should follow as closely as possible form N260.

CPD 13.5(3)

Statement of truth

A statement verifying a statement of case and some other formal documents, without which the document may not be relied upon.

CPR 22
PDP22

Statutory interest

Interest to which the receiving party may be entitled. See chapter 14.

Stay

A stay imposes a halt on proceedings, apart from taking any steps allowed by the Rules or the terms of the stay. Proceedings can be continued if a stay is lifted.

Striking out

When the court orders written material to be deleted so that it may no longer be relied upon.

Substantive costs

The costs of the substantive proceedings (see below), as opposed to the costs of the detailed assessment proceedings (see above).

Substantive proceedings

The main case, which resulted in the order or event giving the receiving party the right to have their costs assessed. See 1.9.

Success fee

See 'percentage increase' above.

Summary assessment

The procedure by which the court, when making an order about costs, orders payment of a sum of money instead of fixed costs or 'detailed assessment.' See chapter 50.

CPR 43.3

Supreme Court Costs Office

A part of the High Court, the main function of which is to assess the costs awarded by any judge of the Court of Appeal, the High Court, a county court and the Principal Registry of the Family Division.

'Without prejudice'

Negotiations with a view to settlement are usually conducted 'without prejudice', which means that the circumstances in which the content of those negotiations may be revealed to the court are very restricted.

Worksheet

An arithmetical calculation or summary. See chapter 5.

PART I
UNDERSTANDING THE COSTS RULES
ABOUT ASSESSMENT AND KNOWING
WHERE TO FIND THEM

CHAPTER 1

Understanding the system

1.1 What are costs?

Costs are sums payable for legal services. They are normally of two kinds:

CPR 43.2(1)(a)

(a) Solicitors' charges

The fees which a solicitor charges to his client for the work he does are traditionally known as 'profit costs' because they include any profit the solicitor makes on the work. Clients probably understand them better if they are described as 'solicitors' charges'. Although normally calculated on a time basis, some solicitors' charges (such as success fees) may be calculated on a percentage basis, while others (such as fixed costs) may be pre-determined scale amounts.

(b) Disbursements

The payments which a solicitor makes on behalf of his client are usually described as 'disbursements' and include court fees, counsel's fees, experts' fees, etc. It is worth noting that:

- in the assessment of costs, particularly in legally aided/LSC-funded cases, counsel's fees are generally presented and dealt with as if they were a separate category; and

- a number of payments that solicitors and the courts habitually describe as 'disbursements' are, for the purposes of the VAT regulations, not disbursements at all, but expenses.

CPD 5.11–12

1.2 Who is responsible for paying them?

(a) In civil litigation

When court proceedings are taken then, with the possible exception of fixed costs, no party to those proceedings has an automatic right to payment of his costs by another party. The court always has a discretion as to:

CPR 44.3(1)

- whether costs are payable by one party to another;

CPR 44.3(1)(a)

- the amount of those costs; and
- when they are to be paid.

CPR 44.3(1)(b)

CPR 44.3(1)(c)

The costs rules make provision for all these matters.

(b) Between the solicitor and his client

The costs of work done for the client will be payable to the solicitor:

- if the case is being privately funded, according to the terms of the contract between the solicitor and the client ('the retainer'); or

- if the client is legally aided/funded by the Legal Services Commission ('LSC'), according to the regulations made under the Legal Aid Act 1988 and the Access to Justice Act 1999.

The rules about the calculation and assessment of costs between a solicitor and his client, or between a solicitor and the LSC, are to be found partly in the costs rules and partly in other regulations.

1.3 What is meant by 'the costs rules'?

In this book 'the costs rules' mean:

- Parts 43 to 48 of the Civil Procedure Rules 1998 ('the CPR'); and

- the Practice Direction Supplementing Parts 43–48 of the Civil Procedure Rules – generally known as the 'Costs Practice Direction' ('the CPD').

1.4 What kind of costs do they cover?

The costs rules run to over 100 pages and govern almost every aspect of costs relating to civil proceedings. For this purpose, 'civil proceedings' generally means proceedings in:

CPR 2.1(1)

- county courts;
- the High Court; and
- the Civil Division of the Court of Appeal.

CPR 2.1(1)(a)

CPR 2.1(1)(b)

CPR 2.1(1)(c)

However, there are some kinds of proceedings in these courts which do not count as civil proceedings. These are:

CPR 2.1(2)

- insolvency proceedings;
- non-contentious or common form probate proceedings;

- proceedings in the High Court when acting as a Prize Court;

- proceedings before the judge within the meaning of Part VII of the Mental Health Act 1983;

- family proceedings;

- adoption proceedings; and

- election petitions in the High Court.

Although family proceedings do not count as civil proceedings for the purposes of the CPR generally, most of the costs rules now also apply to the costs relating to family proceedings – see Chapter 49.

1.5 Are they comprehensive?

As mentioned at 1.2(b), the costs rules do not contain every rule that applies to civil costs so, depending on the type of case, you may need to refer to other provisions, such as:

- in relation to costs between the solicitor and his client – the Solicitors Act 1974 and the regulations made under it;

- in relation to conditional fees, both between the solicitor and his client, and between the parties – the various statutory provisions, conditional fees orders and regulations made since 1990; and

- in relation to Legal Aid/LSC funding, between the solicitor, his client, and the LSC – the regulations made under the Legal Aid Act 1988 and the Access to Justice Act 1999.

CPR 44.17

1.6 What topics do they cover?

The more important areas covered by the costs rules are:

- the court's discretion as to costs and the orders it can make as to who should pay them;

- the different bases on which costs ordered by the court are to be assessed;

- limitations on the amount of costs that can be allowed in some circumstances;

- the court's powers where there has been misconduct; and

- how the amount of costs is to be ascertained.

5

It is with the last topic – the ascertainment of costs – that this book is chiefly concerned.

1.7 How are they laid out?

Table 1 on page 7 shows the relationship between the relevant parts of the CPR and the CPD and their contents. You should note that:

Table 1

- the six main parts of the CPR which deal with costs are Parts 43–46, each of which covers particular areas or topics;

- the part with which this book is principally concerned is Part 47 – 'Procedure for detailed assessment of costs and default provisions', although we will need to look at some of the other parts as well;

- although it now forms one document, the CPD follows the general scheme of Parts 43–48, and is divided into sections which supplement the particular parts; accordingly this book is mainly concerned with sections 28–49;

- there is also a separate schedule of costs precedents, which includes things such as points of dispute, considered in this book;

- other prescribed costs forms are also published in connection with the CPR and the CPD, and most of these feature in this book; and

- Part 51 and the practice direction supplementing it contain transitional provisions which are of diminishing importance.

1.8 How is the amount of costs to be ascertained?

The costs rules provide four main ways in which the amount of costs payable by one party to another can be ascertained.

(a) 'Ordinary' fixed costs

CPR 45 Part I prescribes the amounts to be allowed for solicitors' charges in particular circumstances, such as:

CPR 45 Pt I

- where a defendant pays a money claim within 14 days of service of the proceedings on him;

- where the claimant enters judgment in default or in other specified situations; or

- where enforcement action is taken.

TABLE 1: LAYOUT OF THE COSTS RULES

The Civil Procedure Rules ('CPR')

PART 43	PART 44	PART 45	PART 46	PART 47	PART 48			PART 51
Scope of costs rules and definitions	General rules about costs	Fixed costs	Fast track trial costs	Procedure for detailed assessment of costs and default provisions	Costs – special cases			Transitional arrangements

The Costs Practice Direction ('CPD')

THE PRACTICE DIRECTION ABOUT COSTS SUPPLEMENTING PARTS 43 - 48 OF THE CIVIL PROCEDURE RULES

| Sections 1 – 6 | Sections 7 – 23 | Sections 24 – 25 | Sections 26 – 27 | Sections 28 – 49 | Sections 50 – 56 | SCHEDULE OF COSTS PRECEDENTS | OTHER PRESCRIBED COSTS FORMS | Practice direction supplementing Part 51 CPR |

This kind of fixed costs applies automatically, ie no specific court order is normally needed for them to be payable. As CPR 45 Part I is self-explanatory, these fixed costs are not covered further in this book.

(b) Fixed recoverable costs in minor road traffic accident cases

A separate system of fixed costs applies where 'costs only' proceedings are issued in cases where the dispute arises from a road traffic accident and damages are agreed at not more than £10,000 – see chapter 52.

(c) Summary assessment

The CPR provide that, where the court orders one party ('the paying party') to pay costs to another party ('the receiving party'), it may either:

CPR 44.7
CPR 43.2(1)(f)–(g)

- 'make a summary assessment of those costs'; or

- 'order detailed assessment of the costs by a costs officer'.

The CPR defines 'summary assessment' as 'the procedure by which the court, when making an order about costs, orders payment of a sum of money instead of fixed costs or "detailed assessment"'.
Summary assessment is considered in chapter 50.

CPR 43.3

(d) Detailed assessment

This book is mainly about detailed assessment, which the CPR defines as 'the procedure by which the amount of costs is decided by a costs officer in accordance with Part 47'.

CPR 43.4

A 'costs officer' can be a costs judge, a district judge or an authorised court officer, and in this book the term will be used to cover all three.

CPR 43.2(1)(c)

Before the coming into force of the CPR on 26 April 1999, this procedure was known as 'taxation of costs'.

1.9 Are the detailed assessment proceedings different from the substantive proceedings?

The costs rules distinguish between:

- the 'substantive proceedings' – the main case itself, which resulted in the order or event giving the receiving party the right to have his costs assessed; and

- the 'detailed assessment proceedings' – the process by which the costs of that main case are assessed.

It is a pity that this distinction is not more clearly spelt out in the costs rules, because:

- if it is not clearly understood, the rationale for some of the costs rules will be difficult to grasp; and

- it has important practical consequences, especially in working out what count as the costs of detailed assessment and who should pay them.

Admittedly, the distinction is not obvious, particularly as the detailed assessment proceedings are conducted under the same claim number as the substantive (or costs only) proceedings that gave rise to them, and are therefore, in that respect at least, logically part and parcel of those substantive (or costs only) proceedings.

However, in many ways detailed assessment proceedings operate as a 'case within a case' and the stages through which they go mirror quite closely some of the stages that are gone through in substantive proceedings.

1.10 When do the detailed assessment proceedings begin?

In a case where costs are claimed between the parties, the detailed assessment proceedings begin only when the receiving party serves on the paying party a notice of commencement of detailed assessment, accompanied by a copy of his bill.

CPR 47.6(1)
CPD 33.3

Although, at first sight, the notice of commencement is the equivalent, in the detailed assessment proceedings, of the claim form that began the substantive proceedings, it is different in that it is not issued by the court. Indeed, the court does not become involved in the detailed assessment proceedings unless and until the receiving party applies for a detailed assessment hearing date, or some other application is made in the detailed assessment proceedings.

Table 2 on page 11 is a flow-chart which, among other things, shows diagrammatically the three different periods through which a receiving party may have to pass in order to get his costs assessed between the parties:

Table 2

- The first period begins with the date of the order or event entitling him to have his costs assessed, and includes the preparation of the bill, the notice of commencement and the supporting documents.

The steps taken in this period are part of the substantive proceedings.

- The second period begins with service of the notice of commencement and includes the service of any points of dispute and replies to them. The steps taken in this period are part of the detailed assessment proceedings, but do not normally involve the court.

- The third period begins with the request for a detailed assessment hearing (or the application for a default costs certificate) and ends with the issue of a default costs certificate or a final order for payment of costs. The steps taken in this period are both part of the detailed assessment proceedings and involve the court.

1.11 What are the costs implications of beginning detailed assessment proceedings?

The date of service of the notice of commencement (see 5.1 about how this date is to be worked out) marks the formal division between the 'substantive costs' (the costs of the substantive proceedings) and the 'costs of detailed assessment' (the costs of the detailed assessment proceedings). This division has some practical consequences:

- The costs of preparing and checking the bill are part of the substantive costs. This is how they are treated both in the 'model' forms of bill in the Schedule of Costs Precedents (see 2.2) and in regulation 119(3) of the Civil Legal Aid (General) Regulations 1989. This point matters to the legally aided/LSC-funded client, because these costs are not exempt from the statutory charge, so might come out of his damages.

- Most importantly, the start of the detailed assessment proceedings marks the point at which the costs of detailed assessment start to be incurred. Those costs can be quite substantial, and the questions of who is to pay them, and how much those costs should be, will be increasingly significant to the parties as the detailed assessment proceedings continue.

While this distinction has become more clear with successive revisions of the costs rules, be aware that inconsistencies still remains in some of them, for example:

- CPD 4.5 states that 'the background information included in the bill of costs should set out ... a brief description of the proceedings

CPD 4.5

CPD 4.13

TABLE 2: PROCEDURE FOR DETAILED ASSESSMENT BETWEEN THE PARTIES

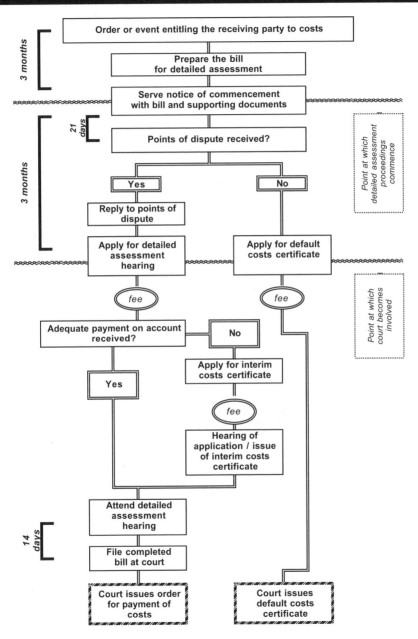

up to the date of the notice of commencement' (which may or may not be capable of including the preparation of the notice of commencement) whereas CPD 4.13 states that 'The bill of costs must not contain any claims in respect of costs or court fees which relate solely to the detailed assessment proceedings other than costs claimed for preparing and checking the bill;'

- CPD 46.2 states that a Part 47.19 offer which, as is explained at 17.7, only relates to the substantive costs and interest, 'should specify whether or not it is intended to be inclusive of the cost of preparation of the bill ...' and

CPD 46.2
CPR 47.19

- the inconsistency between CPR 47.11(3) and CPD 37.8 as to whether the fixed costs payable on the issue of a default costs certificate are costs of the substantive proceedings or of the detailed assessment proceedings – see 11.4(e).

CPR 47.11(3)
CPD 37.8

1.12 What about 'LSC only' detailed assessments?

To add to the difficulties, in a case where costs are to be assessed only against the CLS Fund (an 'LSC only' detailed assessment) there is no notice of commencement. The costs rules therefore provide that the detailed assessment proceedings in such a case begin only with the filing at court of a request for detailed assessment (see 41.2). The work done in connection with the service of the bill on the client, which normally precedes this step, will therefore not form part of the costs of the detailed assessment proceedings.

1.13 Which costs fall into which category where costs are to be assessed between the parties? (A summary)

(a) Substantive costs

These are the costs of everything done *before* the service of the notice of commencement, and include the costs of:

- all the work done in the substantive case;
- preparing the bill;
- checking the bill;
- preparing the notice of commencement;

- preparing the supporting documents;

- serving the notice of commencement; and

- anything else done before service of the notice of commencement.

(b) Costs of the detailed assessment proceedings

These are the costs of everything done *after* the service of the notice of commencement. Although these are often described comprehensively as the 'costs of preparing for and attending the detailed assessment hearing', they may include the costs of:

- requesting a default costs certificate;

- making applications in the detailed assessment proceedings;

- replying to points of dispute;

- making and receiving Part 47.19 offers and negotiating;

- requesting a detailed assessment hearing;

- preparing for the hearing;

- attending the hearing; and

- completing the assessment.

Also forming part of the costs of detailed assessment are the court fees payable:

- on requesting a default costs certificate;

- on requesting a detailed assessment hearing;

- on making applications in the detailed assessment proceedings; and

- on sealing the Legal Aid/LSC Assessment Certificate (form EX80A).

CHAPTER 2

Finding and keeping up to date with the rules and forms

2.1 Where can we find the rules and forms?

Nearly everything that you will need in the way of rules and forms relating to the assessment of costs is available free of charge on the internet, as are some reports of costs cases. However, both the rules and the forms change from time to time, and the case-law is constantly developing, so it is important to try to keep up to date. Although some services offer free e-mail updating, in most cases the onus will be on you to search the various websites periodically to see if there is anything new.

The rest of this chapter sets out the different sorts of information you might need, and tells you where to find it.

2.2 The CPR and the CPD

The whole of the CPR, all the associated practice directions and the schedule of costs precedents can be found on the website of the Department of Constitutional Affairs (formerly the Lord Chancellor's Department):

• www.dca.gov.uk/civil/procrules_fin/index.htm

The costs rules are updated periodically. The most recent update at the time this book was written was No 33, issued on 24 September 2003. The next one was expected to be issued 'early in 2004'.

On the CD-ROM are the following:

• CPR Part 43	**CD-ROM 01.01**
• CPR Part 44	**CD-ROM 01.02**
• CPR Part 45	**CD-ROM 01.03**
• CPR Part 46	**CD-ROM 01.04**
• CPR Part 47	**CD-ROM 01.05**
• CPR Part 48	**CD-ROM 01.06**
• The CPD	**CD-ROM 01.07**

• Precedent E from the Schedule of Costs Precedents (Legal Aid/LSC Schedule of Costs)	**CD-ROM 02.01**
• Precedent F from the Schedule of Costs Precedents (Certificates for Inclusion in Bill of Costs)	**CD-ROM 02.02**
• Precedent G from the Schedule of Costs Precedents (Points of Dispute Served by the Defendant)	**CD-ROM 02.03**

Precedents E, F and G are also reproduced in Appendix II to this book.

2.3 Court forms

These can also be obtained from the website of the Department of Constitutional Affairs:

• www.dca.gov.uk/civil/procrules_fin/menus/forms.htm

The forms considered in this book are listed below, in numerical rather than logical order. Most are reproduced in Appendix II to this book and all the costs forms are on the CD-ROM (with the exception of N255HC which, at the time of writing, was not available, and N253, which only the court will issue).

(a) Costs forms

• N252 – Notice of commencement of detailed assessment.	**CD-ROM 04.01**
• N253 – Notice of amount allowed on provisional assessment.	
• N254 – Request for default costs certificate.	**CD-ROM 04.02**
• N255 – Default costs certificate (county court).	**CD-ROM 04.03**
• N255HC – Default costs certificate (High Court).	
• N256 – Final costs certificate.	**CD-ROM 04.04**
• N256HC – Final costs certificate (High Court)	**CD-ROM 04.05**
• N257 – Interim costs certificate.	**CD-ROM 04.06**
• N258 – Request for detailed assessment hearing.	**CD-ROM 04.07**
• N258A – Request for detailed assessment (Legal Aid/Legal Services Commission only).	**CD-ROM 04.08**
• N258B – Request for detailed assessment (costs payable out of a fund other than the Community Legal Service Fund).	**CD-ROM 04.09**
• EX80A – Legal Aid/Legal Services Commission assessment certificate.	**CD-ROM 04.10**

(b) General forms

- N1 – Claim form.   CD-ROM 05.01
- N1A – Notes for claimant on completing a claim form.   CD-ROM 05.02
- N24 – General form of judgment or order.   CD-ROM 05.03
- N161 – Appellant's notice.
- N161A – Guidance notes on completing the appellant's notice.
- N163 – Skeleton argument.   CD-ROM 05.04
- N208 – Claim form (CPR Part 8).   CD-ROM 05.05
- N208A – Notes for claimant on completing a Part 8 claim form.   CD-ROM 05.06
- N244 – Application notice.   CD-ROM 05.07
- N260 – Statement of costs.   CD-ROM 05.08
- N279 – Notice of discontinuance.   CD-ROM 05.09

2.4 Court fee details

The court fees guides can be obtained from the website of the Court Service:

- www.courtservice.gov.uk

The relevant ones, which are on the CD-ROM, are:

- Guide to Supreme Court Fees – from 1 April 2003.   CD-ROM 03.04
- Guide to County Court Fees – from 1 April 2003.   CD-ROM 03.05

These are based on the various fee orders, which are statutory instruments that can be obtained from the HMSO website:

- www.hmso.gov.uk/acts.htm

For ease of reference, Table 3 on page 19 shows only the fees (as they were at the time of writing) that relate specifically to the assessment of costs.   Table 3

2.5 Supreme Court Costs Office publications

For all the materials listed below, go to:

- www.courtservice.gov.uk/cms/3561.htm

(a) The SCCO Guide

This is large (over 150 pages) and comprehensive. While much of it paraphrases the costs rules, there is useful material that you will not find elsewhere, such as:

- the procedures peculiar to the SCCO;

- guidance on Court of Protection costs; and

- draft orders on costs-related applications.

(b) Guide to the Summary Assessment of Costs

This is referred to in chapter 50. The January 2001 edition (labelled March 2003 on the SCCO website) is on the CD-ROM.

CD-ROM 03.01

(c) Guideline Figures for the Summary Assessment of Costs

These are referred to in chapter 50. The March 2003 edition is on the CD-ROM.

CD-ROM 03.02

(d) Reports of costs cases

This is the best source of free reports of costs cases, and the site provides:

- transcripts of SCCO decisions;

- test cases; and

- case summaries.

2.6 Legal Services Commission publications

An essential (although often confusing) source of information if you do Legal Aid/LSC-funded work is the LSC website:

- www.legalservices.gov.uk

Among the vast amount of material available on it, the following are particularly useful:

(a) LSC Focus

This is a periodical (roughly quarterly) publication for those who do LSC-funded work. Among other things it announces changes to rules and rates and publishes guidance on costs assessment. While it is

TABLE 3: COURT FEES PAYABLE ON DETERMINATION OF COSTS

With effect from 1 April 2003

DESCRIPTION	FAMILY		COUNTY COURT		HIGH COURT	
	Fee No	Amount	Fee No	Amount	Fee No	Amount
On a filing a request for an 'LSC only' detailed assessment [N258a]	8.1	£100	3.1	£100	10.1	£120
On a filing a request for any other detailed assessment (ie either for an assessment between the parties only or for a combined assessment between the parties and against the CLS Fund) [N258] *Note: Where there is a combined assessment, the fee is apportioned between the assessments between the parties and against the CLS Fund on the basis of the amount allowed*	8.2	£160	3.2	£160	10.2	£250
On a request for the issue of a default costs certificate [N254]	8.3	£40	3.3	£40	10.3	£40
On an appeal against a decision made in detailed assessment proceedings	8.4	£100	3.4	£100	10.4	£100
On applying for sealing an EX80A (Legal Aid/LSC detailed assessment certificate) *Note: This is payable when filing the EX80A and is recoverable only against the CLS Fund*	8.5	£30	3.5	£30	10.5	£30
On a request or an application to set aside a default costs certificate	8.6	£60	3.6	£60	10.6	£60

available free on the website, paper copies also appear to be available to anyone free of charge. If you want to go on the mailing list you will usually find the address to which to write at the end of each edition of *Focus*.

(b) Regulations and guidance

There is a mass of material on the website, including:

• the Access to Justice Act 1999 and the regulations and orders made under it;

• Funding Code criteria, procedures and guidance; and

• the Statutory Charge Manual.

(c) Civil Bill Assessment Manual

If you submit CLAIMs 1 or 2 for assessment by the LSC (which is not a topic covered by this book) you need to read this manual, which contains guidance for the LSC's costs assessors.

(d) LSC Forms

All the usual LSC forms are available free of charge. You can either have them in pdf format from the LSC website (see above) or as 'Hot-Docs' from:

• http://lscforms.hotdocs.co.uk

The forms change with alarming frequency, and the LSC will not accept obsolete versions, so it is essential to make sure that the ones you are using are up to date. Once you have installed the Hot-Docs variety you can expect to be notified by e-mail of new versions.

2.7 The Law Society's publications

The website from which to obtain the material mentioned below is:

• www.lawsociety.org.uk

(a) Law Society's Gazette

This is published weekly and is available both in printed form (supplied to every practising solicitor) and also on-line, although the on-line version appears a little later than the paper version. It usually announces changes in the rules and it has occasional articles on costs as well as reports of significant costs cases. The 'Data' page is useful for checking current and historic bank base rates and rates of interest on judgment debts.

(b) Guide to the Professional Conduct of Solicitors

It is sometimes necessary to consult this, for example in questions about retainers, or for the provisions of the Solicitors' Accounts Rules 1998.

(c) Other information

Other useful costs information on this website includes:

• 'Inside Track' – a newsletter on civil litigation;

• 'Dispatch' – a newsletter on Legal Aid; and

• checklists and guidance on conditional fees.

2.8 Practitioners' books and reports

Everything listed in 2.2 – 2.7 is available free of charge, but everything in this section comes at a price. This does not pretend to be a complete catalogue of everything available on the subject of costs and the inclusion of a title here is not to be taken as a recommendation of it.

(a) Greenslade on Costs

A comprehensive loose-leaf publication with periodic updates. For further information visit:

• www.sweetandmaxwell.co.uk

(b) Butterworths Costs Service

Another comprehensive loose-leaf publication with periodic updates. For further information visit:

• www.butterworths.co.uk

(c) Cook on Costs 2004

A guide to legal remuneration in civil contentious and non-contentious business. For further information visit:

• www.butterworths.co.uk

(d) Hoffman: 'Costs Cases – A Civil Guide'

A handbook, arranged alphabetically, summarising the case-law on most of the topics you are likely to encounter in the assessment of costs. For further information visit:

• www.sweetandmaxwell.co.uk

(e) Costs Law Reports

A series of reports concerned exclusively with costs cases. For further information visit:

• www.emispp.com

(f) Lawtel

A database of case reports, articles, statutory instruments etc, which provides daily updates to subscribers. For further information visit:

• www.lawtel.co.uk

(g) The LSC Manual

This is described as 'the main source of guidance and information for contracted suppliers'. For further information visit:

• www.legalservices.gov.uk

PART II
THE PROCEDURE FOR DETAILED ASSESSMENT BY THE COURT OF A BILL CLAIMING COSTS BETWEEN THE PARTIES (WITH OR WITHOUT A CLAIM FOR COSTS AGAINST THE CLS FUND)

CHAPTER 3

The time-table for starting detailed assessment proceedings

3.1 By when should we start the detailed assessment proceedings?

These are the only two time-limits that automatically apply to the receiving party's conduct of the detailed assessment proceedings:

- the time by which detailed assessment proceedings must be commenced is three months after the date of the order or event which entitles the receiving party to the costs; and

  CPR 47.7
  CPD 28.1

- where points of dispute are served, the receiving party must file a request for a detailed assessment hearing 'within 3 months of the expiry of the period for commencing detailed assessment proceedings' (ie within six months from the date of the order or event).

  CPR 47.14
  CPD 40.1

Both dates should be diarised as soon as the order has been made or the event has occurred that confers the entitlement to detailed assessment.

3.2 What kind of order or event entitles us to start detailed assessment proceedings?

The order or event that can provide the legal peg on which to hang the detailed assessment proceedings will be one of the following:

(a) A judgment, direction, order, award or other determination

Here the three-month period starts to run from the date of the judgment etc unless detailed assessment has been stayed (ie suspended) pending an appeal, in which case it starts to run from the date of the order lifting the stay. A stay is not automatic when there is an appeal – it must be applied for.

CPR 47.7
CPR 47.2
CPD 29.1
CPD 40.4(a)

The general rule is that there should be no detailed assessment of costs of any proceedings or any part of the proceedings until they have been concluded, ie when the court has finally determined the matters in issue in the claim, whether or not there is an appeal. Although it is usually clear when this has happened, it will also be regarded as hav-

CPR 47.1
CPD 28.1(1)

ing happened:

- when there has been an award of provisional damages under CPR 41; or   *CPD 28.1(2)*

- when the court orders, or the parties agree in writing that, although the proceedings are continuing, they will nevertheless be treated as concluded.   *CPD 2.5*
CPD 28.1(3)

A costs judge or a district judge may make an order allowing detailed assessment proceedings to be commenced where there is no realistic prospects of a claim continuing.   *CPD 28.1(5)*

If a paying party considers that detailed assessment proceedings have been started without entitlement, he may apply to a costs judge or to a district judge to determine the issue. The court may order the detailed assessment proceedings to continue, may set aside the notice of commencement, or may make other orders.   *CPD 28.1(4)*

Although the date of an order is usually easy enough to find, you might be unsure of the effective date of a consent order in the county court, drawn up and dated by the parties, because the court seal bears no date. In such a case, you have to work on the basis that the effective date is the one inserted in the order by the parties, even though the court seal was not applied until later.   **CPR 40.2(2)**

(b) Discontinuance under Part 38

This is where the Defendant has a right to costs because the Claimant has discontinued his claim. A costs order is deemed to have been made on the standard basis.   **CPR 38.6**
CPR 44.12(1)(d)
CPD 40.4(d)

The three-month period starts to run from the date of service of notice of discontinuance unless there has been an application to set it aside, in which case it starts to run from the date of the dismissal of the application to set it aside.   **CPR 47.7**

(c) Acceptance of an offer to settle or a payment into court under Part 36

This is where the Claimant has a right to costs because he has accepted the Defendant's Part 36 offer or payment into court. A costs order is deemed to have been made on the standard basis.   **CPR 36.13(1)**
CPR 44.12(1)(d)
CPD 40.4(c)

The three-month period starts to run from the date of the acceptance. Note that an offer which might be described as a 'Part 36 offer,' but which is made and accepted without the issue of substantive proceedings, is not a real Part 36 offer, so acceptance of it does not give you   **CPR 36.2(4)** the right to start detailed assessment proceedings. In such a case, if the costs cannot be agreed, you will need to start 'costs only' proceedings (see chapter 51). If all goes well, those proceedings will result in an order for detailed assessment, and that order will be the peg on which the detailed assessment proceedings can be hung.

(d) Striking out of claim for non-payment of court fees

This is where the Defendant has a right to costs because the Claimant's claim has been struck out for non-payment of court fees. A costs order is deemed to have been made on the standard basis.

The three-month period starts to run from the date of the notice served under CPR 3.7 where a claim is struck out under that rule.

CPR 3.7
CPR 44.12(1)(a)
CPD 40.4(b)
CPR 3.7

(e) Other events and circumstances

A miscellaneous collection of orders and events capable of giving rise to detailed assessment proceedings is set out at CPD 40.4(e)–(j).

CPD 40.4(e)–(i)

3.3 When exactly does the three-month period end?

'Month' means a 'calendar month', so you count from the number of the day of the order or event to the same numbered day three months hence (eg order dated 5 March, bill to be served by 5 June). If the expiry date is not a working day you should assume that the three months are up on the last working day before that date.

CPR 2.10

3.4 What paperwork do we need to start the detailed assessment proceedings?

The detailed assessment proceedings are started by the receiving party serving on the paying party:

CPR 47.6(1)
CPD 33.3

• 'a notice of commencement in the relevant practice form', and

• a copy of the bill of costs.

The relevant practice form is form N252. Chapter 8 explains how to complete it.

Form N252
CD-ROM 04.01

Until the bill of costs has been prepared you are not in a position to start the detailed assessment proceedings. The time taken to complete the substantive work and prepare the bill often make it difficult to meet the three-month deadline.

In addition to the bill other supporting documents must be served with the notice of commencement. Chapter 9 identifies them.

3.5 What if we are not going to meet the deadline?

If you are not going to miss it by very much, it may be easiest to say nothing unless and until the paying party starts pressing for service of the bill.

Alternatively, either as a first move or in response to pressure from the paying party, ask them to agree an extension of time. If you are going to do this: **CPR 2.11**
CPD 33.1

• give the reason for the delay (eg large and complex bill, need to retain the papers for implementation work or related proceedings, several firms of solicitors involved, sickness of vital people, any of the usual office disasters);

• be realistic in your request, asking for enough time for the costs draftsman to prepare the bill and for the fee-earner to check it; and

• if the paying party agrees, make sure that you get their agreement in writing.   **CPR 2.11**

You can normally expect a paying party to grant you a reasonable extension of time without any particular conditions attached. However, if you encounter difficulties with them, either because of the length of the extension you need, or because they are simply uncooperative, as the price for securing the extension you may need to offer to waive some of the interest to which the receiving party would otherwise be entitled. For example, if you are three weeks late in serving the bill, you could offer not to claim any interest for those three weeks. This deprives the paying party of their main objection to the delay, while probably not costing the receiving party anything significant, as most claims for costs are settled for a global figure which includes, but does not quantify, the interest.

Chapter 14 explains the right to interest.

3.6 When do we need to ask the court for an extension of time?

If you cannot get the paying party to agree to an extension, and you do not want them to apply for an order compelling you to start detailed assessment proceedings (see 3.7(b)) you will need to apply to the court for an extension. You should make the application 'as soon as it becomes apparent that it is necessary or desirable to make it', although it is difficult to see that there would be much point in making the application very much before the expiry of the three-month period, as you are not at risk of an application by the paying party until then. The   **CPR 3.1(2)(a)**
CPD 33.2
PDP23 2.7

court can grant you an extension even if you make the application after the three-month period has expired. Chapter 4 explains the procedure.

3.7 What if we have already missed the deadline?

(a) If the paying party has not said anything

If the paying party has not said anything, serve the notice of commencement as soon as you can. You do not need permission from the court to serve it out of time.

CPD 33.4

(b) If the paying party makes an application

If you have missed the deadline (either as set by the costs rules or by a court order) the paying party can apply for an order requiring you 'to commence detailed assessment proceedings within such time as the court may specify'.

CPR 47.8(1)
CPD 34.1

For this purpose, the costs rules put the LSC in the position of a paying party, so that it can compel the commencement of detailed assessment proceedings. It might wish to do this where it knows that a case has come to an end, it has made payments on account to the solicitor which it would like repaid, and perhaps counsel is pressing for payment of his fees.

CPR 47.8(4)

Although this application is 'in the detailed assessment proceedings' the procedure and the form of the application notice are as used in the substantive proceedings, so they will need to file an 'ordinary' application notice in form N244 and also comply with the provisions of CPR 23 and PDP23 – see chapter 25.

CPD 34.1(1)

Because the costs rules provide specifically that you are entitled to seven days' notice of any hearing, this is presumably not an application that the court would usually grant without a hearing.

CPD 34.1(2)

If you receive such an application it suggests that the paying party is unlikely to be willing to resolve the matter by a consent order, but if you have any reasonable proposals it would be sensible to put them as:

- if they are accepted you can apply for an order in the agreed terms (see 25.4); or

CPR 40.6(5)

- if they are rejected, the fact that you tried to negotiate a settlement may help you in any argument about costs if the application goes to a hearing.

CPR 44.5(3)(a)(ii)

29

(c) What the court may do

Whether or not the paying party makes an application, if you are late in serving the notice of commencement, the court may disallow all or part of the interest that would otherwise be payable on the costs.

CPR 47.8(3)

• That is only likely to happen if the paying party makes an issue of it, either by making an application, or by raising it in the points of dispute and at the detailed assessment hearing.

• Even then you can argue that the disallowance should be restricted to the interest attributable to the period of delay, eg that if you were three weeks late serving the bill, you should only be deprived of three weeks' interest.

The court must not impose any other sanction unless:

CPR 47.8(3)

• you 'failed to conduct detailed assessment proceedings in accordance with Part 47' (which, presumably, for the purpose of CPR 47.8(3) means in some respect other than just being late in serving the notice of commencement) or with a direction of the court; or

CPR 44.14(1)(a)

• there has been 'unreasonable or improper conduct' by you or the client before or during the substantive proceedings (see 35.6).

CPR 44.14(1)(b)

If the court finds either or both of those things, it can:

• disallow all or part of the costs being assessed; or

CPR 44.14(2)(a)

• order you or the client to pay the costs which the paying party has been caused to incur (although it does not say so specifically, presumably this could include the paying party's costs of the substantive proceedings).

CPR 44.14(2)(b)

If the court makes such an order against the receiving party, and they are not present when the order is made, you must notify them in writing of the order no later than seven days after you receive notice of the order.

CPR 44.14(3)

The court can order that, unless you begin detailed assessment proceedings within the time specified by the court, all or part of the costs to which the receiving party would otherwise be entitled will be disallowed. You should try to persuade the court not to make such an 'unless' order in the first instance.

CPR 47.8(2)

If, however, the court makes an 'unless' order and you fail to meet the deadline set by it, the disallowances prescribed by the order will take effect automatically.

If the court does not make an 'unless' order, and merely sets a dead-

CPR 44.14

line without specifying the penalty for missing it, if you then go on to miss it, the paying party can return to court to invoke Part 44.14 (see 3.7(b) and 35.6), and you might lose all or part of the costs you were to claim as well as be ordered to pay any costs to which the paying party has been put.

CPR 47.8(3)

3.8 What should we do next?

The next step is to prepare the notice of commencement. This is explained in chapter 8.

CHAPTER 4

Applying for an extension of time for serving the notice of commencement

4.1 Is an application essential?

The court may extend the time for serving notice of commencement, and you should normally make such applications as soon as it becomes apparent that it is necessary or desirable to do so. However, in practice, you will need to make an application only if:

CPR 3.1(2)(a)
CPD 33.2
PDP23 2.7

• you are about to miss or have already missed the deadline; and

• the paying party has refused you an extension of time for serving the notice of commencement;

CPD 33.1

• you do not want them to apply for an order compelling you to start detailed assessment proceedings (see 3.7(b)).

4.2 To which court do we apply?

The court to which to apply is the District Registry or county court where the substantive case was proceeding or, in any other case, the SCCO.

CPR 47.4(1)
CPD 31.1

4.3 What type of application is it?

As the detailed assessment proceedings have not begun, the application will technically be in the substantive proceedings. This has no significance so far as the procedure and the form of the application notice are concerned, as these are the same whether an application is made in the substantive proceedings or in the detailed assessment proceedings. The procedure is prescribed by CPR 23 and the practice direction which supplements it. The application notice is in form N244, which is reproduced in Appendix III and is also on the CD-ROM.

CPR 23
PDP23
Form N244
CD-ROM 05.07

4.4 How do we complete the application notice?

(a) The court heading

You can take these details from the pleadings in the substantive case. The 'warrant number' box will not apply.

PDP23 2.1

(b) Listing information

The rules say that you should either ask for a hearing or ask that the application be dealt with without one. A hearing is probably best avoided as, whatever the outcome, the paying party is likely to ask for an order that the receiving party pay his costs of preparing for and attending it. Therefore, unless there are particular reasons for seeking a hearing, tick box 1(c) and complete items 5 and 6. | **PDP23 2.1(5)**

(c) Parts A and B

The notes on the form explain what is required. The rules say that you should state exactly what order you are seeking (it is generally best to do this by attaching a draft order) and, briefly, why. On the CD-ROM is a specimen draft order. | **CPR 23.6** **CD-ROM 06.01**

You can set out the evidence on which you base your application in Part C of the application notice.

(d) Part C

If you think it will help, exhibit relevant copy correspondence, eg between you and the paying party, showing that you made a reasonable request for an extension which he unreasonably refused.

Do not exhibit or refer to any 'without prejudice' correspondence or discussions.

(e) Signature

The application notice is verified by a statement of truth, which can only be signed by a party or his legal representative. | **PDP22** **CPR 32.14**

If drafted by a 'legal representative' (which means 'a barrister or a solicitor, solicitor's employee or other authorised litigator ... who has been instructed to act for a party in relation to a claim'), the document should bear his signature. If drafted by a legal representative as a member or employee of a firm it should be signed in the name of the firm. | *CPD 1.5* **PDP5 2.1** **CPR 2.3(1)**

While an 'in-house' costs draftsman actually employed by a firm of solicitors would be considered a 'legal representative,' so could properly sign in the name of the firm, this would not apply to a free-lance costs draftsman.

(f) Receiving party's address for service

This should be straightforward to complete. The court address should also be completed at the bottom of the first page of the form.

4.5 What is the fee?

The fee is currently £60 whether the application is in the High Court (fee number 2.4) or the county court (fee number 3.2). The cheque should be made payable to 'H M Paymaster General'.

4.6 Should we prepare a statement of our costs?

Because this is the kind of application the costs of which are likely to be summarily assessed, you should prepare, file and serve a statement of your costs – see chapter 50. You may think it unlikely that the court will award you the costs of the application, and if you fail to comply with the rules about statements of costs that will be the almost inevitable result.

4.7 What about filing and service?

On the CD-ROM is a draft covering letter to the court, filing the application. **CD-ROM 07.01**

It is for the court to serve the application and whether it does will depend on whether it decides to deal with the application without notice to the paying party. **CPR 23**
PDP23

4.8 Will there be a hearing?

If you have asked for a hearing, the court should fix a date and time for it, and notify you. **PDP23 2.2**

If you have asked for the application to be dealt with without a hearing, the district judge or master will decide either:

- that the application is suitable for consideration without a hearing, in which case he will either go ahead and make an order, and notify the parties, or give directions for the filing of evidence; if an order is made without a hearing the paying party can apply to have it set aside or varied; or **CPR 23.9** **PDP23 2.3–2.4** **CPR 23.10**

- that the application is not suitable for consideration without a hearing, in which case he will notify the parties of the date, time and place fixed for the hearing, and may at the same give directions as to the filing of evidence. **PDP23 2.5**

4.9 What orders might the court make?

The court has very wide powers. So far as the extension of time is concerned, it might order that:

CPR 3.1(2)(a)

- the receiving party should have the extension of time requested; or

- the receiving party should have some lesser extension of time (with or without any particular conditions); or

- the application should be refused.

As for the costs of the application, the court might order that:

- the paying party should pay the receiving party his costs of the application;

- the receiving party should pay the paying party's costs of the application;

- there should be no order as to costs;

- [if the receiving party is legally aided/LSC funded] that there should be 'LSC only' assessment of the receiving party's costs.

If there is a hearing 'The parties must anticipate that … the court may wish to review the conduct of the case as a whole and give any necessary case management directions.'

PDP23 2.9
CPR 3.1

4.10 What should we do next?

Assuming that the court grants your application, diarise the deadline set by it for you to begin detailed assessment proceedings. If there is time, take stock of the costs claim as suggested (see chapter 6) and consider making a pre-emptive offer (see chapter 7). However, if you do not have much time, prepare the notice of commencement (see chapter 8).

CHAPTER 5
Keeping track of the figures

5.1 How can we simplify things?

For all purely arithmetical issues (eg calculating the total due to date, working out the implications of offers etc) the bill itself is likely to be of limited use.

It is better to abstract from the bill the essential totals and to set up a series of concise summaries that are easy to refer to and easy to update.

These summaries can be set up and used manually or with a word-processing program on your PC. However, if you are able to use a spreadsheet program such as Microsoft Excel, this is by far the easiest way of creating and using them. That is how the specimen summaries in Appendix I and on the CD-ROM have been prepared. Following the Excel terminology, an individual summary is called a 'worksheet' and the collection of summaries for a particular matter is called a 'workbook'.

5.2 What kind of worksheets are most useful?

The number and type of worksheets you need will depend on the nature of the case and the steps that have to be taken in the detailed assessment proceedings, but the following are typical, worked examples of which are illustrated in Appendix I and blank copies of which are on the CD-ROM:

- No 1: Total costs claimed between the parties — **CD-ROM 10.01**
- No 2: Implications of pre-emptive offer — **CD-ROM 10.05**
- No 3: Amount payable under default costs certificate — **CD-ROM 10.06**
- No 4: Implications of paying party's offer — **CD-ROM 10.10**
- No 5: Valuation of paying party's points of dispute — **CD-ROM 10.11**
- No 6: Implications of varying degrees of success by paying party — **CD-ROM 10.12**
- No 7: Implications of complete success by paying party — **CD-ROM 10.13**
- No 8: Implications of receiving party's counter-offer — **CD-ROM 10.14**
- No 9: Updated total claimed for interim costs certificate — **CD-ROM 10.15**

• No 10: Possible transfers to claim against CLS Fund **CD-ROM 10.16**

• No 11: Result of final settlement **CD-ROM 10.17**

Each of these will be considered at the point in the explanation of the detailed assessment process where it is most relevant.

5.3 What about the costs of detailed assessment?

Although most of the work done in the detailed assessment proceedings is fee-earning work by nature, the costs of which may ultimately be recovered from the paying party (or perhaps from the CLS Fund), there is still a reluctance on the part of both solicitors and costs draftsmen to record the actual time spent on it and to claim proper remuneration for it. There is a tendency to treat such work as part of the firm's overheads.

To achieve the best possible recovery of costs it is essential to record this time accurately, so that a proper claim for the costs of it can be made. Of course, not all the time spent will be recoverable, particularly when both a solicitor and a costs draftsman work on a case jointly, but if all the time spent is recorded, a sensible decision can be made later about how much to claim, and the claim so made will be much easier to sustain.

A further worksheet (No 12, which is also reproduced in Appendix I) **CD-ROM 10.18**
provides a means of recording the actual time spent as the matter progresses. It enables those parts of the time spent that are probably not chargeable to be discounted and calculates the total value of the remainder. It has two particular benefits:

• that total chargeable time can easily be carried to those other worksheets that include a calculation of the costs of the detailed assessment proceedings; and

• it provides the basis of the statement of costs of preparing for the detailed assessment hearing (see 32.4).

CHAPTER 6
Taking stock of the costs claim

6.1 When should we take stock?

To negotiate successfully, and also to reduce the risks of coming unstuck at any detailed assessment hearing, you need to make a reasonably objective appraisal of the strength of your costs claim. As matters unfold, the picture may change, so you should always be prepared to modify your views and re-visit your appraisal.

Carrying out a detailed appraisal can take time, so it is not an exercise you want to repeat more often than is necessary. In the usual sort of case, it should be sufficient to do this at three distinct stages:

• before serving the notice of commencement;

• when replying to points of dispute; and

• shortly before the detailed assessment hearing.

6.2 How should we take stock?

If you were not involved with the conduct of the substantive case or with the preparation of the bill, you should try to discuss it with the fee-earner who was responsible. At the very least you should read the bill. If it is well drawn, it will tend to give a positive picture of the case. To make sure that there are no significant negatives, it is helpful to have a quick look at the files. The correspondence with the client and with the opponent, instructions to counsel and counsel's advice can be particularly instructive.

As you do this you may find it helpful to do a 'SWOT analysis', ie to note the bill's Strengths and its Weaknesses as well as the Opportunities and the Threats presented by the situation.

(a) Strengths

These could include:

• well-drawn bill;

• modest charging rates;

• efficient fee-earner;

• little reliance on counsel, considering the type of case;

• total costs low in proportion to the complexity of the issues, the value of the claim etc;

• every head of claim proving successful;

• all the evidence obtained being used; or

• inexplicable delays, lack of co-operation, unreasonable behaviour or even misconduct by the paying party and/or his solicitors.

(b) Weaknesses

These could include:

• badly drawn bill;

• problems with your retainer (eg difficulty in proving compliance with the conditional fee agreement regulations or the indemnity principle);

• high charging rates;

• slow, inefficient, non-specialist, closely supervised or frequently changing fee-earners;

• heavy reliance on counsel, considering the type of case;

• level of costs apparently disproportionate to the issues and the amount at stake or recovered;

• failure of some of the heads of claim;

• evidence having been obtained that you could not use; or

• apparently well-founded allegations of delay, lack of co-operation, unreasonable behaviour or even misconduct by the client and/or the firm.

(c) Opportunities

These could include:

• opponent willing to negotiate (perhaps better still if they are willing to do so without involving costs negotiators!);

• opponent who was reasonable in the substantive proceedings;

- previous experience of negotiations with this opponent and of the level at which he is likely to settle;

- counsel willing to discount his fees to achieve a quick settlement;

- client amenable to bearing some or all of any shortfall between costs claimed and costs recovered;

- no desperate need to get the costs in without delay; or

- court with jurisdiction over the detailed assessment known to be efficient, speedy and reasonable.

(d) Threats

These could include:

- opponent unwilling to negotiate or who has already involved unreasonable costs negotiators;

- opponent who was unreasonable in the substantive proceedings;

- no previous experience of negotiations with this opponent;

- counsel not willing to discount his fees to achieve a quick settlement;

- client not amenable to bearing any of the shortfall between costs claimed and costs recovered;

- cash-flow problems on the part of the client or the firm; or

- court with jurisdiction over the detailed assessment known to be inefficient, slow and unpredictable.

6.3 What should we do next?

You should now be in a position to decide whether this is a case in which to make a pre-emptive offer of settlement.

- If you decide that it is, see chapter 7 for an explanation of how to proceed.

- If you decide that it is not, you will need to prepare the notice of commencement – see chapter 8.

CHAPTER 7

Making a pre-emptive offer of settlement

7.1 Why consider making a pre-emptive offer?

By a 'pre-emptive offer' is meant an offer in settlement of the costs that you put to the paying party at the same time as you serve the notice of commencement. Although you might have tried to agree a figure for costs before this point (eg on the strength of a simple break-down of the work done) the difference is that here you are reinforcing the offer with the service of a full bill and the start of the detailed assessment proceedings, which shows that you mean business.

If the offer is accepted by the paying party, you can:

- avoid the delays in getting to a detailed assessment hearing, which can be considerable, and therefore help the firm's cash-flow;

- avoid incurring the costs of the detailed assessment proceedings, which could be substantial and which you might not recover from the paying party; and

- preserve the goodwill of the client by achieving a rapid resolution of the costs issues.

Even if it is rejected by the paying party, your pre-emptive offer may speed up the negotiations, by forcing them to pitch their opening offer at a higher figure than that at which they might otherwise have started.

7.2 Is it always a good idea to make one?

Not every case will be suitable for the making of a pre-emptive offer. Factors which might incline you not to make one could include:

- a bill which includes the costs of previous solicitors, who will not agree to offer a discount for early settlement;

- a bill for assessment both between the parties and against the CLS Fund where you will want to claim from the CLS Fund any shortfall between the costs as claimed and as recovered between the parties which will result from a settlement at a discount. Here you will need to be able to identify specific items objected to by the paying party and that can normally only be done once you have received points of dispute.

7.3 How do we work one out?

At this stage instinct can be as important as arithmetic, so the first step is to take stock of the costs claim generally – see chapter 6. This should give you at least some idea of how vulnerable the bill might be to attack by the paying party, and to assessing down by the costs officer.

Three particular points which are in your favour now, but which might not be so for much longer, are:

• The paying party has an interest in concluding the matter as quickly as possible, if only to reduce his liability to interest.

• The paying party might wish to avoid the expense of engaging a costs draftsman or negotiator to prepare points of dispute.

• Unless you are already on bad terms with the paying party, his opposition to your bill might be less entrenched now than it will be if he has points of dispute prepared.

Your offer needs to give the paying party a discount which is big enough to encourage him to settle now, thereby avoiding liability to increasing interest, the expenses of instructing his own costs draftsman and the risk of having to pay just as much at the end of a detailed assessment, if only because of the costs of the detailed assessment proceedings.

On the other hand, if you offer too big a discount it might look as though you have little confidence in your claim, and if the offer is not accepted, the paying party's counter-offer may be lower than would otherwise have been the case.

There is no 'right' discount, so this book cannot give you any rule of thumb for working it out. That is why you need to do your own SWOT analysis (see 6.2). If the bill has to be assessed by the court you know that, however reasonable it may be, some reductions will almost certainly be made by the costs officer. Depending on the bill, the costs officer and various imponderables, in an ordinary case those reductions might be anything from 5 to 20 per cent of the profit costs, perhaps more, perhaps less.

If counsel was involved in the case, you may find that his clerk is willing to discount his fees in return for a speedy settlement. It is always worth speaking to him to find this out. The advantages of early payment are obvious, and if you are only asking counsel to offer the same discount on his fees as you are offering on yours, the arrangement is fair.

Although the pre-emptive offer does not have to be for a round sum, it often seems tidier to put one forward.

Worksheet 2 enables you to see the implications for the firm's profit costs of settling on the basis of a pre-emptive costs offer. **Worksheet 2** **CD-ROM 10.05**

- It is similar to worksheet 1, which calculates the total claimed, but it ends with the round sum which is to be put as the pre-emptive costs offer. **Worksheet 1** **CD-ROM 10.01**

- Both the profit costs and counsel's fees have been discounted to arrive at the offer figure. The percentages discounted are shown.

- Interest is, of course, now calculated on the substantive costs as discounted.

- Nothing is included for the costs of the detailed assessment proceedings, as no such costs can start accruing until the notice of commencement is served.

Do not show this calculation to the paying party. Leave him to guess how you arrived at the amount of the offer. Also, for reasons explained in chapter 14, you may want to avoid earmarking any particular part of the offer figure for interest.

7.4 When and how do we put the offer?

Make the offer at the same time as you serve the notice of commencement. This reduces the risk of the paying party getting on with preparing points of dispute before considering the offer.

The offer should be in writing. On the CD-ROM is a draft letter. Note that: **CD-ROM 08.01**

- The letter is headed 'without prejudice save as to the costs of the detailed assessment proceedings'. This means that the letter cannot be shown to the costs officer except at the end of any detailed assessment hearing, when he is considering who should pay the costs of the detailed assessment proceedings. **CPR 47.19(1)**

- There is a deadline for its acceptance. It avoids confusion if this is the same as the deadline for service of points of dispute. That gives the paying party 21 days to consider it, which is a reasonable period. If you give too short a period, he does not accept and the offer is eventually considered by the costs officer in deciding who should pay the costs of the detailed assessment proceedings, the costs officer may decide to ignore it.

- It provides for the automatic withdrawal of the offer even earlier than that, if the Defendant serves points of dispute.

- It sets out terms for the formal acceptance of the offer and payment of the agreed sum.

7.5 What should happen next?

As the pre-emptive offer will normally be made at the same time as the notice of commencement is served, see chapter 8 about the preparation of the notice.

If the pre-emptive offer causes the paying party to negotiate, see chapter 18.

If the pre-emptive offer is accepted, see chapter 19 for ways of securing the settlement and details of what needs to be done if there is a remaining claim for Legal Aid/LSC only assessment.

CHAPTER 8

Preparing the notice of commencement

The notice of commencement is the document that enables the receiving party to start the detailed assessment proceedings. The prescribed form is N252, which is reproduced in Appendix III and is also on the CD-ROM. This chapter tells you how to complete it.

Form N252
CPR 47.6(1)
CPD 32.8(1)
CPD 33.3
CD-ROM 04.01

8.1 The court heading

Take this from the pleadings in the substantive case.

8.2 The paying party

Delete whichever of 'claimant' or 'defendant' does not apply. If neither applies delete both, and in the space that follows insert the correct description of the paying party (eg 'appellant', 'respondent').

8.3 The order or event entitling you to detailed assessment

Insert a brief description and the date of the authority for detailed assessment (see 3.2); you should find both of these in the title to the bill. Examples are:

- 'order dated 16 December 2003'

- 'judgment dated 7 January 2004'

- 'notice of discontinuance served on 5 December 2003'

- 'acceptance on 22 January 2004 of a Part 36 payment into court made on 14 January 2004'

8.4 The total claimed by the bill

CPD 32.8(2)(a)

This is the total of all profit costs, counsel's fees, disbursements and VAT claimed in the bill between the parties.

You should find it in the summary at the end of the bill, but different costs draftsmen use different layouts, so make sure that you are looking at the correct figure. Be particularly careful if the bill claims some costs against the CLS Fund (with which you are not concerned at this point), as there should be a separate total for these. Be careful not to overlook the VAT, as in some bills this is not added to the other elements to show an overall total.

8.5 The figure if you succeed at a detailed assessment hearing

This figure is the bill total that you have just shown, plus the court fee payable on filing the request for detailed assessment. At the time of writing this is £160 for a county court case or £250 for a High Court one. **Table 3**

This figure presupposes that you would achieve 100 per cent success at a detailed assessment hearing, but – as the form makes clear – does not include either interest or the costs of the assessment hearing, to which you would almost certainly be entitled in those circumstances. It therefore gives the paying party no real idea of his potential liability should he contest the bill but achieve no significant reductions.

8.6 The deadline for serving points of dispute

The rules provide that this should be 'not less than 21 days from the date of service of the notice'. **CPR 47.9(2)** **CPD 32.9(2)**

To enable you to work out the correct date for the deadline, you need to know by what method you are going to serve the paying party. You will normally send the notice to their address for service by a method that you know will be acceptable to them. The rules are detailed and you need to check that you are complying with them. **CPR 6.1–6.7** **PDP6**

Noting that 'business day' means any day except Saturday, Sunday or a bank holiday; and 'bank holiday' includes Christmas Day and Good Friday, here is how you work out the date of service: **CPR 6.7(3)**

- **If you are serving the notice personally on the paying party before 5:00 pm on a business day:** service is effective that day. **CPR 6.4**

- **If you are serving the notice personally on the paying party after 5:00 pm on a business day or at any time on a Saturday, Sunday or a Bank Holiday:** it will be treated as served on the next business day. Thus, if you serve it at 6:00 pm on a Friday, and the following Monday is a bank holiday, it is deemed to have been served on the following Tuesday. **CPR 6.7(2)**

- **If you are serving the notice by delivering it to the paying party's address for service:** service is deemed to have taken place the day after you delivered it. Thus, if you deliver it on Monday, it is deemed to have been served on Tuesday. **CPR 6.7(1)**

- **If you are serving the notice by first class post:** service is deemed to have taken place on the second day after posting. Thus, if you post it on Monday, it is deemed to have been served on Wednesday.   CPR 6.7

- **If you are serving the notice by document exchange:** service is deemed to have taken place on the second day after it was left at the DX. Thus, if you put it in the DX on Monday, it is deemed to have been served on Wednesday.   CPR 6.7(1)

- **If you are serving the notice by faxing it before 4:00 pm on a business day:** service is deemed to have taken place that day.   CPR 6.7(1)

- **If you are serving the notice by faxing after 4:00 pm on a business day or on a non-business day:** service is deemed to have taken place on the next business day   CPR 6.7(1)

- **If you are serving the notice by 'other electronic method' (eg e-mail):** service is deemed to have taken place the second day after the day on which it is transmitted. Thus, if you e-mail it on Monday, it is deemed to have been served on Wednesday.   CPR 6.7(1)

The 21 days are 'clear days', ie you leave out the day on which the notice was served and the last day of the period, so if the notice is served on 2 October the last day for service of points of dispute is 24 October.   CPR 2.8

If in doubt, add an extra day for safety; it is better to be generous at this stage than to find you have applied for a default costs certificate prematurely.

The time limit can be extended by agreement or by order of the court (eg if you do not agree and the paying party has to make an application).   CPR 2.11
CPR 3.1(2)(a)
CPD 35.1

There are special rules for calculating the time limit if you are serving someone outside England and Wales.   *CPD32.9*

8.7 Other persons on whom you serve the notice

You must serve the notice of commencement on 'any other relevant persons specified in the costs practice direction'. This means: CPR 47.6(2)
CPD 32.10

- Any person who has taken part in the proceedings which gave rise to the assessment and who is directly liable under an order for costs made against him (eg a co-defendant or a third party).   *CPD 32.10(1)(a)*

- Any person who has given you written notice that he has a financial interest in the outcome of the assessment and wishes to be a party accordingly.   *CPD 32.10(1)(b)*

• Any other person whom the court orders to be treated as such.   *CPD 32.10(1)(c)*

You should give the name and address for service of every other per-   *CPD 32.3(e)*
son on whom you are serving the notice of commencement, otherwise   *CPD 32.4(d)*
you will have to provide this information in a separate statement – see
9.5(g).

The rules enable you to apply to the court for directions if you are not   *CPD 32.10(2)–(3)*
sure whether a person is a 'relevant person'.

An LSC-funded client who has an interest in the detailed assessment   **CPR 47.6(2)**
(ie because costs not recovered from the paying party might be recov-   *CPD 32.10*
ered from the CLS Fund and therefore eventually be borne by him)
does not seem to fall within the definition of a 'relevant person', so
you do not need to name him in the notice of commencement.
Nevertheless, it can be convenient to serve him with the notice of commencement at this point – see 10.3.

8.8 The figure if you obtain a default costs certificate   *CPD 32.8(2)(b)*

This is the bill total that you have shown as the first figure in the form,   *CPD 37.8*
plus £120 (ie the court fee of £40 payable on applying for a default   **Table 3**
costs certificate plus fixed costs of £80). The court fee and fixed costs
are the same whether the case is in the county court or the High Court.

8.9 Signature

To avoid repetition later in this book, it is worth looking in detail now
at the question of who may validly sign formal documents in the
detailed assessment proceedings.

Most such documents may be signed by the party or by his legal   **CPR 2.3(1)**
representative, which means 'a barrister or a solicitor, solicitor's
employee or other authorised litigator … who has been instructed to
act for a party in relation to a claim'.

According to CPD 1.5, in respect of any document required by the   **PDP 22**
CPD to be signed by a party or his legal representative, PDP22 will   **CPR 32.14**
apply as if the document in question was a statement of case (CPD 1.5   *CPD 1.5*
uses the phrase 'statement of truth', apparently in error).

Because a statement of case should be verified by a statement of
truth, the effect of the signature is the same as if the document
contained a statement of truth (which means that a person who signs
without an honest belief in the truth of the document is liable to proceedings for contempt of court).

A document drafted by a 'legal representative' should bear his signature. If drafted by a legal representative as a member or employee of a

firm it should be signed in the name of the firm.

While an 'in-house' costs draftsman actually employed by a firm of solicitors would be considered a 'legal representative', so could properly sign in the name of the firm, this would not apply to a free-lance costs draftsman.

Note that special rules apply to:

• the certificates in the bill of costs;

• points of dispute; and

• replies to points of dispute.

These must be signed either by the party or by his solicitor. Signature by a non-solicitor employee will not do.

8.10 Dating

Do not forget to date the form (and also your file copy of it, as you will need to produce complete copies if you later apply for a default costs certificate or for a detailed assessment hearing).

8.11 What should we do next?

You will now need to prepare the supporting documents to serve with the notice of commencement; this is explained in chapter 9.

CHAPTER 9

Assembling the supporting documents

9.1 What has to be served with the notice of commencement?

To know what has to be served with the notice of commencement – form N252 – you first need to know what kind of costs are being claimed against the paying party. The bill might claim:

• base costs only;

• an additional liability only; or

• both base costs and an additional liability.

'Base costs' means just the ordinary costs claimed from the paying party, ie all the costs other than an additional liability.   *CPR 43.2(1)(a)*
  'Additional liability' means: *CPD 2.2*

• the success fee payable under a conditional fee agreement; and/or   *CPR 43.2(1)(l)&(o)*

• the premium payable for 'after the event' insurance against liability for costs in the proceedings; and/or   *CPR 43.2(1)(m)&(o)*

• the 'additional amount in respect of provision made by a membership organisation.'   *CPR 43.2(1)(n)&(o)*

You should be able to find out from the bill which kind of case it is. The details of funding arrangements given in the background information should, at least, tell you whether there was a conditional fee agreement. You may need to hunt elsewhere in the bill to find exactly what kind of additional liabilities are claimed.
  If the conditional fee agreement was made before 1 April 2000 you cannot recover the additional liability from the paying party, so it should not be shown in the bill, which should claim base costs only.

9.2 If base costs only are to be assessed

You will need to serve with the N252 a copy of: *CPD 32.3(a)*

• The bill.   *CPD 32.3(b)*

• The order or authority for detailed assessment.

• Counsel's fee-notes (if counsel was used).   *CPD 32.3(c)*

- Experts' fee-notes (if any).   *CPD 32.3(c)*

- Evidence of any other disbursements over £250.   *CPD 32.3(d)*

- 'A statement giving the name and address for service of any person   *CPD 32.3(e)*
  upon whom the receiving party intends to serve the notice of commencement.'

9.3 If additional liabilities only are to be assessed

You will need to serve with the N252 a copy of: *CPD 32.4(a)*

- The bill.   *CPD 32.4(b)*

- The order or authority for detailed assessment.

- Relevant details of the additional liability.   *CPD 32.4(c)*

- 'A statement giving the name and address for service of any person   *CPD 32.4(d)*
  upon whom the receiving party intends to serve the notice of commencement.'

9.4 If both base costs and additional liabilities are to be assessed

You will need to serve with the N252 a copy of: *CPD 32.7*

- The bill.

- The order or authority for detailed assessment.

- Counsel's fee-notes (if counsel was used).

- Experts' fee-notes (if any).

- Evidence of any other disbursements over £250.

- Relevant details of the additional liability.

- 'A statement giving the name and address for service of any person
  upon whom the receiving party intends to serve the notice of commencement.'

9.5 How should we prepare the supporting documents?

It is good practice to prepare a front-sheet for each supporting docu-   **CD-ROM 06.02**
ment or bundle, as this makes it easier for both the costs officer and
you to identify them in the heat of a detailed assessment hearing. An

example is on the CD-ROM. The bill should already have its own title page or front-sheet.

You never need to supply originals at this stage, so make sure that you keep the original bill and the originals of the other supporting documents in the file in case you need to prepare further copies later (either for the court or for the client).

(a) The bill

CPD 32.3(b)

Before taking a copy for service check that the title page shows:

- the full court heading, with the correct case number; — *CPD 4.4(1)*

- whose bill it is, ie who the receiving party is; — *CPD 4.4(2)*

- the authority for detailed assessment (see 3.2); — *CPD 4.4(2)*

- if the client was legally aided/LSC funded, the reference number of his certificate, the date it was issued, the dates of any amendments and the date of discharge or revocation (if it has happened); and — *CPD 4.4(4)*

- your firm's VAT registration number. — *CPD 4.4(3)*

CPD 5.2

Also check the certificates at the end of the bill to make sure that:

- The relevant ones have been included and have been ticked/deleted/modified as necessary. The references below are to the certificates in the form in which they appear in Precedent F in the Schedule of Costs Precedents. Your bill may have been supplied with these certificates tailored to the particular case. — *CPD 4.15* **Precedent F** **CD-ROM 01.09**

- Those certificates which can sensibly be signed at this stage – certificates (1) 'as to accuracy' and (2) 'as to interest and payments' – have been signed. The certificates may be signed either by the receiving party or by his solicitor. It is no longer essential to have a bill signed by a partner; a solicitor employed by the firm will do. However, although most documents used in detailed assessment proceedings may now be validly signed by a non-solicitor employee of the firm – see 8.9 – this concession does not apply to the bill itself. — **PDP 22** **CPR 32.14** *CPD 1.5*

- If the bill claims the costs of previous firms of solicitors, it includes the relevant certificate as to accuracy signed by them.

Finally, check that any schedule of times spent, if not attached to the bill, accompanies it. — *CPD 4.12*

(b) The authority for detailed assessment

• Include a copy of every order in the proceedings that specifically entitles the client to costs. If there were any orders for the summary assessment of costs you may include copies for information.

• Include a copy of the relevant notice if the authority for detailed assessment is in receipt of notice of discontinuance or notice of acceptance of Part 36 offer or payment-in.

(c) Counsel's fee-notes

CPD 32.3(c)

• On the fee-note, mark the individual fees charged by counsel with the relevant item numbers in the bill. This enables you to double-check that all the fees claimed have been included in the bill. The court staff will appreciate this if and when the bill is lodged for detailed assessment, as they would otherwise have to do this themselves.

• It does not matter if counsel's fees have not yet been paid.

(d) Experts' fee-notes

CPD 32.3(c–d)

• 'Experts' means expert witnesses engaged to provide opinions in the case, eg medical experts, engineers, employment consultants. It does not include factual witnesses or the providers of medical records, police accident reports etc.

• Include a copy of every experts' fee-note, whatever the amount.

• Mark each fee-note, or separate fee, with the relevant item number in the bill. This enables you to double-check that all the fees claimed have been included in the bill.

• You do not need to prove at this stage that the fees have been paid, although if they are shown in the bill as 'paid' that is a representation that they have been.

(e) Evidence of other disbursements over £250

CPD 32.3(c)–(d)

• Although the bill may contain a certificate that all disbursements 'which individually do not exceed £500' have been paid, you still need to provide 'written evidence as to any disbursement which is claimed and which exceeds £250'.

• 'Evidence' can include a copy of a letter paying a fee for which the fee-note has been lost.

• The 'evidence' is to show the amount; you do not need to prove at this stage that the fees have been paid, although if they are shown in the bill as 'paid' that is a representation that they have been.

(f) Relevant details of the additional liability

CPD 32.4

If the additional liability is a conditional fee agreement with a success fee, you need to prepare a statement showing:

CPD 32.5(1)

• the amount of costs (if any) which have already been summarily assessed or agreed, and the percentage increase which has been claimed in respect of those costs;

CPD 32.5(1)(a)

• the reasons for the percentage increase given in accordance with regulation 3(1)(a) of the Conditional Fee Agreements Regulations 2000 or regulation 5(1)(c) of the Collective Conditional Fee Regulations 2000 (you should find these reasons set out in the conditional fee agreement itself).

CPD 32.5(1)(b)

• In *Hollins v Russell and others ('The CFA Test Cases')* [2003] EWCA Civ 718 at paragraph 220, the Court of Appeal ruled that a receiving party who relies on a conditional fee agreement, with or without a success fee, will ordinarily have to disclose it to the paying party in the detailed assessment proceedings. It will therefore save trouble if you provide a complete copy for disclosure now.

• If the conditional fee agreement contains information that you can reasonably object to disclosing (eg confidential information relating to other proceedings), you can serve an edited version, omitting the confidential information.

• In any event, to avoid embarrassment later, check the conditional fee agreement very carefully, before disclosing it, to make sure that it complies with the Conditional Fee Agreement Regulations 2000. Since the judgment in *The CFA Test Cases* the only kinds of non-compliance that might cause the agreement to be unenforceable (and prevent you from recovering the profit costs incurred under it) are ones which are considered to have a harmful effect on the protection given to the client or on the administration of justice.

On the CD-ROM is a specimen statement.
If the additional liability is an after the event insurance premium, you

CD-ROM 06.03
CPD 32.5

should provide a copy of the insurance certificate showing:

• whether the policy covers the receiving party's own costs, his oppo- | *CPD 32.5(2)*
nent's costs, or his own costs and his opponent's costs;

• the maximum extent of that cover; and

• the amount of premium paid or payable.

If the additional liability is the additional amount recoverable pursuant | *CPD 32.5(3)*
to s30 Access to Justice Act 1999 (in respect of a membership organi- | *CPD 32.6*
sation), you should provide a statement setting out the basis upon
which the receiving party's liability for the additional amount is calculated. There are limits on the amount recoverable

(g) Statement of persons being served

Provided you have stated in the notice of commencement the name
and address for service of every other person upon whom you are serving it, you will not need to prepare a separate statement with this information.

9.6 What should we NOT serve with it?

If either or both of the next two bundles are appropriate to the circumstances of the case, prepare them now even though you may not be
serving them until later, if at all. This will probably save time overall.

(a) Legal Aid/LSC documents

Keep this bundle back unless and until you need to apply for a detailed
assessment hearing. Even then do not serve it on the paying party, as
they are not entitled to know any details of the client's Legal Aid/LSC
funding beyond the date on which the certificate was issued, the proceedings which it covered, and the date on which it was discharged.
They ought to know those details from the notices served on them during the proceedings. This bundle is purely for the benefit of the costs
officer.

Include in this bundle a copy of:

• The latest version of the Legal Aid/Public Funding certificate, which
should show all the amendments; and

• Any specific authorities issued by the LAB/LSC (eg to instruct
experts and incur their fees). These will be usually be in the form of
letters.

(b) Retainer documents

Keep this bundle back unless and until:

* you need to apply for a detailed assessment hearing; and/or

* there is a disagreement (raised in the points of dispute and not disposed of by the replies) about whether the paying party is liable, under the indemnity principle, for all the costs being claimed.

Include in this bundle a copy of any:

* client care letter or terms of business;

* conditional fee agreement (if you have not already disclosed it – see 9.5(f));

* letters increasing the hourly charging rates; and

* interim bills rendered to the client.

Although, in particular circumstances, you may be able to argue that parts of these documents are privileged from disclosure (see 34.5), recent case law is generally against you – see *Hollins v Russell and others* (*The CFA Test Cases*) [2003] EWCA Civ 718 at paragraphs 51–87. So, if the paying party insists on seeing the retainer documents, you may do better to disclose them voluntarily rather than argue the point at the hearing.

9.7 What should we do next?

The next step is to serve the notice of commencement – see chapter 10.

CHAPTER 10

Serving the notice of commencement

10.1 Why calculate the interest now?

Interest will probably play an important part in any negotiations over the costs, so you need to make sure that the paying party is always aware of how it is mounting up. While the notice of commencement mentions interest, it does not enable you to show the amount of it, so it is helpful to prepare a separate calculation of the total claimed, including interest to date.

Worksheet 1 is a worked example presenting this total. The CD-ROM includes:

Worksheet 1

• this straightforward version;

CD-ROM 10.01

• a version where the paying party has already made a payment on account of costs;

CD-ROM 10.02

• a version for cases where there is a conditional fee agreement providing for a success fee; and

CD-ROM 10.03

• a version for cases where two firms have acted for the receiving party.

CD-ROM 10.04

Note that:

• the costs claim is reduced to its basic ingredients, which you can extract from the bill;

• the total of your calculation should be the same as the total shown in the bill summary as claimed between the parties (although if you are a few pence adrift because of the way the VAT was added in the bill, this does not matter);

• interest is calculated on the substantive costs only. If the order for payment of costs was made before 2 December 2002 you can also claim interest on the costs of detailed assessment – see 14.3(a);

• nothing is claimed at this stage for the costs of detailed assessment, as none can be incurred until the notice of commencement has been served – see 1.13.

Calculate the interest as follows:

• The amount on which you calculate it is the total of the substantive costs.

• The rate at which you calculate it is the statutory rate (currently 8 per cent per annum – see 2.7(a) for how to check this) or such other rate as the court specified in the order for costs.

• The period for which you calculate it begins with the date of the order for costs (unless that order specifies some other date) and ends with the date on which you think you will serve the notice of commencement.

• If you have received a payment on account, you have to do a two-stage calculation, with interest calculated on the full amount up to the date you received the payment on account, and on the balance thereafter.

10.2 What should go in the covering letter to the paying party?

List the enclosures to reduce the risk of omitting any. These will normally be:

• the notice of commencement, signed and dated;

• a copy of the bill;

• the other enclosures – see 9.2–9.4; and

• your calculation of the amount claimed.

If the paying party has not already made an adequate payment on account of the costs, threaten to apply for an interim costs certificate if they do not make a payment on account within the next, say, fourteen days.

• You can ask for as much as you like, but do not expect to get more than 50–75 per cent of the total claimed.

• Ask for the payment to be made 'on the basis that it is not just a payment on account of the amount which will finally be found to be due from your client to ours, but that we are free to apply it in part-payment of the profit costs, counsel's fees, other disbursements and VAT claimed in the bill'. The reasons for this request are explained at 15.3.

There is a draft letter on the CD-ROM.   **CD-ROM 08.02**

10.3 Do we need to serve the client?

(a) If the client is legally aided/LSC funded

They will almost certainly have an interest in the detailed assessment, because the statutory charge may apply to money or property recovered or preserved in the proceedings. This means that they may end up paying some or all of the costs not recovered from the paying party out of their damages. You will therefore have to serve them with a copy of the bill before you can apply for a detailed assessment hearing. Although the rules do not require you to serve such a client with the notice of commencement etc at this stage (see 8.7), it can be a good idea to do it anyway because:

- it saves time to deal with this while you are preparing the documents for service on the paying party;

- it saves a potential delay if you have to apply for a detailed assessment hearing, as you will certainly have to serve the client by that stage, and perhaps also wait for their response; and

- it can help to prepare them for the costs negotiations and, perhaps, enable you to manage their expectations as to the eventual outcome.

(b) If the client is privately paying, or covered by a conditional fee agreement (other than a 'CFA Lite')

They are likely to have to pay some or all of any shortfall between the costs claimed from the paying party and the costs eventually recovered, so will need to be consulted over any proposed settlement. It is therefore generally helpful to involve them in the process from the beginning.

By 'CFA Lite' is meant the type of conditional fee agreement made possible by the Conditional Fee Agreements (Miscellaneous Amendments) Regulations 2003, under which the solicitor is paid only what he is able to recover from the paying party, and the client has no liability in respect of any shortfall.

10.4 What do we need to tell the client?

Because both the bill and the detailed assessment process are complicated, an explanation of both is likely to be long, as it may include:

- An explanation of the layout of the bill.

- Information as to the next steps in the process.

- Forewarnings about objections, offers and negotiations.

- Indications as to what might happen at the detailed assessment hearing.

- If the client is legally aided/LSC funded, an explanation of 'the extent of his financial interest and the steps which can be taken to safeguard that interest' (ie as to the possible application of the statutory charge). See regulation 119(1) of the Civil Legal Aid (General) Regulations 1989.

On the CD-ROM are draft covering letters:

- To a legally-aided/LSC funded client.   **CD-ROM 09.01**

- To a client with a conditional fee agreement.   **CD-ROM 09.02**

- To a privately paying client.   **CD-ROM 09.03**

If you want to use these, adapt them generally, so that they reflect your firm's style and the usual layout of your bills. They can then be saved as standard templates.

Those standard letter templates can then be more easily adapted to suit the circumstances of each particular bill and case.

10.5 Do we need a reply from the client?

Normally, you do not need any response from the client. However, if the client is legally aided/LSC funded it is helpful to have a formal response from him, indicating whether or not he has any comments to make on the bill and whether he would like the court to give him notice of any detailed assessment hearing.

On the CD-ROM is a draft response form, which can be adapted to   **CD-ROM 06.04**
suit the particular case. Although it is addressed to the court, you will want the client to return it to you, so that you can lodge it with the bill etc if you need to apply for a detailed assessment hearing.

10.6 What if we did not serve all the requisite documents?

(a) Omissions generally

The omission of one or more of the supporting documents (eg one of the expert's fee-notes) may not seem particularly serious and will usually be picked up when points of dispute are served and remedied when they are answered. However, if you obtain a default costs certificate on the strength of a notice of commencement that was not served with all the right supporting documents, an application by the paying party to have it set aside may stand a better chance of success. So, if you realise that something was omitted, it might be safest to serve it on the paying party as soon as you can and voluntarily extend his time for service of points of dispute until 21 days after the service of that item.

(b) Omission of relevant details of the additional liability

Failure to serve these details (see 9.5(f)) can put you in a more difficult position, as CPR 44.3B provides that the receiving party may not recover as an additional liability:

CPR 44.3B(1)

• any additional liability for any period in the proceedings during which he failed to provide information about a funding arrangement in accordance with a rule, practice direction or court order; or

CPR 44.3B(1)(c)

• any percentage increase where he has failed to comply with a requirement in the CPD or a court order to disclose in any assessment proceedings the reasons for setting the percentage increase at the level stated in the conditional fee agreement.

CPR 44.3B(1)(d)

You are not able to remedy such a failure by sending on the relevant details later, because this is a case where the sanction imposed by CPR 44.3B takes effect unless you apply for and obtain relief from it by

CPD 10.1

• making an 'ordinary' application (see chapter 25) to the court which is dealing with the case, applying for relief from the sanction; and

• supporting the application with evidence, which should meet the requirements of CPR 3.9.

CPR 3.9

If the amount of any percentage increase recoverable by counsel may be affected by the outcome of your application, you should serve on counsel a copy of the application notice and notice of the hearing as soon as practicable and in any event at least two days before the hearing. Counsel may send in written submissions or may attend and make oral ones.

CPD 10.2

However, if the paying party is co-operative, a cheaper and easier solution would be to obtain his consent to the withdrawal of the bill (see 28.3) or, at least, his agreement that the original service of the notice of commencement was ineffective. This would allow you to serve another notice of commencement, this time with all the requisite documents. You may need to offer some concession on interest as the price of his co-operation (see 3.5).

10.7 What should happen next?

(a) If you are making a pre-emptive offer

If you are making a pre-emptive costs offer (see chapter 7) then, for best effect, you should send it at the same time as you serve the notice of commencement, so:

• diarise the time for its acceptance;

• if it is accepted, decide whether you need to take any further steps to secure the settlement – see chapter 19; or

• if it is not accepted, the paying party will need to serve points of dispute – see (b) below.

(b) Whether or not you are making a pre-emptive offer

Diarise the deadline for service of points of dispute - see 8.6.

If, before the deadline, the paying party serves points of dispute, you will need to:

• check them – see chapter 20;

• value them – see chapter 21; and

• reply to them – see chapter 22.

If the deadline expires and the paying party has not served points of dispute, you can:

• request a default costs certificate – see chapter 11; and

• if there are any costs claimed only against the CLS Fund, proceed with their assessment – see chapter 37.

CHAPTER 11

Requesting a default costs certificate

11.1 What does a default costs certificate do?

A default costs certificate orders a paying party who has not served points of dispute to pay the costs at the amount claimed between the parties in the bill, plus £120 fixed costs and interest. Unless it is set aside by the court (see chapter 13) it brings an end to the detailed assessment proceedings between the parties. **CPR 47.11(2)–(3)**

If you have a bill which includes some costs claimed against the CLS Fund only, you can continue with an 'LSC only' detailed assessment of those costs even if you have obtained a default costs certificate in respect of the costs claimed between the parties – see chapter 37. **CPD 37.5**

However, if the bill claims everything between the parties and nothing specifically against the CLS Fund, there will be no need for a separate 'LSC only' detailed assessment, as there is nothing more for you to recover.

11.2 When can we request one?

You can request a default costs certificate immediately after the 21st day from service of the notice of commencement if you have not been served with any points of dispute. If the time for service of points of dispute has been extended (either by agreement between the parties or by order of the court) the earliest you can request one is immediately after the last day of the extended time. See 8.6 as to calculation of times **CPR 47.9(4)** **CPR 2.11** **CPR 3.1(2)(a)** **CPD 35.1**

If there is more than one paying party, and one of them serves points of dispute in time, but the other does not, you may not request a default costs certificate against the one who is late. However, he will not be entitled to be heard at the detailed assessment hearing without the court's permission – see 20.1. **CPR 47.9(3)** **CPR 47.14(6)**

If you receive a document purporting to be points of dispute, but you suspect that it does not comply with the rules, see 20.2–20.3 for the options open to you.

11.3 How do we request one?

(a) The form

Prepare a request in form N254. This is reproduced in Appendix III **CPR 47.11(1)** and a blank version is on the CD-ROM. The form is the same whether the case is in the High Court or the county court.

CPD 37.1.(1)
Form N254
CD-ROM 04.02

(b) The court

The court at which to file the request is the District Registry or county court where the substantive case was proceeding or, in any other case, the SCCO.

CPD 37.2
CPD 31.1

(c) The court heading

This is the same as in the N252.

(d) Name of paying party

Insert their name in the space provided. This will normally be the defendant, but check the beginning of the N252 if you are not sure.

(e) Details of other parties served

You can copy these from the N252 or, if they were not shown there, from the statement of persons being served – see 9.5(g).

(f) Date of service of N252.

See 8.6 for the rules on working out the effective date of service.

(g) Signature

The request may be signed by the receiving party or his legal representative – see 8.9.

(h) The fee

This is currently £40.00, whether in the county court (fee number 3.3) or in the High Court (fee number 10.3). The cheque should be made payable to 'HMPG'.

Table 3

(i) Attachments

You must attach to the N254 a copy of the notice of commencement and a copy 'of the document giving the right to detailed assessment' – see 3.2.

CPD 37(2)

11.4 Who prepares the default costs certificate?

(a) The choice

Although the court will prepare and serve the default costs certificate, you are allowed to do it yourself – at least in county court cases. This should be quicker and time may be of the essence (see 13.1).

CPR 40.3
CPR 40.4
CPD 37.4

(b) The forms

The default costs certificate is in form N255, of which there are two varieties (to reflect the different enforcement regimes). The county court form (N255) is reproduced in Appendix III and is also on the CD-ROM, although neither this nor the High Court version (N255HC), is now made available by the Court Service. Presumably the court prefers to draw up the certificate.

If you are preparing the form, do so in triplicate.

CPD 37.3
Form N255
CD-ROM 04.03
Form N255HC

(c) The court heading

This is the same as in the N254, except that there is now a box for the date, which you should leave blank for the court to fill in.

(d) The Defendant's solicitors

Delete any inapplicable words and insert their name and address in the box provided. You will find them in the covering letter with which the N252 was served, but check that the defendant has not changed his address for service since then. Sometimes defendants instruct new solicitors at this stage, instructing costs negotiators at the same time.

(e) The total sum payable

Delete the inapplicable party and insert the total sum payable. This is the figure stated in the notice of commencement as the amount for which you will ask the court to issue a default costs certificate, ie it is the total claimed in the bill between the parties, plus fixed costs of £120. These fixed costs consist of:

• The court fee of £40, which you are about to pay.

CPD 37.8

• Costs of £80 (which works out at £68.09 profit costs and £11.91 VAT at the current rate of 17.5 per cent).

CPD 25.1

If the fixed costs have gone up since you served the notice of commencement, you are tied to the amount specified in it.

CPD 25.2

You do not include interest in this calculation, presumably because it is a statutory entitlement, so does not need to be specifically ordered. As mentioned at 1.11, there is an inconsistency between the CPR and CPD as to what these fixed costs are meant to cover:

CPR 47.11(3)
CPD 37.8

- CPR 47.11(3) states that 'Where a receiving party obtains a default costs certificate, the costs payable to him for the commencement of detailed assessment proceedings shall be the sum set out in the costs practice direction', while

CPR 47.11(3)

- CPD 37.8 states that 'The fixed costs payable in respect of solicitor's charges on the issue of the default costs certificate are £80.'

CPD 37.8

CPD 37.8 is the more recent provision and it reflects the general principle (see 1.10) that the costs of the detailed assessment proceedings begin only with service (not preparation) of the notice of commencement. On that basis, the costs of preparing and serving the notice of commencement must be part of the substantive costs, so it would be odd if these fixed costs were to be treated as part of the costs of the detailed assessment proceedings, when they are inevitably incurred before the start of those proceedings.

Until this inconsistency in the rules is removed, perhaps the best approach is:

- to see that the costs of preparing and serving the notice of commencement are routinely claimed in bills as part of the substantive costs (it does not follow from the fact that they are not mentioned in the 'model' forms of bill that it would be wrong to claim them in this way); and

- to treat the £80 fixed costs as the costs merely of preparing and filing the request for the issue of a default costs certificate (which is implied by the wording of CPD 37.8).

CPD 37.8

(f) Date from which entitlement to interest begins

This is usually the date of the order or event giving rise to the detailed assessment, but you will have checked this when calculating the total due when serving the notice of commencement – see 3.2.

(g) Address for payment

Insert the receiving party's address for service.

(h) Court details

Insert the address and telephone number of the court.

11.5 How should we file the request?

On the CD-ROM is a draft covering letter to the court. **CD-ROM 07.02**
As the court must set the default costs certificate aside if points of dispute are received before it has been issued, even if they are received after the time for service has expired, it is best to deliver the request to the court personally and ask if they will seal the default costs certificate on the spot.

11.6 What should happen next?

You should receive the sealed and dated default costs certificate from the court.

If you have not received any points of dispute before the date of the default costs certificate, you should proceed to serve it as explained in chapter 12.

If points of dispute arrive late, check the date on which they were served on you:

- If this was *after* the date on which the default costs certificate was issued, you can ignore them unless and until the paying party succeeds in having the default costs certificate set aside, so proceed to serve it as explained in chapter 12.

- If this was *before* the date on which the default costs certificate was **CPR 47.9(5)** issued, you must apply for the default costs certificate to be set aside – see 13.1.

CHAPTER 12

Serving the default costs certificate

12.1 How much is payable under the certificate?

Worksheet 3 sets out the total claimed, but this is modified from earlier worksheets to show:

Worksheet 3

• the fixed costs awarded on the default costs certificate;

• interest calculated to date (check that no payments on account, or additional payments on account, have arrived since the notice of commencement was served); and

• a daily rate of interest.

The CD-ROM includes:

• this straightforward version;

CD-ROM 10.06

• a version where the paying party has already made a payment on account of costs;

CD-ROM 10.07

• a version for cases where there is a conditional fee agreement providing for a success fee; and

CD-ROM 10.08

• a version for cases where two firms have acted for the receiving party.

CD-ROM 10.09

12.2 What should we say in the covering letter?

You should:

• enclose a sealed copy of the default costs certificate;

• enclose the calculation of the amount due; and

• ask for a cheque for the total due (including interest to the date on which they calculate you will receive their cheque).

On the CD-ROM is a draft covering letter to the paying party.

CD-ROM 08.03

12.3 What if they do not pay?

Payment is due within 14 days from the date of the order. If it fails to arrive, you can take enforcement action, but that topic is outside the scope of this book.

CPR 40.11

CPD 37.6

However, the paying party can apply to have enforcement action stayed (ie delayed). They are likely to do this if they apply to have the default costs certificate set aside, but they might also do it if they simply want time to pay.

12.4 What if there are also 'LSC only' costs?

The issue of a default costs certificate only affects the costs claimed between the parties. If the bill includes some costs claimed against the CLS Fund only, you can continue with an 'LSC only' assessment of those costs (see chapter 43) even if you have obtained a default costs certificate in respect of the costs claimed between the parties.

CPD 37.5

But if you have claimed everything between the parties and nothing specifically against the CLS Fund, there will be no need for a separate 'LSC only' assessment, as there is nothing further to recover.

CHAPTER 13

When a default costs certificate can be set aside

13.1 When *must* the court set it aside?

The court *must* set a default costs certificate aside 'if the receiving party was not entitled to it'.

CPR 47.12(1)

You will turn out not to have been entitled to it if you discover, after the issue of the default costs certificate, that the paying party did not receive the notice of commencement at least 21 days before the issue of the default costs certificate.

CPR 47.12(3)

CPD 38.4

In those circumstances you must:

• file a request for the default costs certificate to be set aside; or

CPR 47.12(3)(c)(i)

• apply to the court for directions.

CPR 47.12(3)(c)(ii)

If you decide to ask for the default costs certificate to be set aside, you can presumably make the request by letter (rather than by filing a formal application notice – on which you would have to pay a fee), as in these circumstances a court officer has authority to set the default costs certificate aside. The matter does not have to go before a costs officer.

CPD 38.1(1)

If the default costs certificate is set aside upon your request, you appear bound to lose both the court fee you paid when applying for the default costs certificate and the fixed costs awarded by it, unless the matter eventually goes to a detailed assessment hearing and you include these items in your claim for the costs of the detailed assessment proceedings in the hope that the costs officer will allow them.

If, instead of requesting that the default costs certificate be set aside, you apply to the court for directions, you could seek an order that the paying party pay your costs thrown away. However, as the court is not bound to make such an order you may conclude that the risk does not justify the work involved in applying for directions if that is the only issue you want to put before the court. Directions cannot be given by a court officer, but must be given by a costs officer.

CPD 38.1(2)

A less risky alternative approach would be to wait until the paying party makes an application to the court for permission 'to be heard further in the detailed assessment proceedings' (see 20.3(c)). When that application is heard you can ask for an order that he pays the costs thrown away on applying for the default costs certificate as well as the costs of his application.

CPR 47.9(3)

If it turns out that you did indeed lodge your application for a default costs certificate prematurely, but that by the time the default costs certificate was issued by the court the full 21 days had elapsed since service of the notice of commencement and the paying party had still had not served points of dispute, you would seem to be under no obligation to ask for the certificate to be set aside. However, the paying party may still apply for it to be set aside – see 13.2.

If, for example, you have a dispute with the paying party over the facts, or they threaten to apply for the default costs certificate to be set aside, you may decide to seek directions.

In these circumstances it would be worthwhile trying to agree the directions, as:

• you will avoid the costs and uncertain outcome of a hearing; and

• the court fee on filing a consent order is currently £30, but the court fee on filing an application notice is £60.

On the CD-ROM are standard forms of order, taken from the SCCO Guide (at Appendix A-4 on pages 143–146), which you may find useful in drafting proposed directions for:

• a conditional order; or — **CD-ROM 06.05**

• an unconditional order. — **CD-ROM 06.06**

If you cannot agree the directions with the paying party, you will need to:

• file a formal application notice;

• pay a court fee of £60;

• supply a draft of the order you would like the court to make.

If you were not entitled to the default costs certificate then, until it has either been set aside or the court has given directions, you can take no further steps in: — **CPR 47.12(4)**

• the detailed assessment proceedings; or — **CPR 47.12(4)(a)**

• the enforcement of the default costs certificate. — **CPR 47.12(4)(b)**

13.2 When *may* the court set it aside?

The court *may* set the default costs certificate aside if the paying party: — **CPR 47.12(2)**

• applies for it to be set aside; and

• supports the application with 'evidence.' *CPD 38.2(1)*

Generally, the court will exercise its discretion in the paying party's favour if he:

• applies promptly; *CPD 38.2(2)*

• shows 'a good reason' for the court to set it aside; and *CPD 38.2(3)*

• files with his application (a) a copy of the bill, (b) a copy of the default costs certificate and (c) a draft of the points of dispute he will serve if his application is granted. *CPD 38.2(3)*

13.3 How should we prepare for the hearing?

(a) Negotiate

If the paying party is at fault, he cannot be sure of getting the default costs certificate set aside, so negotiate hard for a settlement covering:

• the substantive costs claimed in the bill;

• interest on those costs;

• the costs of your application for a default costs certificate; and

• the costs of his application to have it set aside.

See chapter 18 about negotiating.

The paying party always runs the risk that, if the matter ends up with a detailed assessment hearing, he will have to pay the costs of the detailed assessment proceedings. However, if he fails to settle at this point, he runs the additional risks:

• that he will lose the application, and have to pay everything you are claiming in the bill, plus your costs of his application; or

• that he will win the application, but possibly subject to onerous conditions, and might still have to pay the costs of it and spend money on having proper points of dispute prepared.

If these overall negotiations fail, and you think the paying party stands a reasonable chance of succeeding in his application, try to agree directions with him, in order to avoid the costs and uncertainties of a hearing.

(b) Prepare documents to support your case

If the issues are complicated or the facts are disputed, it may be helpful to prepare some or all of the following for use at the hearing:

• a chronology (agreed if possible) of the relevant dates and events;

• a bundle of the relevant correspondence and documents;

• a skeleton argument;

• a statement by the fee-earner responsible for the matter.

(c) Should we prepare a statement of our costs?

If the receiving party is legally aided/LSC funded, or if the other circumstances mentioned at 50.6 and 50.7 exist, the court will not make a summary assessment of his costs, so there is no need to prepare a statement of them.   *CPD 13.9*

In other cases whether you should file and serve your schedule of costs is debatable, as there is an apparent inconsistency in the rules:

• The general rule is that if you intend to claim the costs of a hearing lasting not more than one day, you should file your statement at court and serve it on the paying party not less than 24 hours before the day of the hearing – see 50.8.   *CPD 13.5*

• However, because this application is an application 'in the detailed assessment proceedings' the costs of it are costs of the detailed assessment proceedings and CPD 45.3 states that 'No party should file or serve a statement of costs of the detailed assessment proceedings unless the court orders him to do so.'   *CPD 45.3*

One possible solution would be to write to the court before the hearing:

• pointing out that CPD 13.2 states that 'The general rule is that the court should make a summary assessment of the costs … unless there is good reason not to do so';   *CPD 13.2*

• that the general prohibition on filing and serving a statement of costs contained in CPD 45.3 must constitute 'good reason';   *CPD 45.3*

• that if the court directs you to file and serve a statement you will do so; but

• that if you are successful in your opposition to the application you will ask for an order that the receiving party should be awarded his costs of the application, to be assessed at the detailed assessment hearing.

If the court directs you to file and serve a statement of costs, prepare,   **Form N260** file and serve one in accordance with the rules –see 50.8. Even if the court does not so direct then, unless the receiving party is legally aided/LSC funded, you may want to play safe by preparing a statement of costs which you can take to the hearing just in case the court insists on carrying out a summary assessment.

CD-ROM 05.08
Form N260
CD-ROM 05.08

13.4 What orders can the court make?

(a) Dismissing the application

If the court dismisses the application, it might also:

• stay (ie suspend) enforcement of the default costs certificate;

• award the costs of the application to the receiving party;

• summarily assess those costs and state the date by which they are to be paid;

• order that those costs are to be assessed if not agreed;

• order detailed assessment of either party's costs which are payable out of the CLS Fund.

On the CD-ROM is a standard form of order, taken from the SCCO Guide (Appendix A-4, page 146).

CD-ROM 06.07

(b) Adjourning the application

If the court adjourns the application it is likely also to order that enforcement of the default costs certificate should be stayed (ie suspended) until the application is finally decided, or until the court makes some other order.

On the CD-ROM is a standard form of order, taken from the SCCO Guide (Appendix A-4, page 146).

CD-ROM 06.08

(c) Granting the application on conditions

The court may, for example:

CPR 3.1(3)

• order the paying party to pay to the receiving party (or into court) a particular sum on account of the costs claimed in the bill (note (a) that this is done under CPR 44.3(8) and is not the same as issuing an interim costs certificate – see chapter 16 – and (b) the fact that the costs judge may not have been the judge who made the substantive order for costs does not matter);

CPR 44.3(8)
CPD 38.3

- order that only when that payment is made will the default costs certificate be automatically set aside;

- give directions for the future conduct of the detailed assessment proceedings (the court must give directions, even though they will be conditional upon the setting aside of the default costs certificate); **CPD 38.4**

- provide for a stay in the enforcement of the default costs certificate until the date by which the paying party is to make payment;

- award the costs of the application to the receiving party;

- summarily assess those costs and state the date by which they are to be paid;

- order that those costs are to be assessed if not agreed;

- order detailed assessment of either party's costs which are payable out of the CLS Fund.

On the CD-ROM is a standard form of order, taken from the SCCO Guide (Appendix A-4, pages 143–144). **CD-ROM 06.05**

(d) Granting the application unconditionally

The court may, for example: **CPR 3.1(3)**

- set aside the default costs certificate and order the receiving party to return it to the court office;

- give directions for the future conduct of the detailed assessment proceedings (the court must do this); **CPD 38.4**

- make an order as to who should pay the costs of the application;

- summarily assess those costs and state the date by which they are to be paid;

- order that those costs are to be assessed if not agreed;

- if the costs of the application are awarded to the paying party, provide for the costs so assessed or ordered to be set off against any costs payable by him to the receiving party;

- order detailed assessment of either party's costs which are payable out of the CLS Fund.

On the CD-ROM is a standard form of order, taken from the SCCO Guide (Appendix A-4, page 145). **CD-ROM 06.06**

13.5 What should happen next?

(a) If the default costs certificate is set aside

If the default costs certificate was set aside, either because it was issued prematurely, or because the court granted the paying party's application to have it set aside, the detailed assessment proceedings will continue. The next step will be for the paying party to serve points of dispute, so check the date by which he should do this. It will either be:

• the 21st day after the service of notice of commencement; or

• such other date as the court has ordered.

If the points of dispute have still not been served when that time limit expires, there is nothing to stop you from applying again for a default costs certificate (in which case revisit chapter 11), or from doing whatever else is permitted by any court order.

If, however, points of dispute are served within the appropriate time:

• check whether they are adequate – chapter 20 explains how to do this and what to do if they appear to be inadequate;

• if they are adequate, reply to them – see chapter 22.

If the paying party serves points of dispute, but not within the appropriate time, remember that he 'may not be heard further in the detailed assessment proceedings unless the court gives permission' – see 20.1 for a possible tactical approach to this situation. CPR 47.9(3)

(b) If the default costs certificate is not set aside

See 12.3 about enforcing the order and 12.4 if there is to be an 'LSC only' costs assessment.

CHAPTER 14

Interest on costs

14.1 When is the receiving party entitled to interest?

(a) High Court cases

If an order or event (see 3.2) entitles the receiving party to his costs of proceedings, then he will usually be automatically entitled to interest on those costs. This is because the costs are treated as part of the judgment debt which is due to him, and judgment debts in the High Court (regardless of their size) automatically carry interest because of sections 17 and 18 of the Judgments Act 1838.

(b) County court cases

By section 74 of the County Courts Act 1984 and by the County Courts (Interest on Judgment Debts) Order 1991, the position in the county court is exactly the same as in the High Court (see (a) above), provided the judgment:

- is for not less than £5,000 (which presumably includes the costs as well as the substantive judgment debt);

- is not for the recovery of money due under an agreement regulated by the Consumer Credit Act 1974; and

- does not grant a suspended order of possession to the landlord or mortgagee of a dwellinghouse.

14.2 From what date does interest run on the substantive costs?

Interest usually runs from the date of the order or event conferring the entitlement to costs, rather than from the date of assessment of those costs – see *Hunt v R M Douglas (Roofing) Ltd* [1988] 3 WLR 975; [1988] 3 All ER 823; (1988) Costs LR (Core Vol) 136.

However, in cases with split trials, where a first costs order is made at the end of the liability trial and a second one at the end of the quantum trial, interest probably only runs from the date of the second order – see *Thomas v Bunn* [1991] 2 WLR 27; (1990) Costs LR (Core Vol) 161

CPR 40.8(1)

CPR 44.12(2)

Note that the court has power to order that interest should run from a date other than the date of judgment, including a power to order that it should run from a date before judgment.

CPR 40.8(2)

14.3 What about interest on the costs of detailed assessment?

(a) Costs orders or events before 2 December 2002

Interest ran on the costs of detailed assessment from the date of the order or event conferring entitlement to the costs of the substantive proceedings, even though the costs of detailed assessment would obviously not be incurred until after that date – see *Hunt v R M Douglas (Roofing) Ltd* (referred to at 14.2).

If you obtained an order for a specific sum of costs during the course of detailed assessment proceedings (eg on the issue of an interim costs certificate) interest on that sum would presumably only run from the date of that order. However, if the order was for 'costs in the detailed assessment', which meant that they would not be quantified until the end of the detailed assessment hearing, you could argue that interest on the whole of the costs of detailed assessment should be calculated from the date of the order or event that concluded the substantive proceedings.

(b) Costs orders or events after 1 December 2002

The 29th Supplement to the CPR, released on 1 October 2002, added a new paragraph 45.5 to the CPD, which provides that: 'In respect of interest on the costs of detailed assessment proceedings, the interest shall begin to run from the date of the default, interim or final costs certificate as the case may be.' Note that this provision:

CPD 45.5(1)

• applies only to the costs of the detailed assessment proceedings themselves; the costs of the substantive proceedings continue to be governed by rule 40.8(1);

CPR 40.8(1)
CPD 45.5(2)

• came into force on 2 December 2002 so presumably does not affect cases where the order or event conferring entitlement to the costs of the substantive proceedings was made before that date.

CPD 45.5(1)

14.4 What is the rate of interest?

The standard rate, ie the one that applies automatically, has been 8 per cent per annum since 1 April 1993 – see the Judgment Debts (Rate of

Interest) Order 1993 (SI 1993 No 564). You can check the interest rate on the 'Data Page' periodically published in the *Law Society Gazette* (see 2.7). Look under 'Interest on Judgment Debts'.

However, where a claimant is awarded more at trial than the sum at which he had previously made a Part 36 offer of settlement the court can (a) award him costs on the indemnity basis from the latest date when the defendant could have accepted the offer without needing the permission of the court and (b) award him interest on those costs at a rate not exceeding 10 per cent above base rate. Note that:

CPR 36.21

* it is not just a matter of higher interest, but interest starting from a date before judgment;

* you can check the base rate on the 'Data Page' periodically published in the *Law Society Gazette* (look under 'Bank Base Rates');

* the base rate was 4 per cent from 8 November 2001 to 5 February 2003, 3.75 per cent from 6 February 2003 to 9 July 2003, 3.5 per cent from 10 July 2003 and 3.75 per cent from 6 November 2003; and

* it follows that if the base rate is 3.75 per cent, the court needs to award more than 4.25 per cent above base if the receiving party is to do better than the statutory rate of 8 per cent.

14.5 Can the right to interest be taken away?

Although entitlement to interest is automatic (see 14.1), if the receiving party fails to commence the detailed assessment proceedings or to request a detailed assessment hearing within the time-limits set by the rules, the court can disallow some or all of the interest that would otherwise be payable – see 3.7(c).

14.6 Who is entitled to keep the interest?

(a) Privately funded cases

Unless there is an agreement between the solicitor and the client saying that the solicitor can keep the interest, interest on the profit costs belongs to the client and interest on unpaid disbursements belongs to the persons to whom the disbursements are ultimately paid – see *Hunt v R M Douglas (Roofing) Ltd* (1988) at 14.2 .

You will need to check the contentious business agreement or client care letter to see if anything is said about this.

(b) Conditional fee agreements

The principle is the same as in (a) above, but the terms of the conditional fee agreement may allow the solicitor to keep the interest. Check the agreement to make sure.

(c) Legally aided/LSC-funded cases

The LSC's starting point is that they are in the position of the client and so interest on Legal Aid costs belongs to them and not to the solicitor. Para 3.47 of Part D of the *LSC Manual* (see 2.8(d)) gives full details of the lines they take in various circumstances. These are the main points:

If the certificate was issued before 25 February 1994, or if the costs relate to work done in the Court of Appeal or the House of Lords, all the interest specifically identified as interest belongs to the LSC, as civil prescribed rates do not apply.

In all other cases, ie those to which civil prescribed rates apply, if you recover interest that is specifically identified as interest it must be apportioned between the solicitor and the LSC.

The LSC schedule will have shown what the costs as *claimed* between the parties would have been if recalucalted at civil prescribed rates, but you must work out what the costs you *recovered* between the parties would have been if recalculated at civil prescribed rates. If you have to do this, you may find worksheet 5 useful. It is the interest on that sum that is due to the LSC. The rest belongs to the solicitior – see regulations 92(1)(b) and 107B(4) of the Civil Legal Aid (General) Regulations 1989.

The theory behind this approach is that the solicitior owns any costs recovered between the parties in excess of the total that would be payable to the solicitor by the LSC.

If there are any pre-certificate costs, you must make a further apportionment to exclude the interest on them from the calculation of the amount due to the LSC. The excluded interest will belong to the client unless the contentious business agreement or client care letter provides otherwise.

When reporting to the LSC on form CLAIM 2 at the end of a case, they may reject your claim if you do not give full details of the costs and interest recovered.

You should pay over to the LSC 'forthwith' whatever interest is due to them.

Although the client will never be entitles to receive any of the interest paid to the LSC, the amount of it will be shown as a credit on his

Worksheet 5

CD-ROM 10.11

account with the LSC for the purposes of calculating the amount due under the statutory charge.

14.7 Using interest in negotiations

Make full use of interest in negotiations; always include it in your calculations of the amount claimed:

• this serves to increase the total prospectively payable by the paying party, which is useful in negotiations; and

• it reminds them that the longer settlement is delayed, the more interest will be payable.

However, most settlements are for a 'global' figure inclusive of all the various elements claimed (namely profit costs, counsel's fees, disbursements, the costs of drawing and checking the bill and possibly the costs of detailed assessment, VAT and interest) without indicating any apportionment between these elements.

14.8 Accounting for the money recovered

If a settlement is reached for a global sum in this way, neither the client nor the LSC could easily assert that any particular part of the agreed sum ought to be earmarked as interest. If that is so the overall recovery for the firm will be improved, as more money will be available for application as profit costs.

CHAPTER 15

Voluntary payments on account

15.1 Why do paying parties make them?

Paying parties know that they are liable to pay interest on the costs, generally from the date of the order or event entitling the receiving party to the costs (see 14.4). The statutory rate is a penal one, so the interest they must pay will be more than the interest they could hope to gain by keeping the money in their bank account. By making a payment on account of the costs that will eventually be agreed or assessed they reduce the amount of interest that will eventually be payable. They often accompany the payment on account with an offer of settlement of the same amount, in the hope that the receiving party will be tempted to settle for the money in hand.

15.2 When can we expect one?

Sometimes a payment is made as soon as the substantive proceedings have finished, and before you have served notice of commencement.

More often, a payment is made only after you have served notice of commencement, when the paying party will know exactly how much you are claiming and be better able to judge the amount to pay.

Sometimes no payment is made until you have prompted the paying party.

15.3 What can we do with the money?

The money is not much use to the firm if it just has to sit in client account until the costs are finally agreed or assessed. You want to be able to clear any outstanding disbursements and take the balance for profit costs and VAT as quickly as possible.

However, there is a potential problem with the Solicitors Accounts Rules ('SAR'). Rule 19(4) and note (i)(d) to rule 13 SAR provide that a payment on account of costs generally is 'client money'. Rule 15(1) says that such money must be held in client account except where the rules provide to the contrary.

Unfortunately the SAR seem to assume that payments on account will usually come from the client. They contain no specific rule that entitles you to take as profit costs and VAT a voluntary payment on account made by a third party in a non legally-aided case.

Neither the CPR nor the CPD make any provision for voluntary payments on account.

The essence of the problem seems to be that, until there has been some conclusive determination of the amount of the costs either by the court (by way of detailed assessment) or by the parties (reaching a binding agreement), it is not possible to say to whom the money paid on account belongs – it is similar to 'stakeholder' money.

A suggested solution is to ask the paying party to make a payment on account 'on the basis that it is not just a payment on account of the amount which will finally be found to be due from your client to ours, but that we are free to apply it in part-payment of the profit costs, counsel's fees, other disbursements and VAT claimed in the bill'.

This is the approach taken in the letter serving the notice of commencement –see 10.2.

Do not be surprised if paying parties fail to understand why you are asking this, or even if they fail to understand your explanation. However, they usually seem happy to agree to your using the money in the terms indicated, provided you also give them an assurance that 'if the amount finally found to be due from your client to ours is less than the amount so paid on account, we will forthwith refund the difference'.

15.4 What about legally aided/LSC-funded cases?

Rule 21 of the SAR, which seems intended to deal only with final payments of costs by third parties, and not to cover payments on account, tells the firm to keep in client account a sum equal to the payments on account made by the LAB/LSC and to take the balance for costs, disbursements and VAT. See also:

• In the case of Legal Aid certificates issued under the Legal Aid Act 1988 (ie generally before 1 April 2000), 'Note for Guidance' 14-13 in the *Legal Aid Handbook*.

• In the case of LSC funding certificates issued under the Access to Justice Act 1999 (ie generally after 31 March 2000), rule 6.8 of the *General Civil Contract*.

Provided you have the paying party's agreement to the use of their payment on account 'in part-payment of the profit costs, counsel's fees, other disbursements and VAT claimed in the bill', it is difficult to see how you could be considered not to have complied with the SAR.

15.5 Is there a problem with interim costs certificates?

If you obtain an interim costs certificate (see chapter 29), it is arguable that - in relation to the sum that it covers - it is of the same nature as a final order. That sum would then count as money 'paid in full or part settlement of the solicitor's bill' (rule 19 SAR) or as costs 'subsequently settled by a third party' (rule 21 SAR) and could properly be used in part-payment of the profit costs, counsel's fees, other disbursements and VAT claimed in the bill.

But remember in legally aided/LSC-funded cases to keep in client account a sum equal to the payments on account made by the LAB/LSC, in order to comply with rule 21 SAR.

CHAPTER 16

Orders for payments on account

16.1 An important distinction

An order by the court for a payment on account is not the same as an interim costs certificate:

- an interim costs certificate (see chapter 29) is the result of a formal application to the court under CPR 47.15; but CPR 47.15

- an order for a payment on account can be made without the need for any prior application under a general power conferred on the court by CPR 44.3(8). CPR 44.3(8)

16.2 When can the court make an order?

CPR 44.3(8) provides that 'Where the court has ordered a party to pay costs, it may order an amount to be paid on account before the costs are assessed.' CPR 44.3(8)

The power to order a payment on account arises as soon as the court has made an order for costs, for example at the end of the substantive proceedings. While that may be the usual time for the exercise of this power, there is nothing to stop the court from making such an order at any point in the detailed assessment proceedings.

16.3 When ought the court to make an order?

The general approach to be taken by the courts was set out extensively by Jacob J in *Mars UK Ltd v Teknowledge Ltd* (No 2) [1999] 2 Costs LR 44 and he concluded (at page 47): 'So I hold that where a party is successful the court should on a rough and ready basis also normally order an amount to be paid on account, the amount being a lesser sum than the full likely amount'. CPD 12.3

While most of what Jacob J said was concerned with the situation at the end of the substantive proceedings, the principle declared by him is equally applicable to detailed assessment proceedings.

While the court might not be willing to use its jurisdiction in circumstances where you could reasonably be expected to have made a formal application for an interim costs certificate there are other circumstances, chiefly when it is giving directions or dealing with applications in the detailed assessment proceedings, in which it would be worth seeking such an order.

16.4 What form should the order take?

The order should state the amount.   *CPD 8.6(1)*

  If it does not specify some other date the payment on account will be   **CPR 44.8(a)**
payable within 14 days of the date of the order.   *CPD 8.6(2)*

CHAPTER 17

Part 47.19 offers

17.1 What is a Part 47.19 offer?

It is an offer to settle the costs of the substantive proceedings. Its significance lies in the costs consequences that may follow if it is not accepted. Where it is made in accordance with the costs rules the court will take it into account in deciding who should pay the costs of the detailed assessment proceedings.

CPR 47.19(1)
CPD 46.1

It is not the same as a Part 36 offer, although you will sometimes see it incorrectly described as such, or even as a *Calderbank* offer, which it is not either. Table 4 on pages 96–97 shows some of the main differences between Part 36 and Part 47.19 offers.

CPR 36
Table 4

17.2 Why is the paying party likely to make one?

The paying party will almost always make a Part 47.19 offer. He will do so because it gives him the hope of:

• settling the costs for less than the amount demanded by the receiving party;

• settling the costs quickly, so avoiding further liability to interest;

• avoiding the risks of a detailed assessment hearing; and

• avoiding his almost automatic obligation to pay the costs of the detailed assessment.

The offer is designed to put pressure on the receiving party. It does so by providing incentives and by making a threat.
The incentives are:

• an early settlement, avoiding the wait (of perhaps many months) for a detailed assessment hearing; and

• avoidance of the need to incur further, possible irrecoverable, costs in the detailed assessment proceedings.

The threat comes from the risk to which the offer exposes the receiving party. If the matter goes to a detailed assessment hearing, but the receiving party recovers no more than the amount of the offer, the paying party will probably ask the court to order the receiving party to pay both sides' costs of the detailed assessment proceedings.

TABLE 4: SOME DIFFERENCES BETWEEN PART 36 AND PART 47.19 OFFERS

Part 36 offers	Part 47.19 offers
Timing of offer May be made at any time after the substantive proceedings have started – CPR 36.2(4).	No actual rules as to timing, although some guidance is given – *CPD 46.1.*
Time allowed for acceptance Must ordinarily give 21 days for acceptance – CPR 36.5(6).	No particular time need be given for acceptance.
Court's decision on liability for costs If made less than 21 days before trial the claimant many only accept it with the permission of the court, if liability for the costs has not been agreed, in which case the court will make an order as to costs – CPR 36.5.	No provision for the court to be involved in deciding who should pay the costs of the detailed assessment proceedings, when an offer has been accepted in relation to the substantive costs – CPD 46.3.
Payments into court A defendant's offer to settle a money claim must be made by payment into court – CPR 36.3.	No comparable requirement; payments are usually made to receiving party, to reduce liability to interest.
Clarification of offer The offeree may ask the offeror to clarify the offer – CPR 36.9.	No comparable provision; CPD 46.2 states how any ambiguities should be resolved.
Entitlement to costs on acceptance Acceptance of a Part 36 offer entitles the claimant to his costs of the proceedings up to the date of acceptance – CPR 36.13–14.	No comparable provision.

Part 36 offers	Part 47.19 offers
Formalities	
Should be marked 'Without prejudice except as to costs' – CPR 36.19(1).	Should be marked 'Without prejudice save as to the costs of the detailed assessment proceedings' – CPR 47.19(1)(b).
Costs consequences of failing to beat defendant's offer	
Where at trial the claimant fails to beat a Part 36 offer or payment then, 'unless it considers it unjust to do so, the court will order the claimant to pay any costs incurred by the defendant after the latest date on which the payment or offer could have been accepted' – CPR 36.20.	Where at detailed assessment the receiving party fails to beat the paying party's Part 47.19 offer then 'the court will take the offer into account in deciding who should pay the costs of those proceedings' – CPR 47.19(1)(b).
Costs consequences of claimant beating his own offer	
Where at trial a claimant beats his own offer, then the court will, unless it considers it unjust to do so, award him higher than usual interest and costs on the indemnity basis – CPR 36.21.	No comparable provision.
Special protection for legally aided/LSC-funded clients	
None.	The offer 'will not have the consequences specified under rule 47.19 unless the court so orders' – CPD 46.4.

17.3 Should the receiving party make one?

The receiving party is also free to make a Part 47.19 offer. If he does, it will be in the hope of:

• settling the costs quickly; and

• avoiding the risks of a detailed assessment hearing.

In making the offer, he will aim to put pressure on the paying party, again in the form of incentives and a threat.
The incentives are:

• settlement for less than the total claimed;

• a quick settlement, ending the liability to pay interest;

• avoidance of the risk of not doing so well at the detailed assessment hearing; and

• avoidance of the risk of having to pay the costs of the detailed assessment proceedings if the matter goes to a detailed assessment hearing.

The threat comes from the increase in the risk, already faced by the paying party, of having to pay both sides' costs of the detailed assessment proceedings. If the matter goes to a detailed assessment hearing, and the receiving party recovers more than the amount of the offer, the paying party will almost inevitably have to pay both sides' costs of the detailed assessment proceedings.

If you put a pre-emptive offer when serving the notice of commencement, you should already have expressed it as a Part 47.19 offer.

However, even if you decided the case was not suitable for the making of a pre-emptive offer (see 7.2), it may nevertheless be appropriate to make a Part 47.19 offer in response to one made by the paying party:

• to encourage the paying party to make a better offer than he had done previously; and

• to speed up progress towards a possible settlement.

17.4 Have the formalities been complied with?

(a) The heading

The offer should be expressed to be **'Without prejudice save as to the costs of the detailed assessment proceedings.'**   CPR 47.19(1)

• This phrase is usually put as a heading to an offer letter, but provided it appears somewhere in the letter, the exact positioning does not matter.

• Although the rule is clear, it is often broken in practice (by headings such as 'Part 47 offer'). However, you might have difficulty persuading the costs officer to ignore an offer simply because the heading is wrong, provided the intention is clear.

(b) Clarity

The offer 'should specify whether or not it is intended to be inclusive of the cost of preparation of the bill, interest and VAT. ... Unless the offer states otherwise, the offer will be treated as being inclusive of all these items.'

CPD 46.2

• The costs of bill preparation are probably mentioned specifically because, when the CPR were introduced, and the costs of bill preparation were made recoverable in principle, there was confusion as to whether those costs were part of the substantive costs or the costs of the detailed assessment. That confusion has now been largely resolved – see 1.13(a).

• If the costs are settled, it may suit the receiving party to settle for a global figure inclusive of interest (see 14.8), in which case an offer inclusive of interest is not a problem. However, if the costs are not settled and the matter goes to a detailed assessment hearing, if the offer has to be considered in relation to who pays the costs, someone will have to break it down to show how much of it related to the substantive costs and how much to the interest accrued to the date of the offer. While this is not difficult to do with a spreadsheet (see 17.8) it is difficult to do manually. It is not the sort of thing you will want to do at the hearing itself.

• If the offer is inclusive of VAT it is important that neither side is under any misunderstanding as to the ability of the receiving party to recover the VAT on his costs. This ought, of course, to have been made clear in the bill. However, if the paying party assumes that he must pay the VAT on the receiving party's costs in the usual way, but in fact the receiving party ought not to have claimed VAT from him, the paying party will offer more than he intended.

• Unlike in the case of Part 36 offers, the recipient of a Part 47.19 offer cannot require the maker of it to clarify it or break it down in

CPR 36.9

any particular way. This can be a problem if the receiving party's costs were incurred with two or more firms of solicitors. How is a global offer to be apportioned between them? This may be a point to make in any argument as to whether the court ought to penalise a receiving party for failing to accept a Part 47.19 offer in these circumstances.

(c) Secrecy

'The fact of the offer must not be communicated to the costs officer until the question of the costs of the detailed assessment proceedings falls to be decided.'

CPR 47.19(2)

• Some paying parties lodge a copy of the offer in a sealed envelope at court, but this is not required by the rules.

• There is an apparent inconsistency between this requirement of secrecy and the duty placed on the receiving party to state in the certificates to the bill exactly what payments on account have been received from the paying party. Quite often the payment on account will be the same as the amount offered. The costs officer, who can see the certificate before 'the question of the costs of the detailed assessment proceedings falls to be decided', can no doubt guess this.

17.5 At what point should an offer be made?

'An offer made by the paying party should usually be made within 14 days after the service of the notice of commencement on that party. If the offer is made by the receiving party, it should normally be made within 14 days after the service of the points of dispute by the paying party. Offers made after these periods are likely to be given less weight by the court in deciding what order as to costs to make unless there is good reason for the offer not being made until the later time.'

CPD 46.1

• This guidance is almost always ignored in the course of negotiations. You might make a pre-emptive offer at the same time as you serve notice of commencement. Offers and counter-offers may be made over a period of months. Final offers may be made just before the detailed assessment hearing is due to start or even part-way through it.

• However, this guidance may be worth invoking when you are arguing about who should pay the costs of the detailed assessment proceedings (see 35.2(c)).

17.6 Legally aided/LSC-funded cases

'Where the receiving party is an assisted person or an LSC funded *CPD 46.4* client, an offer to settle without prejudice save as to the costs of the detailed assessment proceedings will not have the consequences specified under rule 47.19 unless the court so orders.'

This provision is designed to leave a legally aided/LSC-funded client free to fight his own corner at a detailed assessment hearing. By that stage, his interests and those of his solicitors may no longer coincide; if there are costs not recovered from the paying party, the solicitors will want them paid out of the CLS Fund, but the client will not want them paid by anybody. He must be able to object to a settlement between the parties that would leave a large amount of costs to be claimed against the CLS Fund and thus out of his damages, without the fear that pursuing his objection might result in an order that he should pay the paying party's costs of the detailed assessment proceedings.

In negotiations, paying parties frequently argue that if they make an offer which a legally aided/LSC funded receiving party rejects and does not beat at detailed assessment, then the receiving party will be in exactly the same position as any other. That is not so. It would be odd if it were, as it would make CPD 46.4 meaningless. There seems to be no reported case above District Judge level to support such an argument and cases decided at that level are unlikely to be regarded as authorities that can properly be cited in argument (see 32.3(d)).

17.7 Can the offer include the costs of the detailed assessment proceedings?

(a) The problem

Part 47.19 seems to assume that an offer will only relate to the substantive costs, so will not include any costs of the detailed assessment proceedings that might have been incurred up to the date of the offer.

The detailed assessment proceedings begin with the service of the notice of commencement, so it is only from that date that the costs of the detailed assessment proceedings can start to accrue – see 1.10.

The rules requiring the maker of the offer to specify what it includes *CPD 46.2* (see 17.4(b)) make no mention of the costs of the detailed assessment proceedings incurred to date.

By the time a Part 47.19 offer is made by the paying party you may have spent a great deal of time replying to points of dispute and negotiating, and may therefore have incurred substantial costs of detailed assessment. On the face of it, if you accept the offer, these costs will be irrecoverable. This has some potentially unfortunate consequences. If, for example, you serve a bill claiming £12,000 and the paying party makes a Part 47.19 offer of settlement at £10,000 plus interest, but by that time you have incurred £500 costs of the detailed assessment proceedings:

- If you accept the offer, you must either write off the £500 or regard your recovery as, say, £9,500 for the substantive costs and £500 for the costs of detailed assessment.

- If you reject the offer, proceed to a detailed assessment hearing, but are awarded substantive costs of only £9,750, and the costs officer is asked to take the paying party's offer into account, he is free to ignore the costs of detailed assessment that you had incurred up to the date of the offer in deciding whether that offer had been beaten. Even though you regard the offer as having been worth only £9,500, he might regard it as worth the full £10,000 and therefore make some order as to the costs of the detailed assessment proceedings other than the usual one (that the paying party should pay them).

(b) A possible way of reducing its impact

If there is no prospect of recovering the costs of the detailed assessment proceedings as part of any settlement, there may seem to be little incentive for spending much time on negotiations if the result will only be to increase your level of irrecoverable costs and to devalue any settlement reached. However, such a conclusion seems out of sympathy with one of the aims of the CPR, which is to encourage parties to settle and to use the court only as a last resort.

The problem may turn out to be more apparent than real if you can persuade the costs officer:

- to give full recognition to the presumption that the receiving party is entitled to his costs of the detailed assessment; **CPR 47.18(1)**

- to accept that even if, on the face of it, you did not beat the paying party's offer, your rejection of it was nevertheless reasonable in the circumstances, taking into account the level of costs of detailed assessment that you had incurred up to that point; and

- to conclude that, in the circumstances, the usual presumption should not be displaced, and that the paying party should pay the costs of the detailed assessment.

If, at the hearing, you have to argue as to why the paying party's offer should not displace the usual presumption, there are several things you can mention (see 35.2(c)). However, you can start to prepare the ground for any such argument while negotiating with the paying party, by educating him as to your costs of the detailed assessment proceedings.

• At every critical point in the negotiations, tell him what your total costs of the detailed assessment proceedings are to date. You can do this most easily by updating your statement of the total costs claimed (using worksheet 1).

Worksheet 1
CD-ROM 10.01

• Do not give him details of the profit costs, except perhaps for the number of hours and the hourly rates applied, as you are not supposed to serve schedules of costs in detailed assessment proceedings.

CPD 45.3

• When putting forward any counter-offer, make clear that it includes the total costs of the detailed assessment proceedings to date. This reduces the total you are claiming for the costs of the substantive case and makes your offer look better.

Keeping your costs of the detailed assessment proceedings constantly in front of the paying party might also:

• improve any offers he makes; and

• cause him to think more seriously about the likely costs of the detailed assessment proceedings he might have to pay if the matter does not settle.

17.8 Working out the implications of an offer

Before deciding either to accept an offer from the paying party, or to put a counter-offer, you should work out its implications for the firm's profit costs and for counsel's fees (if counsel is willing to give a discount).

The easiest way to do this is with worksheet 4, which is similar to the one used for evaluating a pre-emptive offer. If you are using a spreadsheet program, then by using the 'goal seek' tool you can work out what percentage discount on profit costs is represented by the offer. This should help you to assess the offer in relation to your SWOT analysis (see 6.2), which you may need to update to take account of developments since you prepared it originally.

Worksheet 4
CD-ROM 10.10

17.9 If you achieve settlement

For details of the different ways of tying things up, see:

• chapter 19, if you have not requested a detailed assessment hearing; or

• chapter 30, if you have requested a detailed assessment hearing.

CHAPTER 18

Negotiating

18.1 Why negotiate?

The general approach of the CPR is to encourage settlement of cases in ways other than by the asking the court to try them. Even if you believe your bill to be completely reasonable, and even if it is, you may not wish to risk the disapproval of the costs officer by refusing to negotiate.

As most costs assessments settle, and for less than was originally claimed, negotiation is almost inevitable, so it can be prudent to use it to the best possible effect.

18.2 Is there anything different about legal negotiations?

There is no shortage of books and courses on negotiation techniques, and it is not the purpose of this chapter to advocate any particular approach, still less to invent a new one.

It is often assumed that negotiation normally involves face-to-face discussions between people who know each other fairly well, who argue over a number of separate points and eventually make various trade-offs in order to arrive at a final compromise.

However, legal negotiations tend to be different:

- they are rarely conducted face to face;

- you might never have encountered this particular opponent before and might never do so again;

- each side is likely to parade their arguments on paper first;

- it is unusual for individual points to be conceded other than as part of a final settlement;

- the aim is often to arrive at an agreed sum of money; and

- there is usually a 'ghost' (ie the client, the instructing solicitor or the insurers) as an unseen presence at the negotiations, influencing both their course and their outcome.

18.3 How do we set our parameters?

If you have not yet done your SWOT analysis – see 6.2 – do it now. If you did it earlier, revisit it now to see if the situation has changed at all since you did it. You need to arrive at three separate figures.

(a) Your bottom line

Work out the lowest figure at which you would be prepared to settle in order to avoid a detailed assessment hearing. The kind of calculations to make are similar to those used to calculate a pre-emptive costs offer (see 7.3) and you may find worksheet 2 helpful. However, your bottom line will probably be somewhat lower than any figure you worked out for a pre-emptive costs offer.

Worksheet 2
CD-ROM 10.05

(b) Your starting point

Work out a figure at or above the highest amount you reasonably think the paying party might agree. In doing this take account of the facts that:

• the costs officer may not be as impressed with the bill or with the complexity of the case as you are;

• the paying party knows he will get something knocked off if the bill goes to detailed assessment, but

• there is no point in being pessimistic as you will want to leave yourself some room for movement; and

• whatever your starting point, the paying party is bound to offer something less, so setting your starting point too low will almost certainly result in a lower counter-offer and a lower final settlement.

(c) Your realistic target

Work out the figure that you think you ought to be able to achieve and for which you would be content to settle. It will be somewhere between your bottom line and your starting point. Exactly where it is will depend on the circumstances of the case.

18.4 How do things look to the opponent?

(a) Do a SWOT analysis for the paying party

This is a useful exercise, although it inevitably involves guesswork.

Based on the information you have, try to do a SWOT analysis for the paying party, but recognise that there may be significant matters of which you have no knowledge.

(b) Know your opponent

While you may have limited knowledge at this stage, take account of the person with whom you are negotiating:

• Is he solicitor, costs draftsman or costs negotiator?

• Does he have any personal axe to grind (eg is the solicitor who conducted the case now dealing with the costs)?

• What 'ghosts' are at his table (eg clients, insurers)?

• Does he know much about costs?

Consider what your opponent's own costs of contesting this bill are likely to be, particularly if the matter goes to a detailed assessment.

18.5 What is our authority?

Particularly if you are an independent costs draftsman, it is essential that you know the scope of your authority: do you have authority to negotiate a settlement or a particular level of discount without referring to the fee-earner or the firm? This is something that your opponent will probably ask.

A limited authority is not usually a problem, provided you can communicate quickly with the fee-earner or the firm. It can sometimes be a useful thing behind which to hide; saying that you have to take instructions can give you an opportunity to reflect on proposals and avoid being pushed into a settlement for which you are not ready.

Do not forget the possible involvement of the client, where he has an interest in the outcome of the detailed assessment:

• What has he already been told about possible outcomes?

• Has a decision been made about what proportion of any shortfall between costs claimed and costs recovered the firm would expect him to pay?

• Has he agreed to any particular outcome or range of outcomes?

18.6 Who goes first?

Some of the more imaginative costs negotiators will tell you that, to comply with the spirit of the CPR, you must offer a reduction in the costs claimed, otherwise you will be criticised by the costs officer for refusing to negotiate. This is, of course, nonsense. The bill sets out your reasonable claim; it is up to the paying party to provide arguments as to why you should settle for less. So, unless this is a case which you think appropriate for a pre-emptive offer (see chapter 7) let the paying party go first.

18.7 Before speaking to the opponent

It is helpful to note on paper (to remind you to refer to them in your negotiations):

• the strengths of your case;

• the weaknesses of the paying party's case; and

• up-to-date figures for interest and the costs of detailed assessment (so that you can check that the paying party has given proper thought to the consequences of not settling).

You should also note on paper (but not, of course, to tell the paying party):

• your starting point;

• your realistic position; and

• your bottom line – see 18.3.

18.8 How should we conduct the negotiations?

(a) Which medium are you going to use?

Writing may be the best way of setting out your case or making any significant points, but using the phone may be the best way of making progress in negotiations. In costs negotiations there is often a contrast between written and spoken exchanges. It is not unusual for correspondence to appear dogmatic and aggressive (it may be intended as much to impress the 'ghost' as to inform you), while the author of it turns out to be quite reasonable on the phone. This is why it can be unwise to communicate only in writing.

(b) Asking questions

If you have already made your case clearly, there is perhaps not much point in going over it again in discussions with your opponent. It can, however, be useful to ask questions:

- to identify any common ground there may be;

- to learn what your opponent thinks are the strengths and weaknesses of the paying party's case;

- to check that they understand what you say are the weaknesses of the paying party's case; and

- to ascertain the scope of their authority.

(c) Setting the tone

It is generally best to be courteous but firm and to resist the temptation to respond to aggressive correspondence in kind. Remember that you may need to produce the correspondence to the costs officer after the detailed assessment, when arguing over who should pay the costs of the detailed assessment proceedings.

18.9 Offers and counter-offers

During the course of negotiations there may be a series of offers and counter-offers. In each case remember the formalities:

- make it clear at the start of any telephone conversation that it is 'without prejudice', and

- put the words 'without prejudice save as to the costs of the detailed assessment proceedings' on any written offers – see 17.4(a).

18.10 Maintaining progress

(a) Setting deadlines

In most cases, when putting an offer or counter-offer, you will want to set a deadline for its acceptance.

- the standard period to allow for acceptance is 21 days (by analogy with Part 36 offers), and this is normally as much as your opponent can reasonably expect;   CPR 36.11–12

- depending on the circumstances (eg the closeness of the detailed assessment hearing) you might argue that a reasonable period may be less than this – perhaps seven days or even less; but

• the court may not give much weight to a proposal that does not give the paying party adequate time to consider it before the time for acceptance runs out; and

• the later the offer is made in the detailed assessment proceedings, the less weight the court may give to it anyway. *CPD 46.1*

Always diarise deadlines you have imposed or been given for the next step to be taken in the detailed assessment proceedings. Try to apply your deadlines strictly and not to let matters drift.

(b) If you get stuck

If your opponent seems impossible to deal with it may be worthwhile trying to work out why:

• if it is because they (or those instructing them) have unrealistic expectations, you may simply have to force the matter to a detailed assessment hearing;

• if it is because they not understand the costs rules, trying to educate them may be fruitless; see if you can find a way to have the matter dealt with by someone else in their firm with more knowledge or authority, provided you can do this with propriety.

18.11 Timing of settlements

Sometimes matters settle at the very beginning of the detailed assessment proceedings (especially where you have made a pre-emptive offer), if both sides are keen to see an end to it and are prepared to be pragmatic in their approach.

More often they do not settle until after points of dispute and replies have been served. Even then, there may be little movement until a hearing date has been set.

In many cases settlement will not happen until the hearing is imminent – perhaps not until the day of the hearing itself. Among the reasons for last-minute settlement are:

• a reduction in expectations by both sides as they get cold feet about the hearing; and

• a reappraisal of the case by someone instructed for the hearing who has not been involved in the negotiations.

In trying to understand the timing of settlements it can be useful to remember that there is more than one kind of time:

• there is 'clock' or 'calendar' time (eg the date by which points of dispute are to be served); and

• there is also the 'right' time for something to happen (eg the point at which both the paying party and the receiving party are, for reasons of their own, ready to do a deal).

While you should take account of the 'calendar' time when conducting negotiations and working towards the detailed assessment hearing, it can help to recognise that if the calendar time is not also the right time for the parties to settle, no amount of effort at that particular time will yield the result you want, whereas if you leave it for a few days or weeks a settlement might be achieved with remarkable ease. If you were not the fee-earner who had conduct of the substantive case it may be helpful to consult them on matters of timing, as they may have useful insights derived from their experience of the opponent gained during the proceedings.

18.12 What if we reach agreement?

If your negotiations result in a settlement, make sure that its terms are properly secured:

• If you have not yet applied for a detailed assessment hearing, see chapter 19.

• If you have applied for a detailed assessment hearing, see chapter 30.

CHAPTER 19

Agreeing the costs without having requested a detailed assessment hearing

19.1 What sort of terms should we aim for?

If you agree the terms of settlement in a telephone conversation, you should make sure that all the vital points are agreed in that conversation, because you cannot expect the paying party to accept additional terms that you thought of afterwards and tried to include in the confirmatory letter.

Among the points you should aim to agree are:

• the exact amount of costs agreed between the parties;

• whether this is an inclusive figure or whether, for example, interest is to be paid in addition and, if so, who is to work it out and by when;

• the date by which payment is to be made;

• how payment is to be made (in most cases it will be to the receiving party's solicitors, rather than to the party himself);

• what is to happen about interest if payment is late (even if the settlement figure is inclusive of interest, you might want to reserve the right to claim interest in addition if payment is delayed beyond the agreed date); and

• if the terms are to be embodied in a consent order (see 25.4) and, if so, who is to pay the court fee.

19.2 How should we record the terms agreed?

It is essential to record the terms of the settlement in writing, whether by letter, fax or e-mail, as soon as it has been reached. At the very least, you will want to state:

• the date on which the settlement was agreed;

• if you are confirming an agreement made in a telephone conversation, the names of the parties to that conversation and its date and approximate time; and

• such of the points mentioned at 19.1 as are relevant.

On the CD-ROM is a draft letter.

CD-ROM 08.04

19.3 What if we want a final costs certificate?

(a) Can we apply for one?

You can still ask the court to issue a final costs certificate, even though you have not filed a request for a detailed assessment hearing. As this will involve agreeing a consent order and paying a court fee (currently £30.00) you will presumably only do this if:

CPR 47.10(1)
CPD 36.1

• the paying party has agreed to pay the court fee; or

• you are sufficiently uneasy about them honouring the terms of the agreement to make this seem money well spent if it results in an enforceable order.

(b) To which court should we apply?

The court to which to apply is the one that would have dealt with the detailed assessment proceedings – see 23.3.

CPR 47.10(2)

(c) What is the procedure?

The procedure is the general one for applying for a consent order, which is set out in CPR 40.6 – see 25.4.

CPR 40.6
CPD 36.1

19.4 What if the paying party reneges on the agreement?

You can apply for a costs certificate if the paying party has 'in the course of proceedings' agreed to pay costs:

CPD 36.2, 36.3, 40.8

• but will neither pay them;

• nor join in a consent application for a costs certificate.

Presumably 'in the course of proceedings' means 'in a case where substantive proceedings have been issued' rather than just 'in the course of detailed assessment proceedings', and is designed to prevent this provision from being used to obtain a costs certificate where no substantive proceedings were issued. In such a case, the only remedy is the issue of Part 7 proceedings – see chapter 51.9.

CPR 7

19.5 What if the receiving party is legally aided/LSC funded?

(a) Are you happy to accept the agreed costs in satisfaction of all your claims?

If you are happy to accept the costs agreed between the parties without seeking to claim any of the shortfall from the CLS Fund, all you need do from the Legal Aid/LSC funding point of view is to report the outcome to the LSC on form CLAIM 2. How to complete this form is not covered in this book because the forms change so frequently that any guidance given here would be out of date very quickly. You can obtain up-to-date forms and guidance on their completion from the LSC website – see 2.6.

(b) Will you want to make an 'LSC only' costs claim?

On the other hand, if you want to make an 'LSC only' claim against the CLS Fund for any of the shortfall between the costs claimed and the costs recovered from the paying party, it may be helpful in pursuing that claim to have a clear statement in writing from the paying party confirming to which items in the bill he objected on the grounds that they were more properly chargeable to the CLS Fund. Now is your only realistic chance of obtaining this, as the paying party will have no incentive to help you with your 'LSC only' claim at some later date. The points of dispute may be sufficient for this purpose, in conjunction with the information in worksheets 5 and 10.

Worksheet 5
Worksheet 10

If the profit costs, counsel's fees and disbursements of your 'LSC only' costs claim exceed £2,500 before VAT, you will need to apply to the court for an 'LSC only' provisional assessment of the costs claimed against the CLS Fund – see chapter 43. If they do not exceed £2,500 you will have to prepare a CLAIM 2 and have it assessed by the LSC rather than by the court.

(c) Was the certificate issued before 25 February 1994?

If you want to claim any of the shortfall from the CLS Fund, but the Legal Aid certificate was issued before 25 February 1994, the court has no power to carry out a separate 'LSC only' provisional assessment. Instead it must carry out a detailed assessment of the whole bill (see paragraph 24.9(a) of the *SCCO Guide* and *Legal Aid Focus* No 24 at page 14).

It will be necessary to apply for a detailed assessment hearing, both for the assessment of the costs between the parties and against the CLS Fund. One way of approaching this is explained at 30.6(c).

19.6 What should happen next?

(a) Collecting the agreed costs

If you have not applied for a final costs certificate:

• diarise the date for payment of the costs; and

• if they do not arrive by the due date, consider whether to make an application for a final costs certificate – see chapter 31.

If you have applied by consent for a final costs certificate for the costs claimed between the parties, or the court has issued such a certificate other than by consent:

• when it arrives, check that it is correct;

• make sure the paying party has received a copy;

• diarise the date for payment of the costs; and

• consider enforcement action if they do not arrive by the due date.

(b) Asking counsel for an amended fee-note

If counsel was involved in the case, and his clerk has agreed to his fees being discounted (see 7.3) report the settlement to him so that he can issue an amended fee-note.

(c) Applying the costs

Work out how the costs received from the paying party are to be apportioned between profit costs, counsel's fees, other disbursements and VAT, so that the profit costs can be invoiced.

• Start with the total figure for costs agreed between the parties.

• Deduct from this figure all the disbursements and VAT on disbursements claimed in the bill, and any disbursements (such as court fees) incurred in connection with the detailed assessment proceedings. Do not deduct any disbursements which are to be included in any 'LSC only' assessment or which are to be paid by the receiving party or someone else.

• From the resultant sub-total deduct counsel's fees (at any discounted figure agreed with his clerk) and VAT.

• Assuming that you are not treating interest as a separately recovered element (see 14.8) then, subject to the next point, the balance is available for profit costs (which will normally include your costs of the detailed assessment proceedings) and VAT.

• If the receiving party is legally aided/LSC funded, remember that you must earmark and keep in client account an amount equal to the total payments on account received from the LAB/LSC (see 15.4).

(d) If there is to be an 'LSC only' assessment

See chapter 43.

CHAPTER 20

Checking the points of dispute

20.1 Have they been served in time?

The paying party should serve his points of dispute no later than the 21st day from service of the notice of commencement.

See 8.6 as to the calculation of times and also check whether the time for service had been extended by agreement between the parties, or by order of the court.

If the paying party serves points of dispute after the deadline, but before you have obtained a default costs certificate, he 'may not be heard further in the detailed assessment proceedings unless the court gives permission'. Presumably this means that, while the costs officer may look at his points of dispute, the paying party is not entitled to say anything at the detailed assessment hearing.

It is up to the paying party to make an application to the court for permission to be heard. If and when he does, you can ask for an order that he pays the costs of his application. Such an application might also be a useful opportunity to ask the court:

• to give directions for the detailed assessment generally (see 13.4(c) and (d) for possible directions and orders to seek); and

• to order a payment on account of costs (see chapter 16) and avoid the need to apply for an interim costs certificate.

It is quite possible that the paying party is unaware that, because he was late, he has no right to be heard at the detailed assessment hearing without the permission of the court. You will need to decide whether, as a matter of tactics, you would do better:

• to point this out to him now, in order to use his application as a means of obtaining directions and/or a payment on account; or

• to leave him unaware of his problem until very shortly before the detailed assessment hearing, when surprising him with it may help to promote an overall settlement of the costs.

20.2 Are they adequate?

The points of dispute should:

CPR 47.9(2)
CPD 35.4(1)
CPR 2.11
CPR 3.1(2)(a)
CPD 35.1
CPR 47.9(3)

• be short and to the point;	*CPD 35.2*
• follow as closely as possible Precedent G in the Schedule of Costs Precedents (which is reproduced in Appendix II and is on the CD-ROM);	*CPD35.2* **Precedent G** **CD-ROM 02.03**
• identify each item in the bill which is disputed;	*CPD 35.3(1)*
• in each case state concisely the nature and grounds of dispute;	*CPD 35.3(2)*
• where practicable, suggest a figure to be allowed for each item in respect of which a reduction is sought; and	*CPD 35.3(3)*
• be signed by the party serving them or his solicitors.	*CPD 35.3(4)*

20.3 What can we do if they seem inadequate?

(a) If they are not signed at all

Of the requirements at 20.2, the only one that seems to provide virtually no scope for argument as to whether it has or has not been complied with is the requirement that points of dispute must be signed 'by the party serving them or his solicitors'.

CPD 35.3(4)

Where points of dispute are prepared by a costs draftsman for service by the solicitors who (often only nominally) instruct them, they are sometimes sent out unsigned, or signed by the costs draftsman rather than by the solicitor.

If they are not signed at all, there can be little doubt that they are not points of dispute within the meaning of the rules. You can therefore ignore them and, when the deadline for service of points of dispute has passed, apply for a default costs certificate (see 11.3).

Service of the default costs certificate will usually produce an outraged initial response, but the paying party should eventually accept that he has to take steps to have the default costs certificate set aside, and to be allowed to be heard further in the proceedings. This must be done either by means of a consent order or, if you are unable to agree terms, by application to the court.

This situation gives you the opportunity to seek (by consent or otherwise):

• orders that any other apparent failings in the points of dispute should be rectified;

• directions for the future conduct of the detailed assessment (see 13.4(c) and (d));

• an order for a payment on account (see 16.3); and

• orders as to the costs of the application.

(b) If they are signed by the costs draftsman only

This is a slightly more tricky situation, as the rules are complex and not entirely clear. In an article, 'Detailed Assessments' (*Solicitors Journal*, 18 April 2003, pages 442-443), Stephen Boyd argues that a costs draftsman may not sign points of dispute as a solicitor, nor on behalf of a solicitor. See 8.9 for brief details of the relevant provisions.

If you are willing to argue on this basis, you can wait until the deadline for service of points of dispute has passed and then apply for a default costs certificate – see (a) above.

Alternatively, you can wait until the deadline for service of points of dispute has passed and then write to the paying party's solicitors pointing out that his purported points of dispute have not been properly signed, so are invalid. You can ask them:

• to explain by what authority they were signed; or

• to admit that the original signature was inadequate, and re-serve them properly.

If they choose the second option then, when the properly signed points of dispute arrive, you can pursue either of the approaches mentioned at 19.1, namely:

CPR 47.9(3)

• to point out that, because they were received after the deadline, the paying party may not be heard further in the detailed assessment proceedings unless the court gives permission and that they will therefore need to make an application; or

• to keep quiet and spring this information on them nearer the date of the detailed assessment hearing.

(c) If they are inadequate in other ways

Points of dispute often fail to meet some of the other requirements listed at 19.2. While most of these requirements are perhaps matters of style, the need for each point of dispute to be identified and, where practicable, quantified, is more a matter of substance. If the paying party fails to do this, it can be very difficult or even impossible to arrive at an overall valuation of the points of dispute. That is something which you need to be able to do in order to assess their possible effect at a detailed assessment hearing (see 21.1).

While you have the right to apply in the detailed assessment proceedings for orders, eg requiring the points to be quantified, or striking out inadequate points, making an application yourself may be a waste of time and costs, if you pay a court fee and wait a few weeks for a hearing, only to find that the costs judge is reluctant to make orders of any particular severity against the paying party. **CPR 23** *CPD 40.8*

Of course, if the paying party has to seek an order (eg that he should be allowed to be heard further in the proceedings), then this may give you an opportunity to seek the orders you want, at his expense and at the cost of no additional delay.

It may be better to deal with the inadequacies of the points of dispute in your replies to them by:

• identifying exactly how they fail to comply with the rules;

• pointing out the difficulties these failures cause you; and

• indicating that you will be referring to these matters in any arguments as to who should pay the costs of the detailed assessment proceedings, and as to how much those costs should be.

20.4 What should happen next?

(a) Notifying counsel of objections to his success fee in a conditional fee agreement case

If counsel's services were provided under a conditional fee agreement and the points of dispute seek a reduction in the percentage increase (ie the success fee) he is claiming, you must within three days of service of them deliver to counsel a copy of: *CPD 20.4(1)*

• the relevant points of dispute; and

• the bill of costs or the relevant parts of it.

Within ten days after that counsel must tell you in writing whether he will accept the reduction sought, or some other reduction. If he provides any points he wishes to have made in the replies to the points of dispute, you must include them in your replies. *CPD 20.4(2)*

If counsel fails to respond within ten days he will be taken to have accepted the reduction unless the court otherwise orders. *CPD 20.4(3)*

(b) Notifying the receiving party of objections to the solicitor's success fee in a conditional fee agreement case

If you were acting for the receiving party under a conditional fee agreement and:

CPD 20.5

- that agreement provides for a percentage increase (ie a success fee); and

- the paying party seeks a reduction in it; and

- you intend to seek an order that any percentage disallowed between the parties should still be payable by the receiving party;

then you must, within 14 days of service of the points of dispute, give to the receiving party a clear written explanation of:

- the nature of the relevant point of dispute;

- the effect it will have if it is upheld in whole or in part by the court; and

- the receiving party's right to attend any subsequent hearings at court when the matter is raised.

(c) The next steps

Proceed to value the points of dispute – see chapter 20 – and to prepare replies to them – see chapter 21.

CHAPTER 21

Valuing the points of dispute

21.1 Why do we need to do it?

Although, if the bill is large, this can be a long and tedious task, it is usually a good idea to value the paying party's points of dispute, as this will enable you to:

• discover what the best possible outcome of the detailed assessment could be for the paying party, and so be able to see his starting point in negotiations;

• see how any offer made by the paying party relates to his view of the best possible outcome, and so gauge whether he has pitched it particularly low;

• know what the worst possible outcome of the detailed assessment could be for the receiving party; and

• prepare a list of possible ingredients for any claim against the CLS Fund or other funder of the claim for the shortfall between the costs claimed between the parties and the costs recovered.

Some points of dispute are more helpful than others. If points are not quantified, you will have to use guesswork, eg as to the extent to which the paying party is really objecting to a particular item.

21.2 When is the best time to do it?

It can be a good idea to value the points of dispute just before, or just after, drafting your replies to them, because:

• it saves time and therefore costs to revisit the matter in depth no more than two or three times in total, and this is one of those occasions;

• it helps you to assess the extent and the possible implications of particular attacks made by the paying party, so enabling you to decide where best to concentrate your defence; and

• it is an essential part of the stock-taking that you should do before considering a further round of settlement negotiations or applying for a detailed assessment hearing and perhaps for an interim costs certificate.

21.3 How should we do it?

As with most of these figure-work tasks, valuing the points of dispute can be done manually, but it is generally quicker to use a spreadsheet program. In a bill with more than one part, you will reduce the risk of confusion and error by preparing separate calculations for each part. It is also easier if you deal with profit costs, counsel's fees and other disbursements separately.

Worksheet 5 in Appendix I shows the valuation of the points of dispute relating only to the profit costs in a bill for detailed assessment both between the parties and against the CLS Fund. It is also on the CD-ROM.

Worksheet 5

CD-ROM 10.11

This worksheet contains the following columns:

1. Item number in bill.

2. Party/topic etc.

3. Grade of fee-earner.

4. Work-type.

5. Time claimed in bill.

6. Bill charging rates.

7. Costs as claimed at bill rates, without reductions.

8. Paying party's charging rates.

9. Costs as claimed at paying party's charging rates.

10. Time objected to by paying party.

11. Time accepted by paying party.

12. Value of time accepted at paying party's rates.

13. LSC charging rates.

14. Costs objected to, recalculated at LSC rates.

You will not necessarily need or want all these columns in every case. This is their purpose:

• Columns 1–7 simply reproduce the relevant details from the bill itself, to enable you to orientate yourself.

• In column 5 item charges (eg for untimed letters and telephone calls) are converted to their hourly equivalents, for consistency in presentation and calculation.

- The total of column 7 should equal the total profit costs claimed in this part of the bill. This enables you to check your accuracy.

- In column 8 you put the charging rates proposed by the paying party. If any of the bill rates are not disputed, put them in as originally claimed.

- Column 9 shows each item at the amount of time in the bill, but calculated at the rates proposed by the paying party. The total of this column enables you to assess the significance of the paying party's objections to charging rates alone.

- Column 10 shows any times objected to by the paying party and column 11 shows the time accepted, ie the time claimed less the time objected to.

- Column 12 shows the value of that time at the rates proposed by the paying party. By comparing the total of this column with the total of column 9 you will be able to see how much of the reduction sought by the paying party is to do with charging rates and how much to do with other disallowances and reductions.

- Columns 13 and 14 provide the potential ingredients for a claim against the CLS Fund in respect of any costs not recovered between the parties other than enhancements that might be sought.

Having done all this, you can work out the implications of varying degrees of success by the paying party. Worksheet 6 in Appendix I illustrates this by showing the paying party's prospective success as a percentage of the total reductions sought by him. While this sort of calculation is almost entirely speculative, because it takes no account of the merits of the points of dispute, it can nevertheless have some value in building up an overall picture of the range of possible outcomes of a detailed assessment hearing.

Worksheet 6
CD-ROM 10.12

21.4 What should happen next?

(a) If you have major problems

If the points of dispute threaten to reveal a weakness in your claim so fundamental that you cannot or would prefer not to answer them formally, your choice is between:

- negotiating the best settlement you can at this stage (see chapter 18);

• requesting a detailed assessment hearing in the hope that it will persuade the paying party to settle (see chapters 23–24) – a very high risk strategy in these circumstances; or

• discontinuing the detailed assessment proceedings or withdrawing the bill (see chapter 28).

(b) Otherwise

If the points of dispute cause you no serious problems, proceed to reply to them – see chapter 22.

CHAPTER 22

Replying to the points of dispute

22.1 Do we have to reply?

(a) Generally

There is no general obligation to reply. The heading to the rule describes the reply as 'optional.' The *SCCO Guide* states (at page 29) that before replying 'the receiving party should consider whether the expense of a reply can be justified; it probably cannot if the reply will merely deny the points in dispute'.

> CPR 47.13(1)

However, most points of dispute raise some matters of general principle, to which it is usually a good idea to reply. Points of dispute and replies enable the parties (or their costs draftsmen) to get the measure of each other. A good set of replies will often produce an improved offer of settlement, so the time spent preparing them is usually justified.

If you neglect to reply to points of dispute that raise legitimate questions, this may be 'conduct' which the costs officer can take into account in deciding who should pay the costs of the detailed assessment proceedings – see 35.1(d).

> CPD 45.4

(b) Where you are claiming an additional liability

If the paying party includes in his points of dispute a request for information about other methods of financing costs which were available to the receiving party, you must reply because such a request is covered by CPR 18 and its associated practice direction.

> CPD 35.7
> CPD1.18(1)(c)
> CPR 18
> PDP18

22.2 By when should we reply?

In theory, you should reply within 21 days after you have had the points of dispute served on you, but no penalty is prescribed for being late. It is difficult to see how a paying party could reasonably allege that late service of a reply was a breach of CPR 47.13(2) (which is not mandatory) for which the court should punish the receiving party under the powers contained in CPR 44.14.

> CPR 47.13(2)
> CPD 39.1(1)
> CPR 44.14

22.3 What form should the reply take?

(a) Format

You can either:

- add your comments to the points of dispute if a column has been provided for this (although you are only likely to want to do this if you have been supplied with the points of dispute on disk or by e-mail); or

CPD 39.1(2)
CPD 35.6

- prepare a separate document.

It is easier to do the latter, as it gives you freedom to collate the general points of principle that emerge. These are usually taken from a limited repertoire, and the most common ones are listed at 22.6. By grouping these points you avoid duplication in your replies and are half-way to setting the agenda for the detailed assessment hearing

(b) Completeness

There is no point in giving detailed replies to every complaint that too long was spent on a particular piece of work, or that a particular fee was too high. Nobody is likely to read such replies before (or even at) the hearing and you are unlikely to be paid for the considerable time you might spend preparing them.

(c) Signature

CPD 39.1(3)

'A reply must be signed by the party serving it or his solicitor.' Signature by a non-solicitor employee of the firm will not do.

22.4 Using standard replies and skeleton arguments

As most points of dispute include standard objections based on points of principle (see 22.6 for examples) you will save time by having standard replies that – suitably adapted of course – you can give to such points. Try to avoid making your replies look too general and all-purpose, because this may impair your prospects of recovering an adequate amount for the costs of preparing them. Nevertheless, separate standard skeleton arguments may be useful in dealing with larger or more complicated issues.

22.5 Can the paying party reserve the right to raise further points of dispute?

Although many sets of points of dispute end with an assertion by the paying party of his entitlement to raise further points of dispute, the rules say that 'only items specified in the points of dispute may be raised at the hearing, unless the court gives permission'. In your replies you should, therefore, object to any assertions of this kind.

CPR 47.14(7)
CPD 40.6(3)

22.6 Some typical points and possible replies

On the CD-ROM are typical formulations of some points of dispute that are frequently encountered, with outline replies to them. The topics covered are as follows:

No 1: Indemnity principle/disclosure of retainer. — CD-ROM 11.01

No 2: Charging rates generally. — CD-ROM 11.02

No 3: Proportionality. — CD-ROM 11.03

No 4: Additional liabilities. — CD-ROM 11.04

No 5: Charging for letters in. — CD-ROM 11.05

No 6: Items allegedly not recoverable between the parties. — CD-ROM 11.06

No 7: Costs of evidence not disclosed/relied upon. — CD-ROM 11.07

No 8: Routine work with the court and with counsel. — CD-ROM 11.08

No 9: Whether attendance notes are chargeable. — CD-ROM 11.09

No 10: Duplication and supervision. — CD-ROM 11.10

No 11: Rates at which travel and waiting time are claimed. — CD-ROM 11.11

No 12: Costs of bill preparation and checking. — CD-ROM 11.12

No 13: Charging rates for costs draftsmen. — CD-ROM 11.13

These replies are provided as starting points only, and must be carefully adapted to the circumstances of the particular case and updated to reflect any changes in the rules or case-law. None of them is guaranteed to work; indeed some of them fail more often than they succeed. Even though they are believed to be based on a correct interpretation of the law, many costs officers make their decisions on the basis of what they consider to be traditional practice, which may not be quite the same thing.

22.7 When should we concede points?

Unless you are fairly certain that you will fail in defending a particular item (eg where the other side has spotted you claiming the costs of an interlocutory hearing where there was no order for the costs of that hearing) there may be little benefit in formally conceding any disputed items until very shortly before the hearing, if then. The reason is that if you are negotiating, as you probably will be until you reach settlement or arrive at the detailed assessment hearing, you will probably be negotiating in global terms. As you may never come to a conclusion as to which items are recoverable or not, conceding particular items now will only lower your starting point, without necessarily obtaining anything in exchange.

However, if you intend to make a claim against the CLS Fund for some or all of the costs not recovered from the paying party, it may be expedient to concede items which have little or no prospect of being recovered between the parties so that they can be claimed from the CLS Fund. See 19.5.

In deciding whether or not to make any concessions, you should remember that 'in deciding what order to make about the costs of detailed assessment proceedings the court must have regard to the conduct of all parties, the amount by which the bill of costs has been reduced and whether it was reasonable for a party to claim the costs of a particular item or to dispute that item'. **CPR 47.18(2)** *CPD 45.4*

It would be wise to reassess the situation shortly before the detailed assessment hearing, in case you decide that it would be sensible to make some concessions in order to reduce the risk of an adverse costs order.

22.8 What should happen next?

Once you have served replies to the points of dispute you are in a position to do any or all of the following:

• request a detailed assessment hearing (see chapters 23–24);

• apply for an interim costs certificate (see chapter 29);

• start or continue negotiations (see chapter 18).

CHAPTER 23

Deciding when and where to request a detailed assessment hearing

23.1 When should we request it?

The costs rules say that you must file a request for a detailed assessment hearing:

- where points of dispute are served; and

- within three months of the expiry of the period for commencing detailed assessment proceedings.

CPR 47.14(2)
CPD 40.1

It follows that, because the time limit for service of the notice of commencement was three months from the date of the order or event entitling the receiving party to costs, the request for a detailed assessment hearing must be filed within six months of that date. These are the only two time-limits that automatically apply to the receiving party's conduct of the detailed assessment proceedings.

While you do not have to reply to the points of dispute either at all (see 22.1), or before requesting a detailed assessment hearing, if you are going to reply then it may be better to defer making the request until you have replied, so that you can lodge the replies with the request.

If the time-limit for filing the request is about to expire, or has already expired, you may decide that complying with the time-limit is more of a priority than serving your replies.

From the tactical point of view it is usually best to file the request as soon as you can, because:

- this helps to concentrate the mind of the paying party;

- you may have a long wait for a hearing date, so the sooner you can get the case in the queue, the better; and

- if the bill also claims costs against the CLS Fund, but you agree the costs claimed in it between the parties without having filed the request for a hearing, you cannot then proceed to ask the court to carry out an 'LSC only' detailed assessment of the costs claimed against the CLS Fund unless they are more than £2,500 plus VAT. You must instead have them assessed by the LSC – see 19.5 – and their assessment may be less generous than the court's.

However, if your stock-taking (see chapter 6) has made you aware of significant weaknesses in your bill, or of issues in the points of dispute on which the paying party is likely to succeed, you might decide to negotiate hard for a settlement before making your request, which is in some ways a point of no return.

23.2 Does it matter if we are late in requesting it?

If you are late in making the request, the paying party may apply for an order requiring you to file the request 'within such time as the court may specify'. When making such an order, the court may direct that unless you file the request within the time ordered, 'all or part of the costs to which the receiving party would otherwise be entitled will be disallowed'.

CPR 47.14(3)–(4)
CPD 40.7(1)

As with lateness in serving the notice of commencement (see 3.7(c)) if you are late in requesting a detailed assessment hearing, but by the time you do so the paying party has not made an application, the court may disallow all or part of the interest that would otherwise be payable on the costs.

CPR 47.14(5)
CPD 40.7(2)

• This is only likely to happen if the paying party makes an issue of it at the detailed assessment hearing.

• Even then you might argue that the disallowance should be restricted to the interest attributable to the period of delay, eg if you were three weeks late in requesting a detailed assessment hearing, you should only be deprived of three weeks' interest.

• The court must not impose any other sanction unless you have been guilty of misconduct, in which case it can disallow all or part of the costs which are being assessed and order the receiving party or you to pay any costs incurred by the paying party.

CPR 47.14(5)
CPR 44.14
CPD 40.7(2)

23.3 At which court do we file the request?

(a) The usual venue

You will usually file the request at the district registry or county court in which the case was conducted when the order was made or the event occurred (see 3.2) which gave the receiving party the right to assessment of his costs.

CPR 47.4
CPD 31.1(1)

If the case was subsequently transferred to another district registry or county court, then you should file the request at that other court.

CPD 31.1(1)

In every other case, including Court of Appeal cases, the request should be filed at the Supreme Court Costs Office ('SCCO').

CPD 31.1(2)

(b) Transfer to other courts for detailed assessment

If the county court or district registry which would be the usual venue for detailed assessment (see (a) above) is satisfied that the detailed assessment could 'more conveniently or fairly' be conducted in another county court or district registry, it may order (or, in the case of a county court, direct) the transfer of the detailed assessment proceedings to that other court or registry.

CPR 30.2
CPR 47.4(3)
CPD 31.2(1)–(2)

Such an order or direction may be made either:

• upon application (see chapter 25); or

CPD 31.2(1)–(2)

• on the court's own initiative.

CPD 31.2(1)–(2)

If the court proposes to make an order on its own initiative it should first give the parties the opportunity to make representations. CPR 30.3(2) lists the matters to which the court should have regard when considering making an order.

CPD 31.2(2)
CPR 30.3(2)

The court does not have to transfer the substantive proceedings.

CPR 47.4(4)

(c) Transfer to the SCCO for detailed assessment

A county court or district registry may direct that the costs be assessed in the SCCO.

CPR 47.4(2)

Such a direction may be made either:

• upon application (see chapter 25); or

CPD 31.2(1)–(2)

• on the court's own initiative.

CPD 31.2(1)–(2)

If the court proposes to make a direction on its own initiative it should first give the parties the opportunity to make representations.

CPD 31.2(2)

It should only make such a direction if it is appropriate having regard to:

CPD 31.2(3)

• the size of the bill of costs;

• the difficulty of the issues involved;

• the likely length of the hearing;

• the cost to the parties; and

• any other relevant matter.

If you are thinking of applying for a transfer to the SCCO, among the points to consider are:

- the fact that the SCCO costs officers see some very big cases, so they may not think your case is as exceptional as you or a local costs officer might;

- how long you might have to wait for a hearing at the SCCO, compared to the local court – you should be able to check this with both of them; and

- the process of applying for a transfer may in itself increase the delay in getting to a detailed assessment hearing (although it may be possible to have your listing at the SCCO expedited – see section 18 of the *SCCO Guide*).

(d) Borrowing a costs officer from another court

It may be possible to have the detailed assessment carried out in your local court by a costs officer brought in for the purpose from the SCCO or from another county court or district registry. This can save the travelling time and expenses that might otherwise be incurred if the parties' solicitors and costs draftsmen had to travel to the SCCO, particularly if the hearing is likely to last for more than one day.

There seems to be no formal machinery for making such arrangements, so your best starting point is to ask the detailed assessment section of your local court what they are prepared to do.

23.4   What should we do next?

Prepare the request – see chapter 24.

CHAPTER 24

Preparing the request for a detailed assessment hearing

24.1 What form do we use?

The request for a detailed assessment hearing is made in form N258, which is reproduced in Appendix III and is also on the CD-ROM. It contains a check-list of enclosures. These are commented on below.

CPD 40.2
Form N258
CD-ROM 04.07

24.2 The court heading

Take this from the N252 unless, of course, the detailed assessment proceedings have since then been transferred to another court, in which case the name of the court will be different, but the other details will remain the same.

24.3 Particulars of the notice of commencement

You should insert:

• the name of the paying party, and of any other 'relevant party' (see 8.7) who was served with the notice of commencement (you do not need to name a legally aided/LSC-funded client here);

• the date on which the notice of commencement was served.

24.4 The document giving the right to detailed assessment

CPD 40.2(c)

You should already have identified this when assembling the documents to serve in support of the notice of commencement (see 9.5(b)).

24.5 A copy of the notice of commencement

CPD 40.2(a)

Make sure that the copy is complete (with signature and date).

24.6 The bill of costs

CPD 40.2(b)

(a) Original or copy?

Although the form seems to require no more than a copy of the bill, you may wish to file the original at this stage, if only because it looks better than a copy. If you do this, make sure you keep a copy for your file.

(b) General checks

Before filing the bill, make sure that:

• all the checks listed at 9.5(a) were carried out; and

• any schedule of times spent is with the bill.

CPD 4.12

(c) Updating the certificates

Check that the relevant certificates have been included and have been ticked/deleted/modified as necessary. The references below are to the certificates in the form in which they appear in Precedent F in the Schedule of Costs Precedents, which is reproduced in Appendix II. Your bill may have been supplied with these certificates tailored to the particular case; if so, your task should be easier.

CPD 4.15
Precedent F
CD-ROM 02.02

Certificates (1) 'as to accuracy' and (2) 'as to interest and payments' may have been signed and dated when a copy of the bill was taken for service with the notice of commencement, but you will need to update the latter if the paying party has made any, or any additional, payments on account since the date of the notice of commencement. If there is no room for these details in the certificate itself, provide the details in the covering letter to the court (see 24.19).

If the receiving party is legally aided/LSC funded then, if certificate (3) 'as to interest of assisted person ...' was not completed when you served the notice of commencement, it will need to be completed now. Alternatively, you can provide a separate certificate.

CPD 40.2(l)(ii)

If the receiving party has no interest in the detailed assessment, delete the second alternative certificate.

If the receiving party has an interest in the detailed assessment:

• Delete the first alternative certificate.

• Make the necessary deletions in the second alternative certificate.

• If you served a copy of the notice of commencement etc on the receiving party at the same time as you served the paying party you should already know whether he has asked for the costs officer to be notified of his interest and/or for notice of the hearing date to be given to him.

• If you are only serving the receiving party now, you will not yet know how he is going to respond. This need not be a problem; complete the certificate on the basis that he has not made either of the requests mentioned.

• If you later hear from him with either or both of those requests, write to the court saying so, and ask for the necessary notifications to be given.

You cannot, of course complete certificate (4) – 'consent to the signing of the costs officer's certificate' – at this stage.

Arguably you are not required to complete certificate (5) – 'certificate in respect of disbursements not exceeding £500' – at this stage either, but if all the relevant disbursements have indeed been discharged, there is no reason why it should not be signed now.

If certificate (6) – 'as to recovery of VAT' – is relevant to the case, this should be signed now.

The relevant certificates will need to be signed by the receiving party or his solicitor – see 9.9.

CPR 32.14
CPD 1.5

24.7 Annotating the points of dispute

The costs rules require you to annotate the copy points of dispute to show:

CPD 40.2(d)

• which items have been agreed, and their value; and

• which items remain in dispute, and their value.

You must also file 'as many copies of the points of dispute so annotated as there are persons who have served points of dispute'.

CPD 40.2(e)

However, it is quite possible that you will not have agreed or conceded anything with the paying party by this stage (see 22.7) so will have no annotations to make. If the situation changes before the hearing, send the appropriate number of annotated copies to the court, with an explanatory covering letter.

24.8 Replies to points of dispute

CPD 40.2(f)

Make sure that copies of any skeleton arguments and copy documents that were served with the replies are filed with them now.

24.9 Details of those to be notified of the hearing

The relevant people are:

- the receiving party (if he is legally aided/LSC funded and has asked to be given notice of the hearing);

  CPD 40.2(j)(i)
  CPD 40.2(l)(iii)

- the paying party; and

  CPD 40.2(j)(ii)

- any other person who has served points of dispute or who has given notice to the receiving party that he has a financial interest in the assessment and wishes to be a party accordingly.

  CPD 40.2(j)(iii)

The relevant details are:

CPD 40.2(j)

- name;
- address for service;
- reference;
- telephone number; and
- fax number (if any).

If the assessment is taking place in the SCCO, they will want this information set out in a formal statement of parties. An example is on the CD-ROM. In other courts it will probably be sufficient to provide the information in a covering letter.

CD-ROM 06.09

24.10 Details of any additional liability claimed

If this is a case in which an additional liability is claimed, you should already have prepared these details – see 9.5(f).

24.11 Orders for costs

CPD 40.2(g)

You should file 'a copy of all orders made by the court relating to the costs which are to be assessed' but where, as is usually the case, any such order is already included in the bundle of documents giving the right to detailed assessment – see 24.4 – you will not need to do this twice.

24.12 Counsel's and experts' fee-notes etc

CPD 40.2(h)

You should file the bundles prepared as described at 9.5(c), (d) and (e).

24.13 Retainer documents

If there is a dispute about the effect of the indemnity principle, which remains live despite service of replies to the points of dispute, you will need to file the bundle of copy retainer documents – see 9.6(b).

CPD 40.2(i)
CPD 40.2(i)

You may need to make a decision at this point whether to disclose these to the paying party. Doing so now may bring an end to the dispute and save time at the detailed assessment hearing – see 34.5. Privileged information which the paying party need not see can be edited out.

If you act under a standard retainer which applies to many clients (eg members of a particular trade union) for whom the firm conducts claims in a particular court, you may avoid filing copies of the same document repeatedly. You do so by: *CPD 40.3*

• filing one copy of the retainer document at court in connection with one such case;

• stating the number of that case (the rule says that you do this in the N258) when filing requests for detailed assessment hearings in subsequent cases; and

• making sure that the retainer document to which you refer is the latest version and was not filed more than two years ago.

24.14 Legal Aid/LSC funding certificate etc
CPD 40.2(l)(i)

If the receiving party is legally aided/LSC funded you will need to file the bundle containing copies of the certificate and of any specific authorities – see 9.6(a).

24.15 LSC schedule

If the receiving party is legally aided/LSC funded and any costs payable out of the CLS fund are to be assessed at civil prescribed rates the costs rules require you to file an 'LSC Schedule' of the kind prescribed by CPD 49. Precedent E in the schedule of costs precedents shows the model form. This is reproduced in Appendix II and is also on the CD-ROM. *CPD 40.2(l)(iv)* *CPD 49* Precedent E CD-ROM 02.01

Civil prescribed rates (for details of which see the Legal Aid in Civil Proceedings (Remuneration) Regulations 1994, as amended) will apply unless:

• the certificate was issued before 25 February 1994; or

• the costs were incurred in the Court of Appeal or the House of Lords.

The purpose of the LSC schedule is to enable the court to assess the costs payable to the receiving party's solicitors out of the CLS Fund should the paying party fail to pay the costs assessed against him.

In cases where the paying party is represented by insurers, or is a government department, the likelihood of default is minimal, so the preparation and assessment of such a schedule is almost certainly pointless. While it may be tempting to ask the court, in the covering letter with which you file the N258, for permission to dispense with the preparation and filing of such a schedule, you should take account of the facts that:

• the court seems to have no express power to grant such permission;

• should your confidence in the paying party's willingness or ability to make payment be misplaced, you will have to go back to the court for a separate 'LSC only' detailed assessment; and

• the LSC forms CLAIM 1 and CLAIM 2 require you to state the costs recovered between the parties both at 'private' and at civil pre-scribed rates, so if there is no LSC schedule you will have to make the calculations at that stage.

24.16 Certificate in cases with a disputed success fee

In a case conducted under a conditional fee agreement, where the success fee claimed by you and/or counsel is disputed (see 20.4(a) and (b)), you are required to provide a certificate signed by the solicitor, stating: *CPD 20.6*

• that the amount of the percentage increase in respect of counsel's fees or solicitor's charges is disputed; *CPD 20.6(1)*

• whether an application will be made for an order that any amount of that increase which is disallowed should continue to be paid by the receiving party; *CPD 20.6(2)*

• that the receiving party has been given the explanation required by CPD 20.5 (see 20.4(b)); and *CPD 20.6(3)*

• whether the receiving party wishes to attend court when the amount of any relevant percentage increase may be decided. *CPD 20.6(4)*

This certificate does not have to be a separate document; it could be incorporated in the covering letter to the court.

24.17 Time estimate

The form requires you to give a time estimate for the hearing. This should be worked out carefully. For example, you may consider that the following times will be needed:

- For each individual piece of work, counsel's fee or disbursement that is disputed: 2–3 minutes.

- For each major point of principle, eg proportionality, exaggeration: 12–24 minutes.

- For each less complicated point of principle, eg charging rates, whether particular types of work are chargeable between the parties: 6–12 minutes.

- For argument as to who should pay the costs of detailed assessment and how much those costs should be: 24–36 minutes.

- For any 'LSC only' detailed assessment: 12–30 minutes for this (perhaps longer if the receiving party is going to be present).

- For an assessment in a case conducted under a conditional fee agreement, where the receiving party and/or counsel may want to make submissions: 30 minutes or more.

Remember that a court day is usually 5–6 hours and that a detailed assessment in the SCCO is likely to be quicker than an assessment elsewhere.

It is better to ask for too much time rather than too little, as your time estimate will probably be pruned down by the court and it is always unsatisfactory having to adjourn a detailed assessment part-heard.

24.18 The fee

The fee will depend upon the court in which the assessment is to take place:

Table 3

- High Court (fee number 10.2): currently £250.

- County court (fee number 3.2): currently £160.

These fees apply to requests for detailed assessment made after 31 March 2003, even if those requests are based on orders for detailed assessment made before that date (except if the order was made before 26 April 1999, when special transitional provisions apply, for details of which see the relevant fee order).

The cheque should be made payable to 'H M Paymaster General'.

24.19 Signing and dating

The request should be signed by the receiving party or his legal representative – see 8.9.

24.20 The covering letter

Include in the letter to the court:

• a list of the documents you are enclosing;

• a detailed explanation of how you arrived at your time estimate for the hearing;

• whether the time estimate has been agreed with the paying party;

• a list of unavailable dates for you, the fee-earner (if this is someone other than you and if they are attending the hearing) and the client (if he plans to attend) for the next three months; and

• a legally aided/LSC-funded client's response to the bill (see 10.5) if you have received it.

On the CD-ROM is a draft letter.   **CD-ROM 07.03**

24.21 What should happen next?

Upon receiving the request, the court will: *CPD 40.5*

• fix a date for the hearing;

• give directions; or

• fix a date for a preliminary appointment.

The assessment section at the court should be able to tell you what their usual practice is.

24.22 What should we do when we receive notice of the hearing date?

(a) Diarise it

Check that the court has given you at least the 14 days' notice to which   *CPD 40.6(1)*
you are entitled, and diarise the hearing date.

(b) Notify the legally aided/LSC-funded receiving party

If a legally aided/LSC-funded receiving party has asked to be given   *CPD 40.6(1)* notice of the hearing date, the court ought to have done this, but check with the receiving party to make sure.

(c) Notify the receiving party in a conditional fee agreement case

If the receiving party has instructed you under a conditional fee agreement and (see 20.4(6)): *CPD 20.7(1)*

• that agreement provides for a success fee;

• the success fee has been objected to by the paying party;

• you intend to claim from the receiving party the shortfall between the success fee as claimed and as recovered between the parties; and

• you gave the receiving party the notification required by the costs rules after service of points of dispute (see 20.4(6)); then

you must within seven days of receiving from the court the notice of the date of the assessment hearing notify the receiving party of the date, time and place of the hearing.

(d) Notify counsel in a conditional fee agreement case

If counsel's services were provided under a conditional fee agreement and: *CPD 20.7(1)*

• the conditional fee agreement provides for a percentage increase (ie a success fee);

• the points of dispute seek a reduction in the percentage increase;

• you have notified counsel of this (see 20.4(a)); and

• counsel has responded to the notification that he will not accept any or this particular reduction; then

you must within seven days of receiving from the court the notice of the date of the assessment hearing notify counsel of the date, time and place of the hearing.

(e) Check with the paying party

It can also be helpful to check that the paying party has been given notice of the hearing date.

(f) Check the court's requirements

If you are not dealing with your usual court, or with the SCCO, check whether the court has any specific requirements about filing papers etc in advance of the hearing.

(g) Generally

Prepare for the hearing – see chapter 32.

CHAPTER 25

Making applications in the detailed assessment proceedings

25.1 Are there special forms for making applications in detailed assessment proceedings?

There are no special forms of application for use in detailed assessment proceedings. The particular forms that ask the court to issue a default costs certificate or to list a detailed assessment hearing are described as 'requests' rather than as 'applications'.

If you wish to make an application in (or even before) the start of the detailed assessment proceedings, you have to do so in the general way prescribed by CPR 23 and the practice direction which supplements it.

Similarly, you can agree the terms of a consent order in the detailed assessment proceedings, but the manner in which the court will deal with it is the general one prescribed by CPR 40.6.

CPD 40.8
CPR 23
PDP23
CPR 40.6

25.2 When might we need to make applications in the detailed assessment proceedings?

Among the applications you might need to make, where the consent of the paying party has either not been given or not been sought, are those for:

• an extension of time for starting detailed assessment proceedings – see chapter 4;

• relief from the sanctions imposed by CPR 44.3B for failure to serve relevant details of an additional liability – see 10.6(b).

• directions in connection with a default costs certificate – see chapter 13;

• the issue of an interim costs certificate – see chapter 29;

• the issue of a final costs certificate where there has been no request for a detailed assessment hearing – see chapter 31;

• directions in connection with a pending detailed assessment hearing – see chapter 26; and

• a change in the date fixed for the detailed assessment hearing – see chapter 26.

25.3 How do we make an application without the consent of the paying party?

(a) The form of application notice

The application notice is in form N244, which is reproduced in Appendix III and which is also on the CD-ROM.

Form N244
CD-ROM 05.07

(b) The court heading

You can usually take these details from the pleadings in the substantive case, but see 23.3(a) as to venue. The 'warrant number' box will not normally apply.

PDP23 2.1

(c) Listing information

PDP23 2.1(5)

The rules say that you should either ask for a hearing or ask that the application be dealt with without one. If you are having to make the application because of some problem you have, rather than because of some failing on the part of the paying party, you may decide that a hearing is probably best avoided as, whatever the outcome, the paying party is likely to ask for an order that the receiving party pay his costs of preparing for and attending it. Therefore, unless there are particular reasons for seeking a hearing, tick box 1(c) and complete items 5 and 6.

(d) Parts A and B

CPR 23.6

The notes on the form explain what is required. The rules say that you should:

• state exactly what order you are seeking; and

• state briefly why you are seeking it.

It is generally best to attach a draft of the order or directions you are seeking.

(e) The supporting evidence

The evidence in support of your application may:

• be set out in Part C of the application notice; and

PDP23 9.3

• exhibit relevant copy correspondence and documents.

You should not refer to any 'without prejudice' discussions or correspondence nor exhibit any such correspondence.

(f) Signature

The application notice is verified by a statement of truth, which can only be signed by a party or his legal representative.

If drafted by a 'legal representative' (which means 'a barrister or a solicitor, solicitor's employee or other authorised litigator ... who has been instructed to act for a party in relation to a claim'), the document should bear his signature. If drafted by a legal representative as a member or employee of a firm it should be signed in the name of the firm.

While an 'in-house' costs draftsman actually employed by a firm of solicitors would be considered a 'legal representative', so could properly sign in the name of the firm, this would not apply to a free-lance costs draftsman.

PDP 22
CPR 32.14
CPD 1.5
PDP5 2.1
CPR 2.3(1)

(g) Receiving party's address for service

This should be straightforward to complete. The court address should also be completed at the bottom of the first page of the form.

(h) The fee

The fee is currently £60 whether the application is in the High Court (fee number 2.4) or the county court (fee number 3.2). The cheque should be made payable to 'H M Paymaster General'.

(i) What about the costs of the application?

If the court awards you the costs of the application, these may be summarily assessed, or ordered to be the subject of detailed assessment with the other costs.

CPD 13.1–13.13

If the receiving party is legally aided/LSC funded, the court will not make a summary assessment of their costs, so there is no need to prepare a statement of them. There are some other types of case where summary assessment is unlikely to be considered – see 50.3.

CPD 13.9

In cases where summary assessment is a possibility, whether you should file and serve your schedule of costs is debatable, as there is an apparent inconsistency in the rules:

• The general rule is that if you intend to claim the costs of a hearing lasting not more than one day, you should file your statement at court and serve it on the paying party not less than 24 hours before the day of the hearing (see 50.8(c) for the exact meaning of this timing).

CPD 13.5

- However, if you are making an application 'in the detailed assessment proceedings' the costs of it are costs of the detailed assessment proceedings and CPD 45.3 states that 'No party should file or serve a statement of costs of the detailed assessment proceedings unless the court orders him to do so.' *CPD 45.3*

One possible solution would be write to the court when filing your application pointing out that:

- CPD 13.2 states that 'The general rule is that the court should make a summary assessment of the costs ... unless there is good reason not to do so'; *CPD 13.2*

- the general prohibition on filing and serving a statement of costs contained in CPD 45.3 must constitute 'good reason'; *CPD 45.3*

- if the court directs you to file and serve a statement you will do so; but

- if you are successful in your application you will ask for an order that the receiving party should be awarded his costs of the application, to be assessed at the detailed assessment hearing.

If the court directs you to file and serve a statement of costs, prepare, file and serve one in accordance with the rules – see 50.8. **Form N260** **CD-ROM 05.08**
   Even if the court does not so direct then, unless the receiving party is legally aided/LSC funded, or the case is one of the other kinds where summary assessment is unlikely, you may want to play safe by preparing a statement of costs which you can take to the hearing just in case the court insists on carrying out a summary assessment.

(j) The covering letter

A draft covering letter is on the CD-ROM. **CD-ROM 07.04**

(k) Who serves the application?

This is probably best left to the court, as whether it is served in advance of the order will depend on whether the court decides to deal with it without notice to the paying party. **CPR 23** **PDP23**

(l) How may the court deal with the application?

If you have asked for a hearing, the court should fix a date and time for it, and notify you. **PDP23 2.2**
   If you have asked for the application to be dealt with without a

hearing, the district judge or master will decide either:

* that the application is suitable for consideration without a hearing, in which case he will either go ahead and make an order, and notify the parties (in which case the paying party can apply to have it set aside or varied), or give directions for the filing of evidence; or

  CPR 23.9
  PDP23 2.3–2.4
  CPR 23.10

* that the application is not suitable for consideration without a hearing, in which case he will notify the parties of the date, time and place fixed for the hearing, and may at the same give directions as to the filing of evidence.

  PDP23 2.5

(m) How should we prepare for the hearing?

Depending on the circumstances, it may be worthwhile seeing if the paying party will agree to the orders you are seeking, including agreement as to who should pay the costs of the application.

If the application seems likely to be contested, and the background is at all complicated, or the facts are in dispute, it may be helpful to prepare some or all of the following for use at the hearing:

* a chronology of the relevant events;

* a bundle of relevant documents; and

* a skeleton argument.

(n) Who draws up the order?

Although the court is primarily responsible for preparing any order, you are allowed to do it yourself. This may save time. You must comply with the standard requirements as to the contents of orders and the service of them, which are set out in CPR 40.2–40.4.

CPR 40.2–40.4
PDP23 12.1

(o) How should we follow up the order?

When you receive the order, diarise any dates set by it.

If the court made a costs order against the receiving party, and he was not present when the order was made, you must notify him in writing of the order no later than seven days after you receive notice of it, explaining why it came to be made. Although the costs rules contain no sanction for the breach of this requirement, the court can ask you to produce evidence to show that you took reasonable steps to comply with it. If your instructions come from some person other than the client, who is liable to pay your fees (eg an insurer, a trade union or the

CPR 44.2
CPD 7.1-7.3

LSC), you must notify them as well.

25.4 How do we obtain a consent order?

(a) All parties must consent

Where there is more than one paying party remember that a necessary pre-condition to obtaining a consent order is the consent of all parties to the proposed terms.

(b) Preparing the order

The order must:

- be drawn up in the terms agreed;
- be expressed as being 'By Consent', and   **CPR 40.6(7)(a)**
- be signed by the legal representative acting for each of the parties to whom the order relates, or by the party himself if he is a litigant in person.   **CPR 40.6(7)(b)**   **CPR 40.6(7)(c)**

(c) The fee

The fee is currently £30, whether the application is in the High Court (fee number 2.5) or the county court (fee number 2.5). The cheques should be made payable to 'HM Paymaster General'.

(d) Will it be 'rubber stamped' automatically?

Some kinds of consent order may be entered and sealed by a court officer – see CPR 40.6(2) and (3) for details. Other kinds require the approval of the court, so will go before a district judge or master, who may make the order without a hearing. He may also decline to do so and direct that a hearing be listed.   **CPR 40.6**

Note that, once a date has been fixed for the detailed assessment hearing, there are special rules governing consent applications to change directions given for the management of the detailed assessment proceedings or the date – see chapter 26.   *CPD 40.9(4)*

CHAPTER 26

Applying to change the hearing date or to vary directions

26.1 If the paying party does not agree

If you wish to change the hearing date, or to vary any directions given in the detailed assessment proceedings, but the paying party will not agree, you must make an ordinary application to the court under the provisions of CPR Part 23 – see chapter 25.

CPR 23
CPD 40.8
CPD 40.9(3)

26.2 If the paying party agrees

(a) The application

The usual rules about consent applications (see 25.4) apply, except that if the court has already given a date for the detailed assessment hearing you must also file in addition to a consent application:

CPD 40.9(4)(a)

CPD 40.9(4)(a)

• a draft of the directions sought; and

CPD 40.9(4)(b)

• an agreed statement of the reasons why the variation is sought.

CPD 40.9(4)(b)

(b) The court fee

The fee is currently £30 whether the application is in the High Court (fee number 2.5) or the county court (fee number 2.5). The cheque should be made payable to 'H M Paymaster General'.

(c) How the court may deal with the application

On receiving the application the court may:

CPD 40.9(4)(c)

• make an order in the agreed terms;

• make an order in some other terms without a hearing; or

• direct that a hearing is to be listed.

(d) If a hearing is listed

If a hearing is listed, and the circumstances are at all complex, it may be helpful to prepare:

- a chronology of the relevant events; and/or

- a bundle of relevant documents.

For the reasons given at 25(3)(i) you should not file or serve a statement of your costs of the application unless the court orders it.

CHAPTER 27

Varying the bill or replies

27.1 How can we vary the bill or the replies to points of dispute?

You may vary the bill or your replies to points of dispute by preparing an amended or supplementary document and then:

CPD 40.10(1)

• filing a copy with the court;

• serving a copy on the paying party; and

• serving a copy on the client, if he has an interest in the detailed assessment.

Under the same provision the paying party can vary his points of dispute.

27.2 What may the court do?

Although you do not need to ask the court for permission to vary the bill or replies to points of dispute, it may:

CPD 40.10(2)

• disallow the variation; or

• permit it only on conditions (including conditions as to the payment of any costs caused or wasted by the variation).

CHAPTER 28

Discontinuing the detailed assessment proceedings or withdrawing the bill

28.1 Will we ever want to do either of these things?

Although the rules governing the discontinuance of detailed assess- *CPD 36*
ment proceedings and the withdrawal of a bill are set out in the section *CPD 46.3*
of the CPD headed 'Procedure where costs are agreed', it is not normally necessary to do either of these things where the costs have been
agreed between the parties. If a hearing date has been fixed, you simply notify the court, and the date is vacated. The court's only remaining involvement might be the issuing of a final costs certificate.

Presumably you would only otherwise need to discontinue the
detailed assessment proceedings formally or withdraw the bill if something had gone badly wrong from the receiving party's point of view,
for example:

- the discovery of major problems with the application of the indemnity principle, which meant that he was unable to recover any costs
  between the parties;

- a bill drawn so badly that it needed complete re-drafting; or

- the setting aside or overturning of the order which was the peg on
  which the detailed assessment proceedings were hung.

Even in situations such as those, you would presumably only have to
take either of these steps if:

- you had been unable to negotiate with the paying party a less humil-
  iating end to the detailed assessment proceedings; and/or

- he wanted you to pay his costs of those proceedings.

28.2 Discontinuance

(a) What is the procedure?

The procedure is that set out in CPR 38, which provides that 'a *CPD 36.5(1)*
claimant may discontinue all or part of a claim at any time' by: *CPR 38*

- filing a notice of discontinuance; and *CPR 38.3(1)*

• serving a copy of it on every other party to the proceedings.

CPR 38.3(2)

(b) Do we need anyone's consent?

You will need the consent of the court:

• if a detailed assessment hearing has been requested; or

CPD 36.5(3)

• the court has granted an interim injunction or any party has given an undertaking to the court in relation to the claim (by which the rule presumably means the substantive claim).

CPR 38.2(a)

If the receiving party has received an interim payment (again, the rule presumably means an interim payment in the substantive claim, although the rule also covers voluntary payments, and that could be taken to include a payment on account of costs), you will need the written consent of the party who made that payment.

CPR 38.2(b)

If there is more than one claimant, a claimant may not discontinue without the written consent of every other claimant, or the permission of the court.

To obtain the court's consent you must presumably make an application in the usual way – see chapter 25.

(c) The form of notice

The form of notice is N279, which is reproduced in Appendix III and is also on the CD-ROM.

Form N279
CD-ROM 05.09

You need to:

• complete the court heading, in the usual way;

• delete whichever of 'claimant' or 'defendant' does not apply;

• tick the box to indicate that the receiving party discontinues part of the claim;

• identify the part discontinued (eg as 'the detailed assessment proceedings between the parties begun by a notice of commencement served on [date])';

• delete those which are inapplicable in the list of parties against which you are discontinuing;

• complete (if applicable) the details of the permission to discontinue given by the court;

• have the notice signed by the receiving party or his legal representative – see 8.9;

• date the notice; and

• attach the consent of any other party whose consent was required.

(d) What are the consequences?

CPR 38.6(1) provides that 'Unless the court orders otherwise, a claimant who discontinues is liable for the costs which a defendant against whom he discontinues incurred on or before the date on which notice of discontinuance was served on him.'

While this provision would seem to entitle the paying party to all his costs, not just of the detailed assessment proceedings, but also of the substantive proceedings, that is presumably not what would ordinarily be intended. Even if the situation is not one where the court has to give permission for discontinuance, it might be as well to make an application if only to secure an order defining the costs to which the paying party is entitled as a result of the discontinuance.

The paying party may also apply to the appropriate court 'for an order about the costs of the detailed assessment proceedings' if you discontinue before a detailed assessment hearing has been requested. *CPD 36.5(2)*

If there is a claim for costs against the CLS Fund, and it is clear that the discontinuance of the detailed assessment did not include those costs, but only related to the claim for costs between the parties, you will need to continue with an 'LSC only' assessment of those costs – see 19.5(b)–(c).

28.3 Withdrawing the bill

All that the rules say about this is that 'A bill of costs may be withdrawn by consent whether or not a detailed assessment hearing has been requested.' *CPD 36.5(4)*

If a hearing has not been requested, there will be no need to tell the court of the withdrawal unless it has been involved in the detailed assessment proceedings (for example by giving directions following the setting aside of a default costs certificate), in which case it would be as well to notify it.

If a hearing has been requested, you should certainly notify the court as soon as possible, so that the hearing can be vacated.

If the withdrawal of the bill does not affect a claim for costs against the CLS Fund, you will need to continue with an 'LSC only' assessment of those costs – see 19.5(b)–(c).

CHAPTER 29

Applying for an interim costs certificate

29.1 What does an interim costs certificate do?

An interim costs certificate orders the paying party to pay a sum on account of the costs claimed in the bill. Do not confuse it with an order for a payment on account – see chapter 16. — CPR 47.15(1)–(2)

You can reasonably expect that the district judge or master granting an interim costs certificate will also order the paying party to pay the costs of the application for it.

Normally the order will be for the sum to be paid to the receiving party's solicitors, but the court can instead order it to be paid into court. — CPR 47.15(3)

29.2 Why apply for one?

The main purpose of applying is to get in at least some of the costs claimed in the bill, without having to wait for the conclusion of the detailed assessment proceedings, which might be many months away. This is particularly important where the paying party has made:

• no payment on account at all; or

• only an inadequate payment on account (depending on the circumstances, a payment on account of less than 50 per cent of what is claimed may be inadequate).

You may also hope that if the paying party is forced to make a substantial payment at this stage, he may take a more serious and realistic approach to settlement.

Although you may threaten to apply for an interim costs certificate where the paying party has made a payment on account that you cannot use (because he has not given the particular consent requested in the letter that accompanied the notice of commencement – see 10.2) you may have problems persuading the court that it should issue a certificate when a suitable amount has already been paid voluntarily.

29.3 How soon can we apply?

The costs rules prevent you from applying until (or after) you have filed the request for a detailed assessment hearing. — CPR 47.15(1) / CPD 41.1(2)

29.4 How much should we ask for?

While it may seem prudent to ask neither for too much nor for too little, it is difficult to know where the court would consider those extremes to be. The basis on which the costs are to be assessed may influence your starting point. With a normal bill:

- if it is to be assessed on the standard basis, you might reasonably ask for about 80 per cent of the total claimed, including interest;

- if it is to be on the indemnity basis, you might reasonably ask for about 90 per cent of the total claimed, including interest.

If a payment on account has already been made:

- take it into account in your calculation; and

- refer to it in the draft order.

29.5 How do we apply?

You apply by making an 'ordinary' application to the court under the provisions of CPR Part 23, using an application notice in form N244. How to fill in the form and the procedure generally is explained at 25.3 and a specimen completed form is on the CD-ROM | CPR 23 / CPD 41.1(1) / Form N244 / CD-ROM 05.07

It is helpful to exhibit a statement of the total costs claimed to date. This can be similar to the calculation served with the notice of commencement, but now showing the costs of detailed assessment incurred to date, as well as the current figure for interest. Worksheet 9 in Appendix I is an example, which is also on the CD-ROM. | CD-ROM 06.11 / Worksheet 9 / CD-ROM 10.15

29.6 Who drafts the order and the certificate?

(a) Draft order

The standard form of interim costs certificate has no provision for an order that the paying party should also pay the costs of the application, so to recover these you need a separate order. A draft is on the CD-ROM. | CD-ROM 06.11

Although the court is primarily responsible for preparing any order, you are allowed to prepare it yourself. This may save time and is generally encouraged. | CPR 40.3 / CPR 40.4 / PDP23 12.1

(b) Draft certificate

The prescribed form of certificate is form N257, which is reproduced | Form N257 in Appendix III and is also on the CD-ROM. The same form is used whether it is a county court or a High Court case. Again, although the court is responsible for preparing and serving the certificate, you are allowed to do it yourself, although the fact that the form is no longer available on the Court Service website suggests that the court prefers to prepare it.

CD-ROM 04.06

29.7 Who serves the application?

This is probably best left to the court, as whether it is served in advance of the order will depend on whether the court decides to deal with it without notice to the paying party.

CPR 23
PDP23

29.8 What goes in the covering letter?

A draft covering letter is on the CD-ROM.

CD-ROM 07.05

29.9 How may the court deal with the application?

If you have asked for a hearing, the court should fix a date and time for it, and notify you.

PDP23 2.2

If you have asked for the application to be dealt with without a hearing, the district judge or master will decide either:

• that the application is suitable for consideration without a hearing, in which case he will either go ahead and make an order, and notify the parties, or give directions for the filing of evidence. If an order is made without a hearing the paying party can apply to have it set aside or varied;

CPR 23.9
PDP23 2.3–2.4
CPR 23.10

• that the application is not suitable for consideration without a hearing, in which case he will notify the parties of the date, time and place fixed for the hearing, and may at the same give directions as to the filing of evidence.

PDP23 2.5

Because your application can only be made once you have filed the application for a detailed assessment hearing, the district judge or master should be in a position consider the bill, the points of dispute and any replies, all of which should be on the court file, before making an order.

It is a matter for the discretion of the district judge or master for what amount, if any, he issues an interim costs certificate. However, in an ordinary case, it would seem reasonable to expect a certificate for not less than 50 per cent of the amount claimed, and perhaps 70-80 per cent.

29.10 How should we follow up the order?

When you receive the order, diarise the time for payment, which is normally within 14 days of the date of the order.

It may be as well to check that the paying party has received the order.

If the time for payment passes and no money has arrived, you can consider taking enforcement action. That topic is outside the scope of this book.

CPR 40.11

29.11 What can we do with the money received?

As explained at 15.5 above, it can be argued that an interim costs certificate is of the same nature as a final order, at least in relation to the sum that it covers. That sum would then count as money 'paid in full or part settlement of the solicitor's bill' (rule 19 Solicitors' Accounts Rules) or as costs 'subsequently settled by a third party' (rule 21 Solicitors' Accounts Rules) and could properly be used in part-payment of the profit costs, counsel's fees, other disbursements and VAT claimed in the bill.

However, remember in legally aided/LSC-funded cases to keep in client account 'a sum equal to the payments on account made by the LAB/LSC'.

29.14 What should happen next?

Unless the issue of the interim costs certificate helps bring about an overall settlement of the costs (in which case, go to chapter 30), the next stage in the progress towards detailed assessment will be preparation for the hearing – see chapter 32.

CHAPTER 30

Agreeing the costs after requesting a detailed assessment hearing

30.1 What sort of terms should we look for?

If you agree the terms of settlement in a telephone conversation, you need to make sure that all the vital points are agreed in that conversation, because you cannot expect the paying party to accept additional terms that you thought of afterwards and tried to include in the confirmatory letter.

Among the points you should aim to agree are:

• the amount of costs agreed between the parties;

• whether this is an inclusive figure or whether, for example, interest is to be paid in addition and, if so, who is to work it out and by when;

• the date by which payment is to be made;

• how payment is to be made (in most cases it will be to the receiving party's solicitors, rather than to the party himself);

• what is to happen about interest if payment is late (even if the settlement figure is inclusive of interest, you might want to reserve the right to claim interest in addition if payment is delayed beyond the agreed date); and

• that both parties will write to the court confirming the settlement and any other points required by the particular circumstances of the case (see, for example, 30.6(c)).

30.2 How should we record the terms agreed?

It is essential to record the terms of the settlement in writing, whether by letter, fax or e-mail, as soon as it has been reached. At the very least, you will want to state:

• the date on which the settlement was agreed;

• if you are confirming an agreement made in a telephone conversation, the names of the parties to that conversation and its date and approximate time; and

- such of the points mentioned at 30.1 as are relevant.

On the CD-ROM is a draft letter. **CD-ROM 08.05**

30.3 When should we cancel the court hearing?

The costs rules require the receiving party to give notice to the court immediately 'if detailed assessment proceedings are settled'. *CPD 40.9(2)*

However, the proceedings cannot be considered to be settled until the terms of settlement have been agreed in writing (see 30.1). Only then is it safe to notify the court.

If you have doubts about the willingness or ability of the paying party to pay the agreed amount and settlement has been reached and the money will be due long before any date fixed for the detailed assessment hearing, you may be tempted to delay notifying the court of the settlement until the money has been received. However, in those circumstances it would probably be better to ask for a final costs certificate – see chapter 31.

30.4 How and what should we tell the court?

The costs rules say that notice should be given preferably by fax. While this is the receiving party's obligation, the court may want the paying party to confirm settlement as well. *CPD 40.9(2)*

The fax should come from the solicitors for the parties rather than from their external costs draftsmen (who are not on the court record).

If you want the court to issue a final costs certificate (see 30.5 and chapter 31), now is the time to ask. To enable the court to get the certificate right, you should state:

- the amount for which the costs have been agreed between the parties;

- any amounts paid voluntarily on account;

- any amounts paid pursuant to an interim costs certificate, with the date of that certificate;

- the balance payable;

- the date by which the balance is to be paid, if this is other than the usual 14 days from the date of the certificate; and

- the date from which any entitlement to interest runs (see 14.2).

If the receiving party is not legally aided/LSC funded, there will be nothing more for the court to do, so you should ask for the hearing to be cancelled.

If the receiving party is legally aided/LSC funded and you want the court to carry out an 'LSC only' assessment of some or all of the costs not recovered between the parties then, depending on the circumstances (about which see 30.6 below), you should ask the court either:

- to use some of the time originally allocated for the hearing for the 'LSC only' detailed assessment (give an estimate of how long will be needed, if you can); or

- to cancel the hearing altogether and to carry out a provisional assessment of the 'LSC only' costs at a later date.

On the CD-ROM is a draft letter including all the above options.

CD-ROM 07.06

30.5 Do we need a final costs certificate?

A final costs certificate can be issued by the court on the application of either party if the amount of costs has been agreed.

CPR 47.10

You do not have to ask for one, but you may decide that you want one if you have doubts about the paying party paying on time or at all.

The costs rules require a formal consent order (and fee) for the issue of a costs certificate. See 25.4 for the procedure.

CPD 36.1

See Chapter 31 for the final costs certificate forms and how to prepare them.

30.6 What if the receiving party is legally aided/LSC funded?

(a) Are you happy to accept the agreed costs in satisfaction of all your claims?

If you are happy to accept the costs agreed between the parties without seeking to claim any of the shortfall from the CLS Fund, all you need do from the Legal Aid/LSC funding point of view is to report the outcome to the LSC on form CLAIM 2. How to complete this form is not covered in this book because the forms change so frequently that any guidance given here would be out of date very quickly. You can obtain up-to-date forms and guidance on their completion from the LSC website – see 2.6.

(b) Will you want to make an 'LSC only' costs claim?

On the other hand, if you want to make an 'LSC only' claim against the CLS Fund for any of the shortfall between the costs claimed and

Worksheet 5
Worksheet 10

the costs recovered from the paying party, it may be helpful in pursuing that claim to have a clear statement in writing from the paying party confirming to which items in the bill he objected on the grounds that they were more properly chargeable to the CLS Fund. Now is your only realistic chance of obtaining this, as the paying party will have no incentive to help you with your 'LSC only' claim at some later date. The points of dispute may be sufficient for this purpose, in conjunction with the information in worksheets 5 and 10.

So far as the hearing is concerned, you have two choices:

- to use some of the time allocated for the hearing by turning up in person for the assessment of the 'LSC only' claim; or

- to cancel the hearing and ask the court to deal with the 'LSC only' claim as a provisional detailed assessment.

Unless the receiving party wants to attend the hearing, or there are some other complications, the second option is probably the easier one to take.

If the total amount of the 'LSC only' claim is less than £2,500 plus VAT, you can still have it assessed by the court. It is only if the costs claimed between the parties are settled without a detailed assessment hearing having been requested that an 'LSC only' claim below that figure has to be assessed by the LSC – see 19.5(c).

(c) Was the certificate issued before 25 February 1994?

If you want to claim any of the shortfall from the CLS Fund, but the Legal Aid certificate was issued before 25 February 1994, the court has no power to carry out a separate 'LSC only' provisional assessment. Instead it must carry out a detailed assessment of the whole bill (see paragraph 24.9(a) of the *SCCO Guide* and also *Legal Aid Focus* No 24 at page 14).

Provided both the court and the paying party co-operate, and there are no circumstances (such as a receiving party who wants to attend) making it necessary to have an actual hearing, it may still be possible to achieve the result you want by writing to the court:

- identifying the procedural problem;

- confirming the figure at which the costs have been agreed between the parties, subject to the approval of the court;

- asking it to assess the costs between the parties at the agreed figure;

- asking it to carry out a provisional assessment of the 'LSC only' costs (which you should identify clearly – see chapter 37); and

- asking for your attendance to be excused.

The paying party should also write to the court:

- confirming the figure at which the costs have been agreed between the parties, subject to the approval of the court;

- consenting to it assessing the costs between the parties at the agreed figure; and

- asking for his attendance to be excused.

30.7 What should happen next?

(a) Collecting the agreed costs

If you have not asked the court to issue a final costs certificate:

- diarise the date for payment of the costs; and

- consider applying for a final costs certificate (see 30.5) if they do not arrive by the due date.

If you have asked the court to issue a final costs certificate for the costs claimed between the parties:

- when it arrives, check that it is correct;

- make sure the paying party has received a copy;

- diarise the date for payment of the costs; and

- consider enforcement action if they do not arrive by the due date.

(b) Asking counsel for an amended fee-note

If counsel was involved in the case and his clerk has agreed to his fees being discounted (see 7.3), report the settlement to him so that he can issue an amended fee-note.

(c) Applying the costs

Work out how the costs received from the paying party are to be apportioned between profit costs, counsel's fees, other disbursements and VAT, so that the profit costs can be invoiced.

- Start with the total figure for costs agreed between the parties.

- Deduct from this figure all the disbursements and VAT on disbursements claimed in the bill, and any disbursements (such as court fees) incurred in connection with the detailed assessment proceedings. Do not deduct any disbursements which are to be included in any 'LSC only' assessment or which are to be paid by the receiving party or someone else.

- From the resultant sub-total deduct counsel's fees (at any discounted figure agreed with his clerk) and VAT.

- Assuming that you are not treating interest as a separately recovered element (see 14.8) then, subject to the next point, the balance is available for profit costs (which will normally include your costs of the detailed assessment proceedings) and VAT.

- If the receiving party is legally aided/LSC funded, remember that you must earmark and keep in client account an amount equal to the total payments on account received from the LAB/LSC (see 15.4).

(d) If there is to be an 'LSC only' assessment

See chapter 37 for details of how to deal with this.

CHAPTER 31

Applying for a final costs certificate

31.1 Do we really need a final costs certificate?

A final costs certificate can be issued by the court on the application of either party if the amount of costs has been agreed.

CPR 47.10

You do not have to ask for one, but you may decide that you want one if you have doubts about the paying party paying on time or at all.

The certificate will be issued in form N256 if the case is in the county court or N256 HC if it is in the High Court. Both forms are reproduced in Appendix III and are on the CD-ROM.

Form N256
CD-ROM 04.04
Form N256 HC
CD-ROM 04.05

31.2 Can we apply for one if we have not requested a detailed assessment hearing?

(a) When might we wish to do so?

You can ask the court to issue a final costs certificate, even though you have not filed a request for a detailed assessment hearing. As this will involve agreeing a consent order and paying a court fee (see 25.4) you will presumably only do this if:

CPR 47.10(1)
CPD 36.1

• the paying party has agreed to pay the court fee; or

• you are sufficiently uneasy about them honouring the terms of the agreement to make this seem money well spent if it results in an enforceable order.

(b) To which court should we apply?

The court to which you should apply is the one which would have dealt with the detailed assessment proceedings – see 23.3.

CPR 47.10(2)

(c) What is the procedure?

The procedure is the general one for applying for a consent order, which is set out in CPR 40.6 – see 25.4.

CPR 40.6
CPD 36.1

31.3 Who prepares the final costs certificate?

Although the court is primarily responsible for preparing any order,

CPR 40.3

you are allowed to prepare it yourself. This may save time but the fact that the forms N256 and N256 HC are no longer available on the Court Service website suggests that the court prefers to prepare them itself. The certificate should show:

CPR 40.4
PDP23 12.1
CPD 42.7

• the amount of any costs agreed between the parties or allowed on detailed assessment; and

CPD 42.7(a)

• where applicable, the amount agreed or allowed in respect of VAT on those costs.

CPD 42.7(b)

31.4 When is payment due?

The certificate normally includes an order to pay the costs to which it relates and payment is normally due within 14 days of the date of the order.

CPR 40.11
CPR 47.16(5)

Enforcement of the order is outside the scope of this book. The paying party may apply for an order staying enforcement of the certificate.

CPD 42.11

CHAPTER 32

Preparing for the detailed assessment hearing

32.1 When should we prepare?

In replying to points of dispute and taking stock of the claim you have already done much of the basic preparation. It is generally best to leave the final preparation until very shortly before the hearing, as most cases settle, often very close to the hearing date. However, if the hearing is to be in the SCCO, or in another court that requires the papers to be lodged before the hearing, you will need to do your preparation before parting with the papers.

32.2 Who will be attending the hearing?

In many cases it will be enough either for the fee-earner or for the costs draftsman, but not both, to attend. However, in larger cases, or ones where the points of dispute raise issues about the way they were conducted, it can be a good idea to have both present:

• the costs draftsman can deal with the costing points; and

• the fee-earner can deal with the issues in the substantive case and with the way it was conducted.

Only in cases of any size or complication are you likely to be awarded the costs of both attending, but that is not, in itself, a reason for not having both present in other cases. Provided both can make a significant contribution, the value of the substantive costs preserved may exceed the cost to the firm of the time of the second person.

The decision as to who is to attend ought to have been made before requesting the detailed assessment hearing, to enable the relevant unavailable dates to be given to the court.

If both the costs draftsman and the fee-earner are to attend, they should prepare together, in order to:

• decide who will do what at the hearing;

• rehearse the arguments on any major points;

• review the SWOT analysis in the light of any recent developments; and

• be prepared for last-minute settlement negotiations.

32.3 How should we prepare generally?

(a) Mark up a copy of the bill

Highlight on the copy bill each item disputed.

Next to the item disputed make a brief note of the grounds of the dispute (eg 'too much', 'not recoverable') and of any sum offered by the paying party. This saves constant cross-reference to the points of dispute at the hearing.

(b) Flag and collate the relevant documents

Ideally you should identify each document, attendance-note, letter etc which is relevant to the points of dispute, and flag it with a self-adhesive tab. Mark on the tab the number of the item, or of the point of dispute, to enable you to identify it quickly.

So far as possible, make sure that all the loose documents to which you will want to refer are assembled in a way that will reduce the time spent looking for them at the hearing.

The perfectionist's approach is to copy all the relevant documents and assemble the copies in a logical sequence, for example in a ring-binder, with one copy for the costs officer and one for you. This saves the scrabbling through files, which is, unfortunately, a feature of most detailed assessments.

While the purpose of this flagging and collating is to save time at the hearing, it can be very time-consuming to do, so in a case where the paying party has challenged hundreds of small items it may prove disproportionate to flag each one of them. It is, however, essential to be able to locate every document which is the subject of a significant point of dispute.

(c) Tidy the files and prepare front-sheets

It is good practice to prepare a front-sheet for each bundle, to identify its contents. This makes it easier for you and the costs officer to find what you need at the detailed assessment hearing, and also reduces the risk of bundles going astray in the court office in cases where the documents have to be filed before the hearing – see chapter 33. The front-sheets can be similar in style to those used for the bundles served with the notice of commencement – see 9.5. The front-sheet to each bundle of correspondence should indicate the period covered by it.

CD-ROM 06.02

(d) Prepare your authorities

If there are any cases you intend to rely upon at the hearing, take three copies of each of them – one for the costs officer, one for the paying party and one for you. Highlight the particular passage(s) on which you intend to rely.

Bear in mind that many of the cases cited in connection with detailed assessments are not ones that count as 'authorities' within the terms of the *Practice Direction (Citation of Authorities) 2001* – [2001] 2 All ER 510 : [2001] 1 WLR 1001 – because they are decisions at too low a judicial level. While you may wish to use this practice direction to oppose the paying party's attempts to cite particular cases as authorities, it would be as well to check first whether those on which you wish to rely are similarly open to attack.

(e) Give notice of your authorities to the paying party

Although not compulsory it is good practice to give the paying party notice of the authorities on which you intend to rely, and to do so at least 24 hours before the hearing. You do not need to supply the copies of the cases at this stage; it is enough to give their names and citations.

Unless the court has specifically asked you to do so, or you know that the papers will be looked at by the costs officer before the hearing, there is little point in lodging copies of your authorities at court before the hearing, as they may not reach the file in time. It is better to take them with you to the hearing

(f) Prepare and serve any additional skeleton arguments

If the issues raised by the points of dispute justified it, you will probably have served any skeleton arguments with replies to the points of dispute. However, other points may have arisen in negotiations on which you want to prepare a skeleton argument, both to save time at the hearing and to make sure you get your point across.

If this is so it is good practice to serve a copy of any skeleton argument on the paying party at least 24 hours before the hearing.

Again, unless the court has specifically asked you to do so, or you know that the papers will be looked at by the costs officer before the hearing, there is little point in lodging a copy of your skeleton argument at court before the hearing, as it may not reach the file in time. It is better to take it with you to the hearing

(g)   Make notes for the hearing

These notes do not need to be very full, but they should remind you of the main points that you need to deal with, particularly if they are not obvious from the points of dispute and the replies. It is a good idea to start with a check-list of the documents you will want to make sure that the costs officer has at the start of the hearing.

32.4 How do we prepare our statement of the costs of the detailed assessment?

(a) The form of statement

You will need to prepare a detailed statement of the costs of all the work done in the detailed assessment proceedings, from the point at which they began (when the notice of commencement was served). This can be done in the standard form, N260, which is reproduced in Appendix III and is on the CD-ROM. However, it can be helpful to provide additional details, perhaps in the form of a schedule, of exactly how all the time was spent. It is essential to do this thoroughly, as proper recovery of your costs of the detailed assessment proceedings can make a significant difference to the overall result.

Form N260
CD-ROM 05.08

If you have been maintaining a detailed record (such as worksheet 12) of the time spent on the detailed assessment proceedings, it should be quite easy to work this up into a formal statement. An example is on the CD-ROM.

Worksheet 12
CD-ROM 10.18
CD-ROM 06.12

Where both the fee-earner and the costs draftsman have been involved in the detailed assessment proceedings, the statement should include the time spent by them both.

As you will not be serving it before the hearing, you can finalise the statement as late as possible, so that all the last-minute preparation is included.

(b) What hourly charging rates should be claimed for the costs draftsman?

Paying parties usually argue that a costs draftsman's time should be charged as if he were the lowest possible grade of fee-earner. However, in setting 'guideline' rates for different grades of fee-earner, the SCCO does not indicate any particular grade as appropriate for costs draftsmen, and its general approach is to look both at formal qualifications and at years of relevant litigation experience. On this basis, it is entirely reasonable for an experienced costs draftsman's time to be charged at a rate similar to that for solicitors and legal executives. There is a specimen point of dispute and reply on this point on the CD-ROM.

CD-ROM 11.13

(c) Does the indemnity principle apply to the charge for work done by free-lance costs draftsmen?

An independent costs draftsman is treated for charging purposes as if he were an employee of the solicitor – *Smith Graham v LCD* [1999] 2 Costs LR 1. An employee's time is charged as profit costs. Profit costs are intended to include a profit, therefore the solicitor can charge more for the costs draftsman's time than the costs draftsman has charged him. The indemnity principle no more applies to this kind of arrangement than it applies to the arrangements between a firm of solicitors and its actual employees. See also *Stringer v Copley* (HH Judge Michael Cook, 11 June 2002), Lawtel document AC0103889.

(d) What can a costs draftsman claim for travelling time and expenses?

Because an independent costs draftsman is deemed to be an employee of the firm, it follows that his journey to court is deemed to start from the solicitor's office, not from his own, and if this is within 10 miles of the court you should only claim the time and not the expenses. This time may be claimed at the hourly rate claimed generally for the costs draftsman. *CPD 4.16(3)*

(e) Be ready to work out the costs of the day itself

Your statement of costs should have spaces for the time spent on the day itself. You will need to note these times as the day goes on.

(f) Remember the costs of the post-hearing work

There will inevitably be work to be done following the hearing – see chapter 39. There is no reason why you should not include reasonable estimates of the time and costs of this work in the statement. *CPD 4.13*

(g) When to produce your statement of costs

Never serve it on the other side or lodge it at court before the hearing unless the court orders you to do so. Only produce it at the end of the hearing, when the costs of the detailed assessment are considered. *CPD 45.3*

32.5 What preparation should we make for arguments as to who should pay the costs of the detailed assessment proceedings?

(a) Prepare a chronology of the detailed assessment proceedings

This is useful when arguing over the costs of the detailed assessment proceedings, and should include brief details of all the offers and counter-offers made. If it seems likely to help your case, include any instances of behaviour by the paying party which may be relevant, such as delays or failures to meet deadlines.

If any offers, whether received or made by you, are inclusive of interest and/or the costs of detailed assessment to the date they were made, you should prepare a breakdown of each of them to show the amount attributable to the substantive costs. It is with this figure that the costs officer will probably have to compare the total costs assessed in order to see whether the offer has been beaten.

Do not serve the chronology or file it at court (because it contains information about offers that the costs officer must not see before the hearing). Instead, keep it in the file to produce at the end of the hearing, when liability for costs is being considered.

(b) Hope for the best, but prepare for the worst

In case you should fail to beat an offer made by the paying party, make notes of the successive fall-back positions which you will want to argue – see 35.2(c).

32.6 What should happen next?

Agree with those who are to attend the hearing with you where and when to meet.

A legally aided/LSC-funded receiving party may attend and be heard by the court in relation to any costs claimed against the CLS Fund.

Counsel who acted under a conditional fee agreement providing for a success fee, to which the paying party has objected, may attend or be represented and may make oral or written submissions. | *CPD 20.7(2)*

Otherwise the only parties who may be heard, unless the court gives permission, are: | **CPR 47.14(6)**

• the receiving party;

• the paying party; and

• any party who has served points of dispute under CPR 47.9. | **CPR 47.9**

CHAPTER 33

Filing the supporting papers at court

33.1 Assessments in the SCCO

(a) What papers must we file?

CPD 40.12

If the claim is for base costs only, without any additional liability, you must file:

- counsel's papers ('instructions and briefs arranged in chronological order together with all advices, opinions and drafts received and responses to such instructions');

  CPD 40.12(a)(i)

- medical and other experts' reports and opinions;

  CPD 40.12(a)(ii)

- any other relevant papers;

  CPD 40.12(a) (iii)

- pleadings ('a full set of any relevant pleadings to the extent that they have not already been filed in court');

  CPD 40.12(a) (iv)

- correspondence and attendance notes.

  CPD 40.12(a)(v)

If the claim is for an additional liability only, you must file such of the papers listed above 'as are relevant to the issues raised by the claim for additional liability'.

CPD 40.12(b)

If the claim is for both base costs and an additional liability, you must file the papers listed above together with any papers relevant to the issues raised by the claim for additional liability.

CPD 40.12(c)

(b) When must we file them?

Unless the court makes some other direction, you must file the papers:

CPD 40.11

- not less than seven days before the date of the detailed hearing; and

- not more than 14 days before that date.

(c) How should we present the papers?

The papers should be tidied and secure and each bundle should be provided with a front-sheet, as explained at 32.3(c). In your covering letter to the SCCO list the bundles that you are filing.

33.2 Assessments in other courts

Although the presumption is that you should follow the SCCO practice unless the local court otherwise directs, most other courts seem to have made general directions to this effect, so will not want you to file any papers in advance of the hearing other than those that you filed with the N258. *CPD 40.11*

If you are not sure, check with the assessment section of the court what their usual practice is. Do this in plenty of time, in case they require the supporting documents to be filed, in which case the period for filing them will normally be as set out at 33.1(b).

Even if the papers do not need to be filed in advance, you should still ensure that they have been arranged in bundles as explained at 32.3(c).

33.3 Directions to file additional papers

The court (whether the SCCO or another court) 'may direct the receiving party to produce any document which in the opinion of the court is necessary to enable it to reach its decision'. Such a direction may be made in advance or at the hearing itself. It is most likely if there is a dispute over the retainer of the receiving party's solicitor – see 34.5. *CPD 40.14*

CHAPTER 34

Attending the detailed assessment hearing

34.1 A check-list of things to take

(a) The main documents:

• your annotated copy of the bill and any schedules of time spent;

• the LSC schedule (if any);

• a copy of each of the bundles filed with the request for a detailed assessment hearing – see chapter 24;

• the points of dispute;

• the replies to points of dispute;

• any skeleton arguments served with the replies;

• any skeleton arguments served subsequently;

• your authorities (in triplicate);

• your schedule of costs of preparing for and attending the hearing (in triplicate);

• your chronology of the detailed assessment proceedings, with copies of any relevant offers and any necessary breakdowns (see 17.4(b) and 17.7); and

• copies of any applications and orders made during the course of the detailed assessment proceedings.

(b) Other useful documents:

• your notes for the hearing;

• your own correspondence etc relating to the detailed assessment proceedings; and

• if you prepared the bill, your costing notes.

(c) Spare copy documents

It can be useful to take spare copies of the bill, points of dispute and replies etc in case the originals have been lost in the court office.

(d) Equipment:

• calculator;

• pen, highlighter, pencil, eraser and note-pad; and

• holdall, trolley etc in which to take away the files after the hearing.

34.2 The start of the hearing

(a) Who sits where?

Choose your seat carefully. The usual arrangement is for those representing the paying and the receiving parties to be seated at opposite
sides of a large table, with the costs officer sitting at its head. If both
the fee earner and the costs draftsman are attending, it is best for the
one who is likely to do most talking to sit nearer to the costs officer,
leaving the one sitting further away with the job of managing the supporting documents. Clients and others attending may sit either at the
end of the table opposite the costs officer or, if there is room, next to
those representing them.

(b) Who's who?

Particularly if the client is attending, make sure that the costs officer
knows who's who by making any necessary introductions. Anyone
other than the parties and their representatives may only be present
with the permission of the costs officer.

(c) Setting out your stall

Make sure that you have conveniently to hand all the papers you are
likely to need during the hearing. Keeping the papers in order while
the hearing is in progress is difficult, so it helps to start as you mean to
go on.

(d) Checking that the costs officer has all the papers

Check that the costs officer has all the papers he needs:

• the bill;

• the points of dispute;

• replies to points of dispute;

• any skeleton arguments lodged with the replies.

Check which of these he has read. If he needs to read them before the argument starts, ask if he would like to adjourn at this stage to enable him to do this.

34.3 How should the hearing proceed?

It is for the costs officer to decide how the hearing is to proceed, but there is no reason why you should not make suggestions, for example that any points of principle identified in your replies to points of dispute (eg as to compliance with the indemnity principle) should be dealt with first, as this may eliminate the need for argument on a number of individual items later.

Although decisions on charging rates can conveniently be made at the beginning, where there is argument as to mark-ups and enhancements these may best be considered after the costs officer has gone through the main part of the bill, by which time he should have a better appreciation of the particular issues and of the weight of the case generally.

The paying party will usually want to plod through each point of dispute in sequence, and this is often how it ends up. Unless the costs officer maintains a reasonable pace there is a risk that the paying party will waste time on minor items and that the appointment will prove too short. If that happens, the assessment will need to be adjourned to another date.

34.4 The hard slog

(a) Identifying the point of dispute

The costs officer will normally ask the paying party to identify each point of dispute that he wants to pursue and, if it is not clear from his written points of dispute, to explain why he is objecting to the particular item.

(b) Your reply

He will then ask you if you have anything to say in response. Do not feel diffident about reading out what you have said in your replies to the points of dispute, as the costs officer may not have read them. It is important not to feel pressured into rushing through or down-playing any of your arguments, as you are entitled to say your piece. In particular, resist any (generally irrational) temptation to abandon an argument before you have put it to the costs officer, unless he has already made a finding that means it is bound to fail.

Conversely, if the costs officer finds in your favour on a point of principle, there is no need to rehearse the arguments when it comes up again.

If you find the costs officer, in effect, arguing your point for you with the paying party, sit back and let him do it. Avoid pushing unnecessarily at an open door.

(c) Producing the paperwork

If you can locate the relevant document or attendance note easily, produce it to the costs officer. He may ask you to do this anyway. However, if you simply cannot locate it relatively quickly, you may do better to apologise to the costs officer and either suggest that you can look for it during an adjournment (if it is an all-day hearing), or just ask him to make a finding without seeing it.

(d) The opponent's reply

The costs officer may ask your opponent if he has anything to say in reply. Try not to interrupt him. If in doubt about whether you can say something more, ask the costs officer.

(e) Noting the decision and the reasons

The costs officer will usually make his decision on each item and will say what that decision is, giving his reasons. He should note any disallowances or reductions on the original bill.

CPD 42.1

You should be sure to note these disallowances or reductions on your own copy of the bill as you go along. Make a separate note on your pad of the reasons given for each decision. If you think you might want to appeal any of these, put a big asterisk next to your note of the decision, as a reminder to deal with this at the end of the hearing.

34.5 The problem of privilege

'The court may direct the receiving party to produce any document which in the opinion of the court is necessary to enable it to reach its decision. These documents will in the first instance be produced to the court, but the court may ask the receiving party to elect whether to disclose the particular document to the paying party in order to rely on the

CPD 40.14

contents of the document, or whether to decline disclosure and instead rely on other evidence.'

This problem has most often arisen in relation to retainer documents – see 9.6(b) above. The frequency with which it arises should be reduced by the decision of the Court of Appeal in *Hollins v Russell and others ('The CFA Test Cases')* – see 9.5(f) – which means both that a receiving party with a conditional fee agreement will ordinarily have to disclose it to the paying party and that paying parties should not raise speculative or trivial challenges to the receiving party's retainer.

If, nevertheless, this issue does arise, section 10 of the SCCO Guide gives detailed guidance on how the court is likely to deal with it.

34.6 Adjournment for negotiations

At some point the costs officer might suggest that you and your opponent should go outside to see if you can agree anything. This might be after he has made findings on significant points of principle.

If you are able to arrive at a comprehensive settlement with your opponent, you will need to go back before the costs officer and ask him to issue a final costs certificate – see 39.5.

If you are able to arrive at an agreed figure for the substantive costs, but are not able to agree on who should pay the costs of the detailed assessment proceedings, and/or how much those costs should be, you will need to go back before the costs officer to ask him to adjudicate on this matter before issuing a final costs certificate.

If you are able to make no progress at all, then as soon as this becomes clear, go back to the costs officer and say so. The detailed assessment will then continue.

34.7 What if we run out of time?

You are entitled to a proper hearing, so if you run out of time it will be necessary for the costs officer to adjourn the detailed assessment hearing to another date. This is unsatisfactory, as time will be wasted at the adjourned hearing while the threads of the previous hearing are picked up again. An adjournment is only likely to be to your advantage if something has arisen on which you need to do some further preparation or if things are obviously going against the paying party and he decides to offer improved terms of settlement.

34.8 Working out the result

Once all the items, other than the costs of the detailed assessment proceedings, have been adjudicated upon by the costs officer, the result will have to be worked out in order to know whether you have beaten any offers made by the paying party. The usual procedure is for you and your opponent to go outside to try to agree the arithmetic. This can take some time. Although you may feel under pressure to get on with it, do not allow yourself to be rushed and risk making mistakes. Once the total for the substantive costs has been agreed, you can go back before the costs officer to tell him the result and to argue over who should pay the costs of the detailed assessment proceedings – see chapter 35.

CHAPTER 35

Arguing about the costs of the detailed assessment proceedings

35.1 Who should pay them?

(a) The general presumption

The presumption is that the receiving party is entitled to his costs of
the detailed assessment. It is important that you do not lose sight of
this point and that the costs officer does not lose sight of it, either.
Paying parties often ignore the presumption in their arguments, assert-
ing instead that if the receiving party has failed to beat an offer made
by them (or even if they have succeeded in getting a significant
amount knocked off the bill) the receiving party should pay their costs
of the detailed assessment proceedings.

CPR 47.18

    These arguments are usually based on a misapplication of the gen-
eral principle that 'costs follow the event', ie that the unsuccessful
party will be ordered to pay the costs of the successful party. The point
that the paying party misses is that, in detailed assessment proceedings, the relevant 'event' that the costs should follow is the receiving
party's success in the substantive claim, rather than success in the
detailed assessment proceedings – see *Chrulew and others v Borm-
Reid & Co* (1991) Costs LR Core Vol 150 at page 158.

CPR 44.3(2)(a)

(b) When the general presumption does not apply

The presumption will not apply if:

- the provisions of any Act, of the CPR or of any practice direction
  provide otherwise; or

CPR 47.18(1)(a)

- if the court makes some other order in relation to all or part of the
  costs of the detailed assessment proceedings.

CPR 47.18(1)(b)

(c) How the court should exercise its discretion

In deciding whether to make some other order, the court must have
regard to all the circumstances, including:

CPR 47.18(2)
CPD 45.4

- the conduct of all the parties;

CPR 47.18(2)(a)

| • the amount, if any, by which the bill has been reduced; and | **CPR 47.18(2)(b)** |

| • whether it was reasonable for a party to claim or to dispute the costs of a particular item. | **CPR 47.18(2)(c)** |

The court is likely to consider making some other order only if invited to do so by the paying party. If that happens, you will need to see that all these matters are considered carefully. Note that the list is not exhaustive. Your chronology (see 32.5(a)) may be useful here, particularly if the paying party's conduct merits criticism. It also leads naturally to a consideration of the overall result in relation to any offers made during the detailed assessment proceedings.

(d) The type of conduct that may be relevant

Do not confuse this requirement of CPR 47.18 that the court should take into account the 'conduct' of all the parties with the specific power given to the court by CPR 44.14 to punish misconduct (either in the detailed assessment proceedings or in the substantive proceedings) by disallowing substantive costs or ordering the guilty party to pay the costs of the other party – see 35.6.

Although CPR 47.18 does not specifically say so, it seems reasonable to assume that the existence of the powers given by CPR 44.14 means that the 'conduct' to be considered under CPR 47.18 is conduct in the detailed assessment proceedings, rather than in the substantive proceedings.

35.2 Are there any offers relevant to the decision?

(a) What offers were there?

If you have not already done so, produce your chronology, on which any offers should be set out clearly. Hand one copy to the costs officer and another to your opponent.

(b) If we have beaten the paying party's best offer

| Unless the costs officer has already stated that there are grounds for criticising your conduct, which are sufficient to justify him making some other order, you can simply ask him to follow the usual presumption and allow you the costs of the detailed assessment proceedings. | **CPR 47.18** |

(c) If we have not beaten the paying party's best offer

You can still argue that the receiving party should be entitled to the benefit of the usual presumption and awarded his costs of the detailed assessment. Try to show why the offer in question should not be taken into account:

- Was it invalid in form (see 17.4(a))?

CPR 47.19

- If the offer was stated to be inclusive of interest and/or the costs of detailed assessment have you really not beaten it if it is unpacked to exclude these elements (see 17.4(b) and 17.7)?

- Have you missed it by only a comparatively small margin?

- Was it made after the recommended time (within 14 days after service of the notice of commencement)?

CPD 46.1

- If it was made after the recommended time, had you incurred substantial costs of detailed assessment up to that point, which should be taken into consideration when deciding whether your rejection of it was reasonable?

- If it was made very shortly before the detailed assessment hearing, did it give you adequate time to consider it?

- Can you show that it was reasonable for you to have pursued your claims for particular items in the bill even though they were objected to by the paying party and, in the end, disallowed?

Be particularly alert to signs of any confusion, either on the part of the costs officer, or of your opponent, between the consequences of a Part 47.19 offer and the consequences of a Part 36 offer – see 17.1. If necessary, go through the relevant rules in detail.

If all else fails, argue that the worst that should happen is that each side should bear their own costs, on the basis that an order that the receiving party should pay the paying party's costs of the detailed assessment is unusual and should be seen as something of a punishment for conducting the detailed assessment proceedings unreasonably in some way.

35.3 Is the receiving party legally aided/LSC funded?

If the receiving party is legally-aided/LSC funded, you can argue with even greater force that any offer he did not beat should still be ignored, because an offer made in such cases does not ordinarily have to be taken into account by the costs officer – see 17.6.

CPD 46.4

In this context it may be easier to argue that it was reasonable to claim particular items that were disputed and, in the event, disallowed, when the result of disallowance would probably be a transfer of those items to the claim against the CLS Fund. To have done otherwise would have been contrary to the receiving party's interest in the detailed assessment proceedings.

35.4 On what basis should the costs of the detailed assessment proceedings be assessed?

If you have persuaded the costs officer to allow the receiving party his costs of the detailed assessment proceedings, it may be worth addressing the question as to whether they are to be assessed on the standard or the indemnity basis.

(a) Does the final order award costs on the indemnity basis?

If the final order in the substantive proceedings provided for the receiving party's costs to be assessed on the indemnity basis, either throughout, or from, a particular point in the proceedings, you may reasonably argue that the effect of the order is to provide for the receiving party's costs of the detailed assessment proceedings to be assessed on the indemnity basis as well

However, a contrary argument is that, because the practical effect of the costs rules is to make a distinction between the costs of the substantive proceedings and the costs of the detailed assessment proceedings (see 1.9), and because the costs officer is, in effect, making an order about the costs of the detailed assessment proceedings when he decides who should pay them, the costs officer can decide on what basis the costs of the detailed assessment proceedings should be assessed. If that argument prevails, then he can order that the costs of detailed assessment should be assessed on the standard basis even though the costs of the substantive proceedings were assessed on the indemnity basis.

(b) Are there circumstances justifying an order for costs on the indemnity basis?

If the terms of the final order in the substantive proceedings do not conclusively determine the basis on which the costs of the detailed assessment proceedings should be assessed, it must be open to the costs officer to award those costs on the indemnity basis.

The costs rules contain no specific guidance on the circumstances that the court should take into account when deciding the basis of assessment, but it is likely to be influenced mainly by considerations of conduct. If you can argue that the conduct of the paying party in the detailed assessment proceedings merits disapproval by the costs officer, you can reasonably suggest that the costs of the detailed assessment should be assessed on the indemnity basis.

However, because of the rather rough and ready basis on which the costs of the detailed assessment proceedings are assessed, the theoretical basis of assessment may make little practical difference to the outcome (except perhaps in matters such as the reasonableness of having both the fee-earner and the costs draftsman attending the detailed assessment hearing, where 'double-manning' may be allowed on the indemnity basis, but not on the standard basis).

35.5 How are the costs of the detailed assessment proceedings assessed?

The costs officer will normally carry out a summary assessment of the costs of the detailed assessment proceedings at the end of the hearing, although he does have power to order these costs to be decided by another detailed assessment. *CPD 45.1* *CPD 45.2*

Only when he is ready to do this should you produce your statement of the receiving party's costs of the detailed assessment proceedings. The rules say that you must neither file nor serve it unless the court specifically orders you to do so. Hand one copy to the costs officer and another to your opponent. *CPD 45.3*

Take the costs officer through the statement of costs item by item so that he has to decide whether each was reasonable in nature and amount. It is important that you try to discourage him from taking a 'broad brush' approach.

35.6 How may the court punish misconduct?

(a) Where the power arises

This particular power to punish misconduct arises where:

- a party or his legal representative, in connection with a summary or detailed assessment, fails to comply with a rule, practice direction or court order; or *CPR 44.14(1)(a)*

- it appears to the court that the conduct of a party or his legal representative before or during the proceedings which gave rise to the assessment proceedings, was unreasonable or improper (and this includes steps which are calculated to inhibit the court from furthering the overriding objective of enabling the court to deal with cases justly). *CPR 44.14(1)(b)* *CPD 18.2* *CPR 1.1*

(b) What punishment may be imposed?

If the power has arisen in the circumstances set out at (a), the court may:

• disallow all or part of the costs which are being assessed; or

• order the party at fault or his legal representative to pay costs which he has caused any other party to incur.

(c) What procedure should the court follow?

Before making an order under CPR 44.14 the court must give the party or legal representative in question a reasonable opportunity to attend a hearing to give reasons why it should not make such an order.

CPD 18.1

(d) Who is most at risk from the exercise of this power?

Although this power may be used against either party (or maybe even both), it poses more of a danger to the receiving party than to the paying party, because

• if he fails to comply with the time-limits for serving the notice of commencement and/or for requesting a detailed assessment hearing, in addition to the other penalties to which he may be subject (see 3.7(c)) he may also be exposed to the risk of an order made under this power;

• if such an order is made, he faces the potential loss of his substantive costs; and

CPR 44.14(2)(a)

• even if he has behaved impeccably in the detailed assessment proceedings, the costs officer has the power to punish him at this late stage for misconduct during, or even before, the substantive proceedings, which may only have come to light during the detailed assessment proceedings.

CPR 44.14(1)(b)

The paying party is already, on the face of it, liable to pay the receiving party's costs of the detailed assessment proceedings, so if the way he conducts himself in those proceedings causes those costs to be increased, it is likely that he will have to pay those increased costs in the normal course of events. There may therefore be little point in a receiving party trying to persuade the costs officer to make an order against the paying party under CPR 44.14 if the receiving party will be adequately compensated by a proper assessment of his costs of the detailed assessment proceedings.

(e) How does this power relate to the 'wasted costs' jurisdiction?

The court's power to punish misconduct under CPR 44.14 is the equivalent, for detailed assessment proceedings, of the court's power to make a wasted costs order under CPR 48.7. The 'wasted costs' procedure may only be invoked in the substantive proceedings. However, it appears that the procedure under CPR 44.14 is not correspondingly confined to detailed assessment proceedings, because it can also arise in relation to a summary assessment arising during the course of the substantive proceedings.

CPR 48.7
CPD 53.1
CPR 44.14(1)(a)

(f) Notifying the client of the making of an order

Where the court makes an order of the kind mentioned at (b) against a legally represented party who is not present when the order is made, it is the duty of that party's solicitor to notify him in writing of the order no later than seven days after the solicitor receives notice of it.

CPR 44.14(3)

Although there is no sanction for breach of this obligation, the court may either in the order itself, or in a subsequent order, require the solicitor to produce to the court evidence that he took reasonable steps to comply with the obligation.

CPD 18.3

There is no provision to prevent a solicitor from claiming from his client any costs which have been disallowed between the parties under this power.

35.7 What should happen next?

(a) If there is a shortfall in the recovery of a success fee in a conditional fee agreement case

If the receiving party has instructed you and/or counsel under a conditional fee agreement and:

• that agreement provides for a success fee;

• the success fee has been objected to by the paying party;

• you intend to claim from the receiving party the shortfall between the success fee as claimed and as recovered between the parties; and

• you gave the receiving party the notification required by the costs rules after service of points of dispute (see 20.4(b)); then

at the detailed assessment hearing, the costs officer will deal with the assessment of the costs between the parties, including the amount of

CPD 20.8(1)

the success fee, and will provide a final costs certificate for the total costs so assessed.

The costs officer must then decide whether any shortfall between the success fee claimed between the parties and the success fee recovered should be paid by the receiving party.

He can do this immediately if: *CPD 20.8(2)*

- the receiving party and all parties to the relevant agreement agree that the issue should be decided without an adjournment; *CPD 20.8(2)(a)*

- the receiving party (or, if corporate, an officer or employee who has authority to consent on behalf of the receiving party) is present in court; and *CPD 20.8(2)(b)*

- the court is satisfied that the issue can be fairly decided without an adjournment. *CPD 20.8(2)(c)*

Otherwise, the costs officer will give directions and fix a date for the hearing of the application. This will enable the receiving party to be notified of the order sought and to seek separate representation. **CPR 44.16** *CPD 20.3(1)* *CPD 20.8(3)*

(b) If there are 'LSC only' costs

If there are some costs claimed against the CLS Fund, proceed immediately to the 'LSC only' part of the detailed assessment hearing – see chapter 36.

(c) Will you want to appeal?

If you think you might want to appeal against any aspect of the detailed assessment, see chapter 38.

(d) Otherwise

Proceed to complete the bill – see chapter 39.

Dealing with the 'LSC only' part of the detailed assessment hearing

36.1 When will this happen?

The 'LSC only' part of the detailed assessment hearing will only happen where there are some costs claimed against the CLS Fund:

• either because they were only ever claimed against the CLS Fund in the bill, or

• because they had been claimed against the paying party, but were disallowed against him during the detailed assessment hearing.

The usual time for this to happen is immediately after the conclusion of the detailed assessment of the costs claimed between the parties. At that point the paying party, who has no interest in this part of the assessment, will leave.

CPD 49.6

36.2 What is the receiving party's involvement?

The receiving party is entitled to take part if he has an interest in the detailed assessment – see 10.3(a).

The receiving party will not necessarily be present. He is under no obligation to attend, and may well have sent in written observations, which he wants the costs officer to take into account.

Whether the receiving party is present or absent, the costs officer will generally help to look after his interests. Remember that, by this stage in the case, the receiving party's interest in the assessment is not the same as yours. This is because if some item of costs is disallowed between the parties, it will be in your interests to have it allowed against the CLS Fund, whereas if this means it will come out of his damages, it is in the receiving party's interest to have it disallowed completely. It follows that, so far as the 'LSC only' part of the detailed assessment is concerned, you have to look after your own interests.

36.3 What costs are to be assessed?

(a) Items claimed only against the LSC

These are items in the bill that were only ever claimed against the CLS

Fund (eg the costs of a particular application where no order for costs was made between the parties) and not against the paying party.

(b) Items originally claimed against the paying party

These are items originally claimed in the bill against the paying party, but which the costs officer disallowed between the parties in the first part of the detailed assessment hearing. He must now decide whether to award all or part of those items against the CLS Fund. He may well have indicated at the time he disallowed these items between the parties what his intentions were in this respect.

(c) The costs of the 'LSC only' detailed assessment

These are the costs of the detailed assessment proceedings relating to the preparation for, the attendance at and the follow-up of the 'LSC only' detailed assessment.

36.4 How should the assessment be conducted?

To avoid items being overlooked, it may be best if you identify to the costs officer in sequence the items claimed against the CLS Fund. If the receiving party is present, the costs officer should listen to any points he wants to put, and he should also listen to any arguments you may wish to put forward. He should then make his findings.

As in the case of the detailed assessment between the parties, you should make a careful note of his findings, and of any reasons he gives for them.

36.5 How should the results of the assessment be recorded?

(a) Items claimed only against the LSC

Because these items will be clearly identified in the bill, the costs officer can note his assessment of these costs where they appear in the bill itself.

(b) Items originally claimed against the paying party

It can be difficult keeping track of these items, and the 'LSC Schedule' will probably be of little use in this exercise, which is not one for which it was designed. Unless the bill itself is arranged with separate columns or parts to which such items which are allowed against the

CLS Fund can be transferred, there will be no obvious place for the costs officer to note his assessment of those items. In such a case the best course of action is probably for the receiving party to note all these items carefully and to prepare a summary of them later. The costs officer may endorse a note of what was decided on the title page of the bill.

(c) The costs of the 'LSC only' detailed assessment

Finally, the costs officer should decide how much, if any, of the costs of the detailed assessment proceedings to order against the CLS Fund.

36.6 The LSC schedule

The costs officer will need to go through the LSC schedule (see 24.15) approving the items potentially claimed from the CLS Fund, and deleting any that he decides to disallow both between the parties and against the CLS Fund.

If any enhancements are claimed on the basic civil prescribed rates, the costs officer will need to decide whether any enhancements are justified in principle and, if so, at what percentage they should be allowed.

CHAPTER 37

Requesting a semi-detached 'LSC only' detailed assessment

37.1 When is this possible?

Where:

- your bill claims costs against both the paying party and the CLS Fund;

- you have requested a detailed assessment hearing;

- the costs claimed against the paying party are agreed without a hearing;

- you wish to claim some or all of the shortfall (ie the difference between the costs as claimed between the parties and the costs as recovered) from the CLS Fund; and

- the costs agreed between the parties have been paid (this is a requirement of regulation 106A of the Civil Legal Aid (General) Regulations 1989);

you can ask the court to carry out, in effect, a provisional detailed assessment of the 'LSC only' costs. This saves the inconvenience of attending a full hearing to assess what may be a comparatively small amount of costs. It seems safe to assume that the court is not prevented from assessing the costs claimed against the CLS Fund even if they are £2,500 or less. If that were not so, you would have to abandon the detailed assessment proceedings for which a non-refundable court fee had been paid and prepare a CLAIM 2 for assessment by the LSC.

Ordinary (ie free-standing) 'LSC only' provisional detailed assessments are explained in chapter 43. Semi-detached 'LSC only' detailed assessments differ from them only in the way in which they come about – as a semi-detached part of the full detailed assessment hearing originally requested. For this reason, no additional formal request has to be made (eg in form N258A – see 43.2) or fee paid, because the request has already been made and the fee paid in the detailed assessment proceedings between the parties.

Such 'semi-detached' LSC-only detailed assessments are provided for in the costs rules.

CPD 49.7

37.2 When is it not possible?

(a) When a detailed assessment hearing between the parties has not been requested

If you had not requested a hearing for the detailed assessment of the costs claimed both between the parties and against the CLS Fund by the time the costs claimed between the parties were agreed, then what you should do next depends on the amount of costs claimed against the CLS Fund.

If the total costs (ie profit costs, counsel's fees and disbursements) claimed exceed £2,500 (excluding VAT), you may proceed with an ordinary 'LSC only' provisional assessment – see chapter 43.

If the total costs (ie profit costs, counsel's fees and disbursements) claimed do not exceed £2,500 (excluding VAT), the court has no power to assess them and you will have to have them assessed by the LSC, using their form CLAIM 2. How to complete this form is not covered in this book, because the forms change so frequently that any guidance given here would be out of date very quickly. You can obtain up-to-date forms and guidance on their completion from the LSC website – see 2.6.

(b) When the client wants to attend the hearing

If the client has indicated that he wishes to attend the detailed assessment hearing and if you had not requested a hearing for the detailed assessment of the costs claimed both between the parties and against the CLS Fund by the time the costs claimed between the parties were agreed, then:

- if the total costs (excluding VAT) claimed against the CLS Fund exceed £2,500, apply for an ordinary 'LSC only' assessment (see chapter 43), with a request that the court should fix a hearing date rather than make a provisional assessment; alternatively

- if the total costs (excluding VAT) claimed against the CLS Fund are £2,500 or less, the court has no power to assess them and you will have to have them assessed by the LSC, leaving the client to make his representations to them.

37.3 The tailor-made LSC schedule

(a) What is the purpose of it?

It may be unreasonable to expect a costs officer to pick his way through the remains of a bill prepared originally for assessment both between the parties and against the CLS Fund in order to identify and then assess the items which were disputed by the paying party and which form the subject of the final claim against the CLS Fund.

What you cannot do is simply present him with a figure which represents the difference between the costs as claimed between the parties and the costs agreed between the parties, and ask him to decide how much of that sum should be paid out of the CLS Fund. He has to carry out a proper assessment of a properly presented claim.

You should therefore prepare a tailor-made LSC schedule, limited to the specific items you are asking the costs officer to order against the CLS Fund.

(b) What should the schedule contain?

The schedule may be quite short and:

- should contain only the briefest of details, as in the usual kind of 'LSC schedule';

- may refer to or summarise the relevant parts of the paying party's points of dispute, to show that the items you are now claiming were indeed disputed and the grounds of the dispute; and

- should include your claim for the costs of the 'LSC only' detailed assessment.

CPD 49.2-4
Precedent E
CD-ROM 02.01

(c) What about the costs of the 'LSC only' assessment?

It is worth claiming what you reasonably can for the costs of the 'LSC only' detailed assessment, as they will not be subject to the statutory charge, so will not come out of the client's damages.

- Remember what count as 'costs of detailed assessment' – see 1.13 above.

- Claim in full the costs of any work done solely in relation to the claim against the CLS Fund, eg preparing the LSC schedule.

- Claim an apportioned part of any work that can fairly be said to relate both to the claim between the parties and to the claim against the CLS Fund, eg negotiating over the costs, preparing the N258, etc.

- Unless the certificate was issued before 25 February 1994 or the costs relate to work done in the Court of Appeal or the House of Lords, these costs will have to be claimed at civil prescribed rates – see the Legal Aid in Civil Proceedings (Remuneration) Regulations 1994, as amended.

- If the paying party refused to pay any part of the court's detailed assessment fee (which is the implication if he refused to pay any of the costs of the detailed assessment proceedings), you can reasonably claim the whole of it against the CLS Fund. The approach envisaged by the Supreme Court and county court fees orders, that the assessment fee should be attributed to the costs allowed between the parties and the costs allowed against the CLS Fund 'proportionately... on the basis of the amount allowed', can logically apply only where there has been an assessment of the costs claimed between the parties.   **Table 3**

- The fee on sealing the Legal Aid/LSC assessment certificate (form EX80A) – currently £30 – is always and only claimable against the CLS Fund, so be sure to include it.

(d) Do we need the client's consent?

It is always helpful if you can supply the client's written consent to the deduction from his damages of those costs claimed against the CLS Fund that are subject to the statutory charge. Ideally his consent will specify that figure as the amount up to which the client is content to suffer a deduction from his damages. A draft form of consent is on the CD-ROM. This may help to reduce any concern on the part of the costs officer that the claim deserves to be scrutinised minutely and critically.   **CD-ROM 06.13**

(e) What do we ask the court to do?

It can be helpful in the covering letter to explain exactly what needs to be done, as the paperwork can be confusing. A draft letter is on the CD-ROM.   **CD-ROM 07.07**

37.4 What happens next?

(a) If the result of the assessment is acceptable

If the costs officer either assesses the LSC schedule as drawn, or makes reductions that you are prepared to accept, the next step is to accept the provisional assessment – see 44.2.

(b) If the result of the assessment is not acceptable

If the costs officer makes reductions that you are not prepared to accept, the next step is to request an assessment hearing – see 44.3.

CHAPTER 38

Deciding whether to appeal against the detailed assessment

38.1 Why are there two appeal routes?

If you wish to appeal against a detailed assessment, the way in which you launch your appeal, and the way it is decided, depend on the level of costs officer before whom the assessment took place. It will have been either:

- before an 'authorised court officer' (any officer of a county court, district registry or the SCCO who has been authorised to assess costs); or

  CPR 43.2(1)(d)

- before a costs judge or district judge.

38.2 How do we appeal against a detailed assessment by an authorised court officer?

(a) Where do we find the rules about this kind of appeal?

This kind of appeal is dealt with in accordance with the costs rules, rather than in accordance with CPR 52 (which governs all appeals above this level).

CPR 52.1(2)

(b) To whom does the appeal lie?

An appeal from an authorised court officer lies to a costs judge or a district judge of the High Court, who will deal with it by way of re-hearing.

CPR 47.21
CPD 48.2

(c) Do we need permission?

You do not need permission for this kind of appeal, which can be made by 'any party to detailed assessment proceedings'. However, a legally aided/LSC-funded client does not count as a party to detailed assessment proceedings for this purpose, so he cannot use this type of appeal to try to overturn the assessment of 'LSC only' costs with which he is dissatisfied.

CPR 47.20
CPD 47.2

(d) What form should we use?

There is no longer a special form for use in costs appeals. Instead, your notice should be in form N161, 'Appellant's Notice', which is used for appeals in substantive proceedings. The form is long, but comprehensive notes on completing it are available on form N161A. Both because of their length, and because they are forms generally used in substantive proceedings, they are not reproduced in this book.

CPR 47.22
CPD 48.1

(e) What is the time limit for appealing?

You must file the notice of appeal within 14 days after the decision against which you wish to appeal. Note that time starts to run from each individual finding in a detailed assessment, so if the hearing is not completed on the first day and has to be adjourned, make sure that at the end of the first day the authorised court officer makes an order that the time for appealing is extended to 14 days from the conclusion of the detailed assessment. In this way you will preserve your right to appeal and not be required to make an appeal before the detailed assessment as a whole is finished.

CPR 47.22(1)

(f) What record of the detailed assessment do we need?

Although you do not need to seek the authorised court officer's written reasons for making the findings against which you are appealing, you should try to provide a suitable record of the judgment appealed against. If reasons for the decision have been officially recorded by the court, you should submit an approved transcript (not a photocopy). If there is no official record you may instead rely upon:

CPD 47.2
CPD 48.3

• the authorised court officer's comments written on the bill; and/or

CPD 48.3(1)

• advocates' notes of the reasons, agreed by the respondent to the appeal if possible, and approved by the authorised court officer.

CPD 48.3(2)

If you are not able to obtain a suitable record of the authorised court officer's decision within the time in which you must file the notice of appeal, complete the notice so far as you are able. You may amend it later, with the permission of the costs judge or district judge hearing the appeal.

CPD 48.4

(g) What is the court fee?

The fee is currently £100 whether the appeal is in the High Court (fee number 10.4) or the county court (fee number 3.4). The cheque should

Table 3

be made payable to 'H M Paymaster General'.

(h) Who serves the notice?

Once you have lodged the notice of appeal, the court will serve a copy of it on the other parties to the detailed assessment and will also give notice of the date fixed for the hearing of the appeal. | CPR 47.22(2)

(i) How is the appeal hearing conducted?

At the appeal hearing, the costs judge or district judge will: | CPR 47.23

- re-hear the proceedings which gave rise to the decision appealed against; and | CPR 47.23(a)

- make any order and give any directions he considers appropriate. | CPR 47.23(b)

38.3 How do we appeal against a detailed assessment by a costs judge or district judge?

(a) Where do we find the rules about this kind of appeal?

This kind of appeal is dealt with in accordance with CPR 52 and the practice direction supplementing it, which provide a comprehensive code for appeals in substantive proceedings. A detailed consideration of them is outside the scope of this book. It is, however, important to be aware before the detailed assessment hearing of what the appeal route is and of what you have to do if you wish to appeal against a decision in the detailed assessment. | CPR 52 / PDP52

(b) To whom does the appeal lie?

The appeal has to be dealt with in accordance with CPR Part 52. The route of appeal depends upon the level of judge against whom the appeal is made. | CPR 52 / PDP52 2A.1

(c) Do we need permission?

You do need permission to appeal, which you can seek in either of two ways: | CPR 52.3(2)

- Ideally, you should ask for it orally at the end of the detailed assessment hearing, even if you are not sure that you will ultimately decide to pursue the appeal.

- However, if you asked at the hearing and permission was refused, or if you did not ask at the hearing, you must seek permission in writing in your notice of appeal.

Permission will only be given if the court considers that the appeal would have a real prospect of success or there is some other compelling reason why it should be heard.

CPR 52.3(6)

(d) What form should we use?

The form is N161 – see 38.2(d).

(e) What is the time-limit for appealing?

You must file the notice of appeal within 14 days after the decision against which you wish to appeal. See 38.2(e) about what to do if the detailed assessment hearing lasts for more than one day.

CPR 52.4

  Only the appeal court has power to grant an extension of time for filing the appeal notice; this is not something the parties can agree themselves.

CPR 52.6

(f) What record of the detailed assessment do we need?

Form N161 contains a check-list of the documents you must file in support of your appeal. It includes:

• 'a suitable record of the reasons for the judgment of the lower court', and

• 'any relevant transcript or note of evidence'.

If you are not able to obtain a suitable record within the time in which you must file the notice of appeal, complete the form so far as you are able, giving reasons why it is not available and when you expect to have it.

(g) What is the court fee?

The fee is currently £100 whether the appeal is in the High Court (fee number 10.4) or the county court (fee number 3.4). The cheque should be made payable to 'H M Paymaster General'.

Table 3

(h) Who serves the notice?

It is your responsibility to serve the notice on each respondent and to do so within seven days after filing it at court. The respondent to the appeal may serve a respondent's notice (in form N162), but he is not

CPR 52.4(3)
CPR 52.5

obliged to do so if he intends to rely on the reasons given by the court for the judgment being appealed against.

(i) How is the appeal hearing conducted?

The appeal will normally be a review of the decision of the lower court, unless the appeal court considers it would be in the interests of justice to hold a re-hearing.

CPR 52.11(1)

The appeal court will generally allow an appeal if it is satisfied that the decision of the costs judge or district judge was wrong in a matter of principle or construction, or unjust because of a serious procedural or other irregularity. It will be less willing to do so if the appeal challenges details of the assessment, such as the amount of time allowed for particular items of work, where the question is one of judgment rather than principle. 'Permission to appeal should not be granted simply to allow yet another trawl through the bill, in the absence of some sensible and significant complaint' – Buckley J in *Mealing-McLeod v Common Professional Examination Board* [2000] 2 Costs LR 223 at page 224.

CPR 52.11(3)

If it does not dismiss the appeal, the appeal court may:

CPR 52.10(2)

• affirm, set aside or vary any order or judgment made or given by the lower court;

• refer any claim or issue for determination by the lower court;

• order a new hearing;

• make orders for the payment of interest;

• make a costs order.

It may exercise these powers in relation to the whole or part of the order of the lower court.

CPR 52.10(4)

CHAPTER 39

Completing the detailed assessment

39.1 What papers should we take away

Make sure that you take the original bill away from the hearing, as it will be your job to complete it, to show the result of the detailed assessment.

You should also take away all the papers you filed or brought in support of the bill. If you fail to do this, the court is liable to dispose of them without notifying you.

CPD 40.16

39.2 Do we need to tell counsel of any reductions?

(a) In legally aided/LSC-funded cases

In a legally aided/LSC-funded case you must, within seven days after the detailed assessment, tell counsel of any reductions in his fees allowed against the CLS Fund, in case he wishes to make representations to the court – see regulation 112 of the Civil Legal Aid (General) Regulations 1989.

If counsel is dissatisfied with the reduction, he is entitled to enlist your help in appealing against it – see regulation 116 of the Civil Legal Aid (General) Regulations 1989.

(b) In cases funded in other ways

In a case funded privately, or under some types of conditional fee agreement, the receiving party is usually responsible for meeting any shortfall between counsel's fees as claimed and as allowed, and it is quite likely that by the time of the detailed assessment hearing they will already have been paid in full. On the face of it, counsel will not be concerned about any shortfall, although if he has not been paid by that stage you may be able to persuade his clerk to waive all or some of the shortfall.

39.3 How should we complete the bill and LSC schedule?

(a) Dealing with the figures

After the detailed assessment, it is the responsibility of the receiving

CPR 47.16(1)

211

party to complete the bill, ie to 'make clear the correct figures agreed or allowed in respect of each item' and to 'recalculate the summary of the bill appropriately'. If the costs officer has done as he ought, and marked his disallowances and reductions in the body of the bill itself, it seems that you need only recalculate the summary, not every page total (if the bill is in a format that provides page totals).

CPD 42.2

Rather than crossing out the figures in the existing summary for the costs as claimed, and squeezing in the figures for the costs as allowed, you may find it quicker and tidier to substitute a summary of the costs as allowed for the original summary of the costs as claimed.

However, if the bill uses a layout with separate columns for the amounts claimed and the amounts allowed, you may use these columns without needing to cross anything out, either in the body of the bill or in the summary.

If the bill contains a space for the court fees payable in connection with the detailed assessment (either in the body of it or in the summary), you may show them there. The fees in question are:

• the fee you paid when requesting the assessment (see 24.17); and

• any fee you are about to pay for the sealing of the Legal Aid/LSC assessment certificate – form EX80A (see 40.2(i)).

However, because the costs rules state that 'the bill of costs must not contain any claims in respect of costs or court fees which relate solely to the detailed assessment proceedings' it is sufficient for these fees to appear in the final costs certificate and/or the form EX80A and not in the bill at all. If you show these fees in the bill then, to avoid confusion where the court is asked to draw up the final costs certificate, you should mention this in your covering letter.

CPD 4.13

(b) Signing the remaining certificates

Any remaining certificates in the bill will need to be signed by the receiving party or his solicitor – see 8.9. In a legally aided/LSC-funded case, this will be certificate (4) in Precedent F (as to the signing of the costs officer's certificate and the notification to counsel of any reduction in his fees).

Precedent F
CD-ROM 02.02

(c) Vouching for the payment of disbursements

In theory, at the same time as you file the completed bill, you must produce receipted fee-notes for all disbursements other than those covered by the '£500 certificate' in the bill. However, it seems that this is not

CPD 42.4
CPD 5.16

always insisted upon in practice, perhaps because the bundles of copy fee-notes filed with the request for a detailed assessment hearing already show them to have been paid. You are not required to produce the original receipted invoices – photocopies will be accepted.

Also, in theory, the court will not issue a final costs certificate includ- | *CPD 42.8*
ing counsel's fees unless you have produced counsel's fee-notes, duly receipted.

(d) Completing the LSC schedule

If the case is one where an LSC schedule was filed (see 24.15), you | *CPD 49.8*
need to complete this to show the figures allowed in respect of each item and to recalculate its summary.

(e) Taking copies for your file

Before filing the completed bill (and any completed LSC schedule) take copies of them as completed, because you may need these to support any report to or claim from the LSC.

39.4 By when must we do this?

The time-limit for filing the completed bill at court is 14 days after the | **CPR 47.16(2)**
detailed assessment hearing. | *CPD 42.3*

On the CD-ROM is a draft covering letter to the court. | **CD-ROM 07.08**

If you fail to file the completed bill, the paying party can apply for | *CPD 42.6*
'an appropriate order' under the court's case management powers. The | **CPR 3.1**
procedure is the usual one for applications – see chapter 25. | **CPR 23**

39.5 Who prepares the final costs certificate?

The final costs certificate is issued by the court after the completed bill | **CPR 47.16(3)**
has been filed. However, it is open to the court to order that the cer- | **CPR 47.16(4)**
tificate should not be issued until other costs have been paid (eg if the receiving party in the detailed assessment proceedings had an order for costs made against him during the proceedings).

The certificate will:

• state the total costs payable; | *CPD 42.7(a)*

• state the amount of VAT on the costs; | *CPD 42.7(b)*

• state whether these figures were agreed between the parties or allowed on detailed assessment; and

• include an order that the paying party should pay the amount agreed | **CPR 47.16(5)** or assessed, unless the court orders otherwise.

Although the court will prepare the form you are allowed to do it your-self, but the fact that the forms are no longer available on the Court Service website suggests that the court prefers to prepare them itself. These forms are reproduced in Appendix III and are on the CD-ROM. They are:

CPR 40.3
CPR 40.4

• For cases in the county court: Form N256.

• For cases in the High Court: Form N256HC.

The court will serve the certificate on all the parties.

Form N256
CD-ROM 04.03
Form N256HC
CD-ROM 04.04
CPR 47.16(3)

39.6 When is payment due?

Payment is normally due within 14 days of the date of the order, although the paying party can apply for a stay, ie a delay in the enforcement of the order.

CPR 40.11
CPD 42.11

The topic of enforcement is outside the scope of this book, but note that proceedings to enforce a costs certificate may not be issued in the SCCO.

CPD 42.12

CHAPTER 40

Preparing the Legal Aid/LSC assessment certificate

40.1 What is the purpose of the form?

This form, numbered EX80A, is used only in cases where the receiving party has had some or all of his costs assessed by the court to be paid out of the CLS Fund. It is the link between the court's assessment of those costs and the LSC's payment of them. That it exists in a kind of no-man's land between the two institutions is suggested by its numbering, which is neither part of the court's 'N' series nor part of the LSC's library of forms. Although vital in legally aided/LSC-funded cases, this form is barely mentioned in the costs rules and the LSC offers no guidance on its completion. It is reproduced in Appendix III and is also on the CD-ROM.

Form EX80A
CD-ROM 04.10

The EX80A enables the court to certify the amount of the costs it has assessed. These are shown broken down into the categories required by the LSC's CLAIM 1 form, which are designed to separate:

- costs payable at civil prescribed rates (the rates at which the costs are payable by the LSC) from costs payable at 'private' rates (the rates at which the costs are payable by the paying party);

- the costs of the substantive proceedings (which are subject to the LSC's statutory charge) from the costs of the detailed assessment proceedings (which are not); and

- within each of the previous categories, profit costs, counsel's fees, disbursements and any VAT on them, from each other.

It is this need to look at everything from three different angles at once that can make it a little difficult to complete the form correctly.

40.2 How should it be completed?

(a) Court heading

The heading is arranged differently to the headings on the other forms used in the detailed assessment proceedings:

- there is no need to give the paying party's reference, as this form has no relevance to him; but

• you now need to show the LSC reference (which you will find on the title page to the bill).

(b) Identification of court and parties

The tick-boxes are self-explanatory.

(c) Pre-certificate costs

Even though they may not be paying them, the LSC always want to know the amount of any pre-certificate costs (ie 'Legal Help' or privately funded costs incurred before the Legal Aid/LSC funding certificate was issued).

Although the EX80A indicates that the figure should include profit costs, disbursements and VAT, it does not indicate whether the figure required is the pre-certificate costs as claimed, or as recovered. Where the bill claimed costs both between the parties and against the CLS Fund, and the costs claimed between the parties were agreed at a figure inclusive of pre- and post-certificate costs, it may be impossible to say exactly how much of the pre-certificate costs were recovered. Any apportionment of the settlement figure is bound to be speculative. It is therefore easier to put the amount claimed. In a case where the pre-certificate costs were claimed between the parties, these ought to have been shown in a separate part in the bill, so there should be a separate sub-total for them in the bill's summary.

(d) Box A

The purpose of this box is to show the LSC how much to pay you for costs relating to work done while the certificate was in force and which were assessed between the parties, if the paying party fails to pay them. If the costs payable between the parties have been agreed, rather than assessed by the court, you will be unable to complete this box, so leave it blank.

If the costs were assessed by the court, where you will find the appropriate figures will depend upon the date of the Legal Aid/LSC funding certificate:

• If the certificate was issued before 25 February 1994, the costs will have been assessed both between the parties and against the CLS Fund at 'private' rates; the figures to use are those allowed in the bill.

• If the certificate was issued after 24 February 1994, the costs (in the bill) will have been assessed between the parties at 'private' rates and (in the LSC schedule) against the CLS Fund at civil prescribed rates; the figures to use are those allowed in the LSC schedule.

If some or all of the work was done in the Court of Appeal or the House of Lords then the civil prescribed rates will not apply, even if the certificate was issued after 24 February 1994, so the costs of that work will have been assessed at 'private' rates.

Note that you must exclude from these figures:

• any pre-certificate costs;

• any costs outside the scope of the certificate, which were assessed against the paying party only; and

• the 'costs of assessment', which should be interpreted as 'the costs of the detailed assessment proceedings' – see 1.13(b) for a list of what these may include.

Having done that, show the remaining costs broken down between profit costs, counsel's fees, disbursements, and the VAT on each of those elements, and finally show the total for this box.

(e) Box B

The purpose of this box is to show the LSC how much to pay you for the costs assessed as payable only out of the CLS Fund. These costs will be either:

• costs that were originally claimed in the bill only against the CLS Fund (eg the costs of particular applications where the paying party was not ordered to pay them); or

• costs that were originally claimed in the bill against the paying party, but which were not allowed against him and were instead allowed against the CLS Fund.

If the certificate was issued before 25 February 1994 these costs will be calculated at 'private' rates, otherwise they will be calculated at civil prescribed rates (unless they relate to work done in the House of Lords or the Court of Appeal).

Again, you must exclude from these figures:

• any pre-certificate costs;

• any costs outside the scope of the certificate, which were assessed against the paying party only; and

• the 'costs of assessment,' about which see (d).

(f) Box C

The purpose of this box is to show separately from the substantive costs the 'costs of assessment" which again should be interpreted as the 'costs of the detailed assessment proceedings', about which see 1.13(b). They have to be shown separately because they are outside the scope of the LSC's statutory charge, so cannot be charged to the receiving party's contributions and/or property recovered or preserved in the substantive proceedings.

The way the information has to be presented in this box is potentially confusing, because you must:

• show separately the costs of detailed assessment relating to the costs in box A, from those relating to the costs in box B; and

• within each of those two categories, if there are any disbursements other than court fees (eg travelling expenses), you must lump them together with the relevant profit costs to show just one composite figure (before VAT) as the costs of assessment 'For Part A' and another one 'For Part B'.

You must also show separately the court fees relating to the detailed assessment of the costs in box A, from those relating to the detailed assessment of the costs in box B.

• The box A court fees will normally be just the fee paid on requesting the combined detailed assessment between the parties and LSC detailed assessment, although if there were any court fees paid for other requests or applications during the course of the detailed assessment proceedings, they should be included in this figure.

• Although the High Court and county court fees orders envisage the fee paid for a combined detailed assessment being apportioned between the two elements in proportion to the amount allowed it is difficult to see the point of this, so it should be sufficient to show the total fee in relation to part A.

Table 3

• The box B court fees will always include the £30 fee payable on sealing the EX80A (as this is never recoverable between the parties). If the detailed assessment was of an 'LSC only' bill, the fee paid on filing the request for detailed assessment will also be included.

(g) Box D

In this box, show the totals (if any) of each of boxes A, B and C, and then show the grand total of all three boxes.

Although you may wish to check the accuracy of your completion of the form by comparing the grand total of box D with the grand total of the bill as assessed, do not be surprised if they are different. Any such difference should be due to:

• the omission of any pre-certificate costs and/or any costs outside the scope of the certificate; and/or

• the recalculation at civil prescribed rates (in the LSC schedule) of any costs allowed in the bill between the parties at 'private' rates.

(h) Signature and dating

Do not overlook the need for the solicitor to sign and date the form where indicated about one-third of the way down. See 8.9 for the rules about who may sign.

(i) The court fee

The fee is currently £30, whether the case is in the High Court (fee number 10.5) or in the county court (fee number 3.5). The cheque should be made payable to 'H M Paymaster General'.

Table 3

40.3 What should we do next?

(a) Sealing the EX80A

Send two copies of the EX80A to the court for sealing, with the fee. A draft covering letter is on the CD-ROM.

CD-ROM 07.09

(b) Reporting to the LSC

To obtain payment of the costs you will need to send the sealed EX80A to the LSC with a report and claim for costs in form CLAIM 1. How to complete the CLAIM 1 is not covered in this book because the forms change so frequently that any guidance given here would be out of date very quickly. You can obtain up-to-date forms and guidance on their completion from the LSC website – see 2.6.

PART III
THE PROCEDURE FOR THE DETAILED ASSESSMENT BY THE COURT OF A BILL CLAIMING COSTS ONLY AGAINST THE CLS FUND ('LSC ONLY' DETAILED ASSESSMENT)

CHAPTER 41

The procedural time-table

41.1 What is meant by an 'LSC only' detailed assessment?

Part II of this book covered the procedure for the detailed assessment of a bill claiming costs between the parties, whether or not that bill also claimed costs against the Community Legal Service (CLS) Fund. This part of the book covers the procedure for the detailed assessment of a bill that only claims costs against the CLS Fund. Those costs will be for work done under a Legal Aid certificate issued by the Legal Aid Board or a public funding certificate issued by the Legal Services Commission ('LSC'). It is this procedure that is described as an 'LSC only' detailed assessment. The client for whom the work was done is described as an 'assisted person' if it was done under a Legal Aid certificate and as an 'LSC-funded client' if it was done under a public funding certificate. In this part of the book he will simply be referred to as 'the client'.

41.2 How does the procedure for an 'LSC only' detailed assessment differ from the procedure for an assessment between the parties?

The procedure for a detailed assessment between the parties leaves much of the initiative to the parties themselves, with the court normally becoming involved only when a detailed assessment hearing is requested. Those detailed assessment proceedings begin with a step which is taken between the parties – the service of the notice of commencement.

However, an 'LSC only' detailed assessment normally involves only the receiving party's solicitor (perhaps also the client himself) and the court. These detailed assessment proceedings therefore begin with a step which is taken between the solicitors and the court – the filing of a request for a detailed assessment. CPR 47.17(1)

It follows that the work done in connection with the service of the bill on the client, which normally precedes this step, will not form part of the costs of the detailed assessment proceedings.

Although, in reality, taking a bill to 'LSC only' detailed assessment is generally simpler than obtaining a detailed assessment of a bill Table 5 claiming costs between the parties, the procedure offers a number of alternatives and this makes the overall picture look rather complicated – see Table 5 on page 225.

41.3 When can the court assess the costs?

An 'LSC only' detailed assessment by the court can only take place in a case where the client has (or had) a Legal Aid/LSC funding certificate and:

• proceedings have been issued; and

• the total costs (ie profit costs, counsel's fees and disbursements) claimed before VAT exceed £2,500.

If proceedings have not been issued then, no matter how large the claim for costs, it can only be assessed by the LSC – see regulation 105 of the Civil Legal Aid (General) Regulations 1989, as amended by the Civil Legal Aid (General) (Amendment) Regulations 2003. Such assessments are outside the scope of this book.

41.4 What is the authority for detailed assessment?

There must be an authority for 'LSC only' detailed assessment and that authority can be either:

• an order for detailed assessment of the receiving party's costs pursuant to regulation 107A(2) of the Civil Legal Aid (General) Regulations 1989; or

• the termination (by discharge or revocation) of the client's Legal Aid/LSC funding certificate.

An order for 'LSC only' detailed assessment might not be expressed exactly in the terms above, but so long as its intention is clear, it should suffice. The order does not need to state the basis of assessment, because regulation 107A(2) provides that it will be on the standard basis.

41.5 What is the deadline for requesting a detailed assessment?

The request for detailed assessment should be filed 'within three months after the date when the right to detailed assessment arose'.

That right will have arisen on the date of the order or termination referred to in 41.4. If the order is followed by a termination, perhaps

CPR 47.17(2)

CPD 43.2

TABLE 5: PROCEDURE FOR 'LSC ONLY' DETAILED ASSESSMENT

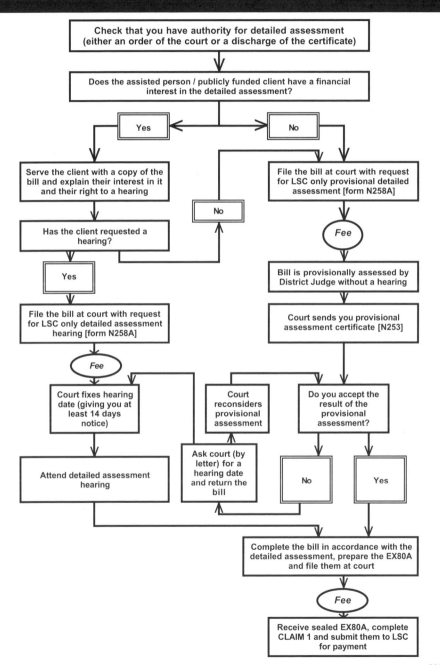

225

logically the date of the order should be taken as the date on which the right arose, but in practice it is unlikely to matter very much.

The LSC's approach, under which it seeks to calculate the three-month period from the date on which the solicitor's retainer was terminated (which might be earlier than the discharge of the certificate), seems only to apply to cases where it is to assess the costs itself and not to cases for assessment by the court.

'Month' means a 'calendar month,' so you count from the number of the day of the order or the termination to the same numbered day three months hence (eg order or termination dated 5 March, bill to be served by 5 June). If the expiry date is not a working day you should assume that the three months are up on the last working day before that date.

CPR 2.10

41.6 What if we miss the deadline?

It may not matter if you miss the deadline. The court is not likely to be interested in when, or indeed whether, you start detailed assessment proceedings and you do not need to ask it for an extension of time.

Although, where costs are to be the subject of detailed assessment proceedings both between the parties and against the CLS Fund, the costs rules put the LSC in the position of the paying party to enable it to apply for sanctions for lateness by the receiving party in beginning detailed assessment proceedings, that provision does not seem to apply to 'LSC only' detailed assessments.

CPR 47.8(4)

CHAPTER 42

Serving the bill on the client

42.1 Do we need to serve the client?

You will need to serve the client if he has a financial interest in the detailed assessment. He will have such an interest if the statutory charge applies to money or property recovered or preserved in the proceedings, ie he may end up paying some of the costs out of his damages or out of any contributions paid by him under the certificate.

CPR 47.17(3)
CPD 43.4

- If the client has no financial interest in the detailed assessment, you can ignore the rest of this chapter and proceed to preparing the request for detailed assessment – see chapter 43.

- If the client does have a financial interest, see 42.2.

42.2 What do we need to serve on him?

Regulation 119(1) of the Civil Legal Aid (General) Regulations 1989 requires you to:

- supply the client with a copy of the bill; and

- inform him 'of the extent of his financial interest and the steps which can be taken to safeguard that interest'.

If he is to be properly informed, you will need to give him an explanation of the contents of the bill, the detailed assessment procedure, the possible outcome from his point of view and how he can protect his interests. On the CD-ROM is a draft letter. If you wish to use it you should adapt it generally to reflect both your firm's style and the usual layout of your bills and specifically to suit the circumstances of the particular case. It is helpful:

CD-ROM 09.04

- to send the client a response form to make it easier for him to say whether he has any comments on the bill and whether he would like to attend the detailed assessment hearing (a blank form is on the CD-ROM); and

CD-ROM 06.04

- to state a date by which you would like his reply, although there does not seem to be any prescribed time within which he has to respond. The nearest analogy is regulation 105A of the Civil Legal Aid

(General) Regulations 1989, which gives such a client 21 days to make written representations to the LSC if the LSC is to assess the costs.

Once you have served the client with the bill and the explanation of his interest in the assessment, you are in a position to request the detailed assessment of the bill. Although you are not obliged to wait for the client to respond, or for the expiry of the deadline you gave him, it is generally best to do so, as the nature of his response will determine the kind of detailed assessment you ask the court to carry out. How to apply for detailed assessment is explained in the next chapter.

CHAPTER 43

Requesting an 'LSC only' detailed assessment

43.1 At which court do we file the request?

See 23.3 for the rules about the normal venue, and about the options for transferring the assessment to other courts.

Note that the SCCO now assesses the costs of cases conducted in the Principal Registry of the Family Division.

43.2 What form do we use?

The request for detailed assessment must be made in form N258A, which is reproduced in Appendix III and is also on the CD-ROM.

CPD 43.3
Form N258A
CD-ROM 04.08

43.3 How do we complete the form?

(a) The court heading

Take the necessary details from the title page to the bill, and add the references.

(b) Provisional assessment or hearing?

If the client has indicated that he wishes to be heard at the detailed assessment, delete the words 'provisionally assess the bill'. If he has not so indicated, delete the words in brackets.

If the client has not responded one way or the other, or if you have not yet served him with a copy of the bill, it is probably best to ask for a provisional assessment. If the client subsequently indicates that he wishes to be heard, you can notify the court and ask for a hearing to be listed. If the provisional assessment has already been made by that point, but you have not accepted it, you can still apply for a hearing.

(c) The enclosures

These should be prepared in the same way as for a detailed assessment between the parties. For suggestions as to general presentation, see 9.5. For detailed commentary, see the paragraph numbers referred to:

- 'The document giving the right to detailed assessment' – see 9.5(b), and note that in an 'LSC only' detailed assessment a termination of the certificate may be the authority.

CPD 43.3(b)

- 'The bill of costs' – see 9.5(a), but note that the only certificates necessary at this stage are (1) 'as to accuracy' and (3) 'as to interest of assisted person', *CPD 43.3(a)*

- 'A statement giving the names, addresses for service and references of all persons to whom the court should give notice of the hearing.' This will usually be the client with a financial interest in the detailed assessment. You should give his postal address so that the court can send him notice of the hearing. This can be given in the covering letter, so long as it is signed by the solicitor, unless the detailed assessment is in the SCCO, in which case you should prepare a separate statement of parties – see 24.9. *CPD 43.3(b)* *CD-ROM 06.09*

- 'A copy of all the orders made by the court relating to the costs of the proceedings which are to be assessed' – if your authority for detailed assessment is an order, include a copy of it and a copy of any other order as to costs, whether or not it provides for 'LSC only' assessment and whether or not it is in the client's favour. *CPD 43.3(c)*

- 'Any fee notes of counsel and receipts or accounts for other disbursements relating to items claimed' – see 9.5(c), (d) and (e) *CPD 43.3(d)*

- 'Written evidence as to any other disbursement which is claimed and which exceeds £250' – see 9.5(e). *CPD 43.3(e)*

- 'All civil Legal Aid certificates and LSC certificates and amendments to them; notice of discharge or revocation and specific Legal Aid authorities' – see 9.6(a). *CPD 43.3(f)*

- 'The relevant papers in support of the bill.' Note that this only applies to cases to be assessed in the SCCO. If this is one of them, see 33.1(a) and (c) *CPD 43.3(g)*

(d) Certificate as to client's wish to attend and time estimate

If the client has indicated he wishes to attend, you are required to certify this and also to give a time estimate. If the client has indicated specific points he wants to raise, this may give you a very rough idea of how long will be needed, but otherwise you will simply have to guess at a figure and leave it up to the court to approve or modify it.

(e) The court fee

The fee will depend upon the court in which the assessment is to take place: *Table 3*

• High Court (fee number 10.1): currently £120.

• County court (fee number 3.1): currently £100.

These fees apply to requests for detailed assessment made after 31 March 2003, even if those requests are based on orders for detailed assessment made before that date (except if the order was made before 26 April 1999, when special transitional provisions apply, for details of which see the relevant fee order).

The cheque should be made payable to 'H M Paymaster General'.

(f) Signature and dating

The request should be signed by someone qualified to do so – see 8.9.

43.4 What do we send to the court?

You should send the court:

• the request for detailed assessment;

• the enclosures listed in it;

• the client's response form if he has made any comments on the bill that he would like brought to the attention of the court, whether or not he also says that he wishes to be given notice of the hearing date.

In your covering letter:

• list the enclosures;

• if there is to be a hearing, give your unavailable dates for the next three months (and the client's, if you happen to know them).

A draft letter is on the CD-ROM.   CD-ROM 07.10

43.5 What should happen next?

If a hearing was requested, wait until you receive notice of the date,   CPR 47.17(4)
diarise it and make sure the client has also been notified of it. Then
prepare for the hearing – see chapter 45.

If a hearing was not requested, await the court's notice of the result of the provisional assessment and consider it carefully when it arrives – see chapter 44.1.

Even if a hearing was not requested, the court can list one anyway if   *CPD 43.4*
it has queries about the bill. However, it is likely to send a request for
further information before deciding whether a hearing is necessary.

CHAPTER 44

Accepting or rejecting a provisional assessment

44.1 How will we be told the result of the provisional assessment?

(a) The notice of amount allowed

If no hearing is required, the court will carry out a provisional assessment of the bill. It is essentially a postal detailed assessment.

The bill, as provisionally assessed, will be returned to you with a 'notice of amount allowed on provisional assessment', in form N253, which is reproduced in Appendix III, and the original bill.

Contrary to the promise in its title, the N253 will not, in fact, tell you the amount allowed. To find this out you have to look at the costs officer's annotations on the bill itself.

CPR 47.17(5)
CPD 43.4
CPR 47.17(6)
CPD 43.5
Form N253

(b) If the bill is assessed as drawn

If the title page of the bill is endorsed 'Assessed as drawn' you will obviously want to accept this outcome, which awards you everything you have claimed, so proceed to 44.2.

(c) If the costs officer has made reductions

If the bill has not been assessed as drawn, you will need to go through it carefully to identify the items reduced or disallowed by the costs officer. From his annotations you should be able to work out the overall amount allowed.

Within 14 days you will need to decide whether to accept the provisional assessment or not. One way of approaching this task is as follows:

• Consider each of the reductions or disallowances made to identify which of them are, in principle, worth arguing and which of them you would be as well to concede.

• Work out the total value of those points that seem to be worth arguing in principle, to see whether it is large enough to justify the delay and the risk that is involved in applying for a hearing.

• If necessary, carry out a kind of SWOT analysis (see chapter 6) to help you make your final decision.

44.2 How do we accept the provisional assessment?

(a) Notifying counsel

If the bill includes a claim for counsel's fees, and any of those fees have been reduced or disallowed, you must tell him of those reductions or disallowances within seven days in case he wishes to make representations to the court – see regulation 112 of the Civil Legal Aid (General) Regulations 1989.

If counsel is dissatisfied with the reduction, he is entitled to enlist your help in appealing against it – see regulation 116 of the Civil Legal Aid (General) Regulations 1989. This will mean that you are not able to accept the provisional assessment after all, so instead proceed as explained at 44.3.

(b) Completing the bill

Complete the bill as explained at 39.3, although the cross-reference to the court fee when applying for the assessment is to 43.3(e). *CPD 43.5* *CPD 43.9*

If the bill has been assessed 'as drawn', there is no need to do any of the figure-work in the body of the bill or in the summary mentioned at 39.3(a), except perhaps in relation to the court fees.

(c) Preparing the EX80A

Prepare the Legal Aid/LSC assessment certificate (form EX80A) as explained in chapter 40. The only difference is that there were no costs claimed between the parties, so box A will be blank.

Form EX80A
CPD 43.9
CD-ROM 04.10

(d) Writing to the court

Send to the court:

• the completed bill (having first taken a copy for your file);

• form EX80A in duplicate; and

• the £30 fee for sealing the EX80A.

A draft letter to the court is on the CD-ROM.

CD-ROM 07.11

(e) Reporting to the LSC

To obtain payment of the costs you will need to report to the LSC on form CLAIM 1. How to complete this form is not covered in this book, partly for reasons of space, but mainly because the forms change so frequently that any guidance given here would be out of date very quickly. You can obtain up-to-date forms and guidance on their completion from the LSC website – see 2.6.

44.3 How do we reject the provisional assessment?

(a) The letter to the court

If you wish to reject the provisional assessment you should write to the court within 14 days of receiving the N253: *CPD 43.6*

• stating that you do not accept the provisional assessment;

• asking for a hearing date;

• giving a time-estimate;

• giving the unavailable dates for the next three months of those who are to attend (see 45.2); and

• returning the provisionally assessed bill.

Take a copy of the bill as provisionally assessed to help you in your preparation for the hearing.
A draft letter is on the CD-ROM. *CD-ROM 07.12*

(b) Is a hearing always necessary?

If, in your letter rejecting the provisional assessment, you identify the particular reductions to which you object, giving reasons for your objection, the costs officer may reconsider and respond by post.
If he restores enough of the items previously disallowed to make you content to accept his revised assessment, proceed as outlined at 44.2.
If you are still not satisfied, respond to the court that you would still like a hearing.

44.4 What should we do once we receive notice of the hearing date?

The court should give you at least 14 days' notice of the hearing date. When you receive this notice: *CPD 43.7*

• diarise it; and

• prepare for the hearing, as outlined in chapter 45.

CHAPTER 45

Preparing for the 'LSC only' detailed assessment hearing

45.1 When should we prepare?

There is no benefit in leaving the preparation until the last minute. The situation is different to that which prevails in a detailed assessment between the parties, where a last-minute settlement is likely. Here, once the hearing date has been fixed, a hearing is almost inevitable.

45.2 Who is to attend the hearing?

Before requesting a hearing a decision should already have been made as to who (apart perhaps from the client) will be attending the hearing. See 32.2 for points to consider in making this decision, and 32.6 for action to take once it has been made, but ignore the references to the paying party that appear there.

45.3 How should we prepare generally?

The guidance for preparation at 32.3(b), (c), (d), (f) and (g) applies equally here, except for the references to the paying party, which are obviously not relevant.

45.4 What about filing the papers?

See chapter 33, which applies equally here, except for the references to base costs and additional liabilities.

45.5 How should we prepare details of our costs?

As the costs of the detailed assessment proceedings are not subject to the statutory charge, you should claim what you reasonably can against the CLS Fund, as it will not affect the client's damages.

The guidance for preparation of your statement of costs at 32.4 applies equally here save that the charging rates will be limited to the civil prescribed rates (unless the certificate was issued before 25 February 1994 or the proceedings were in the Court of Appeal or the House of Lords, in which case 'private' rates may be used). See the Legal Aid in Civil Proceedings (Remuneration) Regulations 1994.

CHAPTER 46

Attending the 'LSC only' detailed assessment hearing

46.1 What should we take?

(a) The main documents:

• your annotated copy of the bill and any schedules of time spent;

• a copy of each of the bundles filed with the request for a detailed assessment hearing – see 43.3(c);

• any skeleton arguments you have prepared;

• your authorities (in duplicate); and

• your schedule of costs of preparing for and attending the hearing (in duplicate).

(b) Other useful documents:

• your notes for the hearing;

• your own correspondence etc relating to the detailed assessment proceedings; and

• if you prepared the bill, your costing notes.

(c) Spare copy documents

It can be useful to take a spare copy of the bill in case the original has been lost in the court office.

(d) Equipment:

• calculator;

• pen, highlighter, pencil, eraser and note-pad; and

• holdall, trolley etc in which to take away the files after the hearing.

46.2 What should we do at the start of the hearing?

(a) Who sits where?

If both the fee earner and the costs draftsman are attending, it is best for the one who is likely to do most talking to sit nearer to the costs officer, leaving the one sitting further away with the job of managing the supporting documents. Clients and others attending may sit wherever is most convenient

(b) Who's who?

If the client is attending, make sure that the costs officer knows who's who by making any necessary introductions. Anyone other than the client and his representatives may only be present with the permission of the costs officer.

(c) Setting out your stall

Make sure that you have conveniently to hand all the papers you are likely to need during the hearing. Keeping the papers in order while the hearing is in progress is difficult, so it helps to start as you mean to go on.

(d) Checking that the costs officer has read the bill

If the hearing is before a costs officer other than the one who carried out the provisional assessment, check that he has read the bill and, if not, whether he would like to do so now.

46.3 How should the hearing proceed?

The client is entitled to take part if he has an interest in the detailed assessment – see 42.1 – and the hearing may be taking place at his request. However, he will not necessarily be present and may instead have sent in written observations, which he wants the costs officer to take into account.

If the client is present, the costs officer should listen to any points he wants to put, and he should also listen to any arguments you may wish to put forward. He should then make his findings.

Whether the client is present or absent, the costs officer will generally help to look after his interests. Remember that, by this stage in the case, the client's interest in the assessment is not the same as yours. This is because if some item of costs is disallowed against the CLS Fund, the firm will lose it, whereas if it is allowed it will come out of the client's damages, so it is in the client's interest to have it disallowed completely. It follows that you have to look after your own interests.

CPD 42.1

The costs officer should make his decision on each item and will say what it is, giving his reasons, noting any disallowances or reductions on the original bill. If the hearing follows a provisional assessment, he should note any variations from his original disallowances or reductions.

Be sure to note these on your copy of the bill as you go along and make a separate note on your pad of the reasons he gives for each item. If you think you might want to appeal any of these, put a big asterisk next to them to remind yourself at the end of the hearing.

46.4 Will we be awarded the costs of the detailed assessment?

CPR 47.18

The general presumption that the receiving party is entitled to his costs of the detailed assessment applies here just as in assessments between the parties.

CPR 47.18(1)(b)

But the court may make some other order in relation to all or part of the costs of the detailed assessment proceedings.

CPR 47.18(2)

In deciding whether to make some other order, the court must have regard to all the circumstances, including:

CPD 45.4

CPR 47.18(2)(a)

• the conduct of all the parties;

CPR 47.18(2)(b)

• the amount, if any, by which the bill has been reduced; and

CPR 47.18(2)(c)

• whether it was reasonable for a party to claim or dispute the costs of a particular item.

Although 'parties' presumably includes the client, it is difficult to see how his conduct should be considered relevant to the question of whether his solicitor should be awarded the costs of the detailed assessment.

A more usual area for the exercise of discretion is the amount by which the bill was reduced; if the judge feels that asking for a full detailed assessment hearing was unnecessary, where you did little or no better than on the provisional detailed assessment, he might decline to allow you any costs for attending the hearing.

46.5 How are the costs of the detailed assessment proceedings assessed?

CPD 45.1

If he is willing to allow you the costs of the detailed assessment pro-

CPD 45.2

ceedings, the costs officer will normally make a summary assessment of them at the end of the hearing, although he does have power to order the costs to be decided by a further detailed assessment.

CPD 45.3

Only when he is ready to do this will you normally produce your statement of costs of the detailed assessment proceedings. Take the costs officer through the statement of costs item by item so that he has to decide whether each was reasonable in nature and amount – try not to let him take a 'broad brush' approach.

46.6 How may the court punish misconduct?

If you or the client have been guilty of misconduct either in the detailed assessment proceedings or in the substantive case itself, the court has powers to punish it – see 35.6.

46.7 How can we appeal?

If you think you will want to appeal then, unless the detailed assessment hearing was conducted by an authorised court officer, you will need permission to appeal. Ideally, you should seek that permission orally at the end of the detailed assessment hearing, but if you fail to do this, or you are refused, you can apply to the court to which you hope to appeal. See chapter 38 for more on appeals.

Before embarking on an appeal in a legally aided/LSC-funded case, you should give careful consideration to regulation 113 of the Civil Legal Aid (General) Regulations 1989. In its present form it provides that the solicitor takes all the risks as to costs, in that the costs of the appeal will only be treated as covered by the certificate if the court so orders. In no circumstances will the client be liable for them.

CHAPTER 47

Completing the 'LSC only' detailed assessment

47.1 What papers should we take away?

Make sure that you take the original bill away from the hearing, as it will be your job to complete it, to show the result of the detailed assessment.

You should also take away all the papers you filed or brought in support of the bill. If you fail to do this, the court is liable to dispose of them without notifying you.

CPD 40.16

47.2 Must we notify counsel?

If the bill includes a claim for counsel's fees, and any of those fees were reduced or disallowed in the provisional assessment, you might at that point have told him of those reductions or disallowances. If you did not, then you must do so within seven days in case he wishes to make representations to the court – see regulation 112 of the Civil Legal Aid (General) Regulations 1989.

If counsel is dissatisfied with the reduction, he is entitled to enlist your help in appealing against it – see regulation 116 of the Civil Legal Aid (General) Regulations 1989.

47.3 How should we complete the bill?

Complete the bill as explained at 39.3, although the cross-reference to the court fee when applying for the assessment is to 43.3(e).

CPD 43.5

47.4 How do we prepare the EX80A?

Prepare the Legal Aid/LSC assessment certificate (form EX80A) as explained in chapter 40. The only difference is that there were no costs claimed between the parties, so box A will be blank.

Form EX80A

CD-ROM 04.10

47.5 What should we send to the court?

Send to the court:

• the completed bill (having first taken a copy for your file);

• form EX80A in duplicate; and

• the £30 fee for sealing the EX80A.

A draft letter to the court is on the CD-ROM.

CD-ROM 07.09

The time-limit for re-filing the completed bill is 14 days after the
detailed assessment hearing

CPR 47.16(2)

CPD 42.3

47.6 How do we report to the LSC?

To obtain payment of the costs you will need to report to the LSC on
form CLAIM 1. How to complete this form is not covered in this book,
because the forms change so frequently that any guidance given here
would be out of date very quickly. You can obtain up-to-date forms and
guidance on their completion from the LSC website – see 2.6.

PART IV
OTHER FORMS OF ASSESSMENT AND 'COSTS ONLY' PROCEEDINGS

CHAPTER 48

Detailed assessment by the court of costs payable out of a fund other than the CLS Fund

48.1 When is this procedure likely to be used?

The costs rules provide a procedure very similar to that for an 'LSC only' detailed assessment for use in cases where the costs are to be paid out of a fund, such as funds administered under the supervision of the Court of Protection.

48.2 Is the procedure the same as for an 'LSC only' detailed assessment?

The procedure is almost, but not quite, the same as the procedure for an 'LSC only' detailed assessment. The main differences are:

• there may be a number of people with a financial interest in the outcome of the assessment (eg a body of trustees), so the court will decide which of them need to be served with a copy of the bill and with details of any hearing; and

• the presumption is that there will always be a provisional assessment of the bill unless the court considers a hearing to be necessary.

48.3 By when should detailed assessment proceedings be started?

The request for detailed assessment should be filed within three months after the date when the right to detailed assessment arose.

CPR 47.17A(2)

48.4 How are the detailed assessment proceedings started?

(a) The request for detailed assessment

The request is in form N258B, which is very similar to the request in form N258A used to begin the detailed assessment of an 'LSC only' bill. Form N258B is reproduced in Appendix III and is also on the CD-ROM.

Form N258B
CD-ROM 04.09
CPR 47.17A(1)
CPD 44.3

It differs from N258A as follows:

- it does not give the receiving party (ie the solicitor) the option of asking at the outset for a hearing, nor does it seek a time-estimate for a hearing; and

- instead of referring to Legal Aid/LSC funding it has provision for details of any additional liability to be supplied.

(b) Documents to be filed with the request

In addition to the items listed in the form itself, you should also file with it: — CPD 44.3

- a statement signed by the receiving party giving his name, address for service, reference, telephone number and fax number (while the SCCO will want this as a formal statement of parties, other courts may well be satisfied if this information is given in the covering letter); — CPD 44.3(a)

- a statement of the postal address of any person who has a financial interest in the outcome of the assessment, to which the court may send notice of any hearing; and — CPD 44.3(b)

- in respect of each person stated to have such an interest, if such person is a child or patient, a statement to that effect (again, this could presumably go in the covering letter). — CPD 44.3(c)

(c) The court fee

The fee will depend upon the court in which the assessment is to take place: — Table 3

- High Court (fee number 10.2): currently £250.

- County court (fee number 3.2): currently £160.

The cheque should be made payable to 'H M Paymaster General'.

48.5 What happens next?

(a) Service of the request

The court will decide whether the request, and copies of the documents accompanying it, should be served on any person who has a financial interest in the outcome of the assessment. — CPR 47.17A(3)

- A person has a financial interest in the outcome of the assessment if — CPD 44.2(a) the assessment will or may affect the amount of money or property to which he is or may become entitled out of the fund.

- Where an interest in the fund is itself held by a trustee for the benefit of some other person, that trustee will be treated as the person having such a financial interest. *CPD 44.2(b)*

- 'Trustee' includes a personal representative, receiver or any other person acting in a fiduciary capacity. *CPD 44.2(c)*

- The court will make its decision as to who should be served having regard to the amount of the bill, the size of the fund and the number of persons who have a financial interest. The court may dispense with service on some or all of them. *CPD 44.4*

- If the court decides that a person with a financial interest should be served, it may direct you to effect service. *CPR 47.17A(3)* *CPD 44.1*

(b) The provisional assessment

Where the court makes an order dispensing with service on all persons with a financial interest it may proceed at once to make a provisional assessment (ie a postal assessment without the attendance of the receiving party). *CPR 47.17A(4)* *CPD 44.5*

After it has provisionally assessed the bill, it will return it to the receiving party, with a notice in form N253, which is reproduced in Appendix III, showing the amount of costs which the court proposes to allow. It will also return the original bill. **Form N253** *CPR 47.17A(5)* *CPD 44.6(1)*

(c) If the provisional assessment is accepted

If the receiving party accepts the provisional assessment, he should complete the bill as explained at 39.3, although the cross-reference to the court fee when applying for the assessment is to 48.4(c). *CPD 44.6(1)* *CPD 44.10*

If the bill has been assessed 'as drawn', there is no need to do any of the figure-work in the body of the bill or in the summary mentioned at 39.3(a), except perhaps in relation to the court fees.

(d) If the provisional assessment is rejected

If, within 14 days after he receives the provisionally assessed bill, the receiving party informs the court that he wants the court to hold a hearing, it will fix a date for one. *CPR 47.17A(6)* *CPD 44.8*

(e) When a hearing may be ordered on the court's own initiative

When the court decides upon whom (if anyone) the bill should be served (see 48.5(a)) it may also decide that a hearing is necessary. Before making that decision it may require the receiving party to provide further information relating to the bill.

CPD 44.5

If it decides that a hearing is necessary, it may give appropriate directions, including directions about the service of notice of the hearing on those whom it has ordered should be served with a copy of the request for assessment.

CPD 44.5

CPD 44.7

(f) Applications in the detailed assessment proceedings

If the receiving party, or any party with a financial interest in the outcome of the assessment, wishes to make an application in the detailed assessment proceedings, he should do so in accordance with the provisions of CPR 23 – see chapter 25.

CPD 44.9

CHAPTER 49

Assessment of costs in family proceedings

49.1 How far do the costs rules apply to family proceedings?

(a) Generally

Family proceedings do not count as civil proceedings, so the general provisions of the CPR do not apply to them, unless there is some specific rule to the contrary. However, most of the costs rules do apply to family proceedings in exactly the same way as they apply to civil proceedings.

(b) The CPR

When the CPR came into effect on 26 April 1999, rule 4 of the Family Proceedings (Miscellaneous Amendments) Rules 1999 (SI 1999 No 1012) revoked the Family Proceedings (Costs) Rules 1991 (SI 1991 No 1832) and made CPR 43, 44, 47 and 48 applicable to family proceedings, except for:

- CPR 44.3(2) – the general rule that 'costs follow the event' ie that the unsuccessful party will be ordered to pay the costs of the successful party;

- CPR 44.9–44.11 – rules about costs relating to the various tracks;

- CPR 44.12 – rules about the cases in which costs orders are deemed to have been made.

Note that CPR 45 (fixed costs) and CPR 46 (fast track trial costs) do not apply to family proceedings.

Rule 16 of the Family Proceedings (Amendment) Rules 2003 (SI 2003 No 184) restated the 1999 provisions and also brought the rules for appeals against costs assessments in family proceedings into line with the system governing appeals in civil cases (see chapter 38).

(c) The CPD

The CPD was made to apply to family proceedings by the *Practice Direction (Family Division: Allocation of Cases: Costs) (1999)* issued by the President of the Family Division on 22 April 1999. Referring to

CPR 44.3(2)

CPR 44.9–44.11
CPR 44.12

CPR 45
CPR 46

the CPD as the 'costs direction' the President directed in a rather general way that 'References in the costs direction to "claimant" and "defendant" are to be read as references to the equivalent terms used in family proceedings and other terms and expressions used in the costs direction shall be similarly treated. References to procedural steps and to other Parts of the 1998 Rules which have not yet been applied to family proceedings are to be read as referring to equivalent or similar procedures under the rules applicable to family proceedings, as the context may permit.'

On 24 July 2000 the President issued the *Practice Direction (Family Proceedings: Costs) (2000)*. This directed that the revised edition of the CPD effective from 3 July 2000 and all subsequent editions should apply to family proceedings.

CD-ROM 03.03

Recognising that the CPD now contain many provisions about conditional fee agreements, the 2000 Direction points out that although family proceedings cannot be the subject of an enforceable conditional fee agreement, the cost of the premium in respect of legal costs insurance or the cost of funding by a prescribed membership organisation might be recoverable.

49.2 What count as family proceedings?

(a) Proceedings that are included

Family proceedings include actions relating to children and wardship conducted under the inherent jurisdiction of the High Court as well as proceedings under the following enactments:

• the Children Act 1989, Parts I, III and IV;

• the Matrimonial Causes Act 1973;

• the Adoption Act 1976;

• the Married Women's Property Act 1882;

• the Matrimonial and Family Proceedings Act 1984, Part III;

• the Family Law Act 1986 and 1996, Part IV; and

• the Child Abduction and Custody Act 1985.

(b) Proceedings that are excluded

Although proceedings under the following enactments may, in some instances, look like family proceedings, they are not. Instead they count as civil proceedings, to which the whole of the CPR apply:

• the Inheritance (Provision for Family and Dependants) Act 1975;

• the Trusts of Land and Appointment of Trustees Act 1996; and

• the Protection from Harassment Act 1997.

49.3 Are the forms the same?

The forms used for detailed assessment in family cases are essentially the same as those used in civil cases, although the parties will be described, for example, as 'petitioner' and 'respondent' rather than as 'claimant' and 'defendant'.

CHAPTER 50

Summary assessment of costs

50.1 What is summary assessment?

The CPR provide that where the court orders one party to pay costs to another party, it may make a summary assessment of those costs. 'Summary assessment' is defined as 'the procedure by which the court, when making an order about costs, orders payment of a sum of money instead of fixed costs or "detailed assessment"'.

CPR 44.7
CPD 12.1(a)
CPR 43.3

An order for costs will be treated as an order for detailed assessment unless it provides otherwise, but (except in a case to which fixed costs apply) the court is directed to consider whether to make a summary assessment.

CPD 12.2
CPD 13.1

50.2 When will the court usually make a summary assessment?

(a) At the end of a fast track trial

At the end of the trial of a case which has been dealt with on the fast track, the court should make a summary assessment not just of the costs of the trial, but of the costs of the whole claim.

CPD 13.2(1)

The costs of an advocate for preparing for and appearing at the trial of a claim in the fast track are subject to a kind of fixed costs regime. This is set out fully in CPR 46, as supplemented by CPD 26 and 27, and is not covered further in this book.

CPR 46
CPD 46–47

(b) At the end of a hearing lasting not more than one day

At the end of any other hearing which has lasted not more than one day, the court should make a summary assessment of the costs:

CPD 13.2(2)

• of the application or matter to which the hearing related; or

• of the whole claim if the hearing disposed of it.

(c) At the end of certain Court of Appeal hearings

There is 'likely' to be a summary assessment at the end of the following types of Court of Appeal hearings:

CPD 13.2(3)
PDP52 14

- contested directions hearings;   PDP52 14(1)

- applications for permission to appeal at which the respondent is   PDP52 14(2)
  present;

- dismissal list hearings at which the respondent is present;   PDP52 14(3)

- appeals from case management decisions; and   PDP52 14(4)

- appeals listed for one day or less.   PDP52 14(5)

50.3 Are there cases when the court should not make a summary assessment?

(a) Is there good reason not to?

In general, the court should not make a summary assessment if there   *CPD 13.2*
is 'good reason' not to do so. Only two examples are provided by the
costs rules:

- where the paying party shows substantial grounds for disputing the
  sum claimed for costs that cannot be dealt with summarily (eg arguments about the application of the indemnity principle); or

- where there is insufficient time to carry out a summary assessment.

If the trial of a multi-track case listed for more than one day only lasts
for one day or less, the court has the power to make a summary assessment. However, unless it was obvious that the case was going to be
resolved so quickly, it is difficult to see how the parties could be criticised for failing to prepare statements of their costs (see 50.8) and
they could reasonably argue that a multi-track case was not suitable for
summary assessment.

(b) Conditional fee agreement cases

At the end of an application during the course of proceedings, the court
may decide to award the costs of the application to a party whose case
is being conducted under a conditional fee agreement. This raises a
potential problem with the indemnity principle. If at the end of the proceedings this party loses the case, he will ordinarily have no liability
to his own solicitor for the solicitors' charges incurred on his behalf. It
follows that the indemnity principle will prevent him from recovering
any of those charges from the other party, including any which were
summarily assessed at an earlier date.
  However, the costs rules state that 'the existence of a conditional fee   *CPD 14.1*

agreement … is not by itself a sufficient reason for not carrying out a summary assessment'.

There are at least two possible ways round the indemnity principle problem:

- The terms of the conditional fee agreement may provide that if the receiving party is successful at an interim hearing (whether or not he later goes on to lose the claim itself), his solicitors are entitled to payment of their base costs, together with a success fee on them if the receiving party is successful overall. In such circumstances there is no breach of the indemnity principle, so the court can make a summary assessment and order payment of the costs so assessed.

- If the terms of the conditional fee agreement do not contain the provision just mentioned, or the court is not satisfied that they do, it may exercise its powers, for example, to defer the date of payment of the costs summarily assessed until the outcome of the case is known – see 50.12(b).

(c) Cases where everything depends on the final order

There will be circumstances where nobody will know until the end of the case which party is actually entitled to the costs of an application during the course of proceedings, for example, where the court wishes to order:

- that the costs should be reserved (ie the decision about who is to pay them should be left to a later occasion); or

- that the costs in question should be costs in the case (ie whoever is awarded costs at the end of the proceedings is entitled to the costs of this earlier part of the proceedings).

If the court nevertheless decides to make a summary assessment, it will need:

- to make an assessment of both parties' costs; and

- to make no order for the payment of the costs so assessed (see 50.12).

(d) Cases where the court's powers are restricted

The court's ability to make summary assessments is also limited by particular rules relating to cases where there is a conditional fee agreement (see 50.4), where the receiving party is legally aided/LSC funded (see 50.5), is a child or patient (see 50.6) or is a mortgagee (see 50.7). These are considered in detail below.

50.4 What if there is a conditional fee agreement or other funding arrangements?

(a) Assessing the base costs only

If there is a conditional fee agreement or other funding arrangement, the court may not make a summary assessment of an additional liability (see 9.1) before the conclusion of the proceedings or the part of the proceedings to which the funding arrangement relates. *CPD 13.12(1)*

However, in such circumstances, the court should still make a summary assessment of the base costs of the particular hearing or application unless there is good reason not to do so. *CPD 14.2*

Where the court makes a summary assessment of the base costs, all statements of costs and estimates put before the judge will be retained on the court file and the costs officer carrying out the final assessment (which will include the additional liability) should be supplied with copies of all the costs orders previously made and also, if required, shown all the previous costs statements and estimates. *CPD 14.9*

(b) Assessing the additional liability

Only when making a summary assessment 'at the conclusion of proceedings' may the court also assess the additional liability. Such an assessment: *CPD 14.7*

• must relate to the whole of the proceedings; and

• include any additional liability relating to base costs allowed by the court in earlier summary assessments.

However, if there are split trials (eg a trial on liability to be followed by a trial on quantum) the additional liability will not normally be assessed, either by summary or by detailed assessment, until all the issues have been tried, unless the parties agree. *CPD 14.5*

If the parties have agreed the base costs, but disagree about the additional liability, the court may summarily assess that liability or make an order for its detailed assessment. *CPD 14.8*

50.5 What if the receiving party is legally aided/LSC funded?

The court should not make a summary assessment of the costs payable *to* a receiving party who is an assisted person or LSC-funded client. However the court may make a summary assessment of the costs payable *by* such a party, although that assessment will not by itself be a determination of that person's liability to pay those costs. That determination has to take place in accordance with the detailed provisions of CPD 21.1 to 23.17, which are outside the scope of this book. *CPD 21.1–23.17*

50.6 What if the receiving party is a child or a patient?

The court should not make a summary assessment of the costs payable *to* a receiving party who is a child or a patient within the meaning of CPR 21, unless their solicitor has waived the right to further costs (in which case there will be no need for a separate assessment of the costs as between the solicitor and the receiving party, so all aspects of these costs can be finalised by way of the summary assessment). *CPR 21* *CPD 13.11(1)* *CPD 51.1(c)*

However, the court may make a summary assessment of the costs payable *by* a child or patient. *CPD 13.11(2)*

50.7 What if the receiving party is a mortgagee?

The court should not make a summary assessment of a mortgagee's costs incurred in possession or other proceedings relating to a mortgage, unless the mortgagee asks for an order that his costs be paid by another party. This is because such costs are generally payable to the mortgagee under the terms of the mortgage itself. There are rules about the costs relating to mortgages at CPD 50.3–50.4, but they are outside the scope of this book. *CPD 13.3* *CPD 50.3–4*

50.8 What should we do before the hearing?

(a) The need to prepare a statement of costs

If you intend to claim costs at a forthcoming hearing, you must prepare a statement of those costs, showing: *CPD 13.5(2)*

• the number of hours to be claimed;

• the hourly rate to be claimed;

• the grade of fee-earner;

• details of any disbursements to be claimed;

• the solicitors' costs to be claimed for appearing at the hearing;

• counsel's fees to be claimed in respect of the hearing; and

• any VAT payable on the profit costs, disbursements and counsel's fees.

(b) The form of the statement of costs

The statement 'should follow as closely as possible form N260'. That form is reproduced in Appendix III and is also on the CD-ROM. **Form N260** **CPD 3.2**

There is scope to improve on form N260, especially by providing additional information in the form of schedules of work done. Giving a full item-by-item account of the ingredients of the costs claimed ought to make it more difficult for the judge making the summary assessment to do so in an arbitrary manner. On the CD-ROM is an example of a statement of costs which, although prepared specifically for a detailed assessment hearing (see 32.4(a)), shows how this can be done. **CD-ROM 05.08** **CD-ROM 06.12**

Where the intended receiving party is, or may be, entitled to claim an additional liability (such as a success fee), the statement should not reveal the amount of it – see 50.4. *CPD 13.5(5)*

(c) Signature of the statement of costs

The statement must be signed by the party or his legal representative (see 8.9 for an explanation of what this implies). This seems to be required in every case. *CPD 13.5(3)*

Form N260 includes a certificate that 'the costs estimated above do not exceed the costs which the *[party]* is liable to pay in respect of the work which this estimate covers'. This is intended to prevent claims being made which breach the indemnity principle. However, if the intended receiving party is legally aided/LSC funded or is represented by his in-house solicitor, this certificate can be omitted. *CPD 13.5(3)*

In a case conducted under a conditional fee agreement which does not contain a provision of the kind mentioned at 50.3(b) entitling the solicitors to payment of any base costs awarded to the client in a hearing during the course of the proceedings, irrespective of the final outcome of the case, it is difficult to see how the solicitor can properly sign such a certificate. However, the costs rules contain no provision allowing it to be omitted in such circumstances. Probably the best solution is to omit it and be prepared to explain the problem to the court should there be a summary assessment.

(d) Filing and service of the statement

The statement must be filed at court, and copies of it served on any *CPD 13.5(4)* party against whom you intend to seek an order for payment of costs, 'not less than 24 hours before the date fixed for the hearing'. Although it is often assumed that these words mean that you must serve the statement not less than 24 hours before the *time* fixed for the hearing, if these words are taken literally, that would be too late, because it is the *date* rather than the time of the hearing that counts. Thus, if you have a hearing fixed for 2:15 pm on Thursday, the latest time for serving your statement is 11:59 pm on Tuesday, as midnight on Tuesday would be exactly '24 hours before the date fixed for the hearing'.

(e) Additional documents to be filed before the final hearing of a case where an additional liability is to be assessed

If the hearing is, or is likely to be, the final one at which the court is expected to make a summary assessment of the costs and that assessment will include an assessment of any additional liability, then a prospective receiving party must prepare and take to the hearing a bundle of documents containing copies of: *CPD 14.9*

• every notice of funding arrangement (form N251) filed by him;   *CPD 14.9(1)*

• every estimate and statement of costs filed by him; and   *CPD 14.9(2)*

• the risk assessment prepared at the time any relevant funding arrangement was entered into and on the basis of which the amount of the additional liability was fixed.   *CPD 14.9(3)*

(f) Consequences of failure to comply with the rules

It is the duty of the parties to help the judge in making a summary assessment, by complying with the rules about the preparation and service of statements of costs.   *CPD 13.5(1)*

If a party fails, without reasonable excuse, to comply with these rules, that failure will be taken into account by the court in deciding what order to make about the costs of: *CPD 13.6*

• the claim, hearing or application; and

• any further hearing or detailed assessment hearing that may be necessary as a result of that failure.

See chapter 35 as to the general presumptions and the powers of the court in relation to liability for the costs of assessment.

50.9 What is the scope and basis of the order?

If the judge makes an order that one party should pay costs to the other, it is important that he makes the scope of the order clear, ie:

- whether it covers the whole case, or only particular parts of it;

- if the order is to be for a percentage of the costs, what that percentage is to be; and

- whether the costs are to be assessed on the standard or the indemnity basis (if the order does not say, the costs will be assessed on the standard basis).   CPR 44.4

50.10 Is there to be a summary assessment?

Having made clear the scope and basis of the costs order and having heard representations from both parties, the judge can consider whether summary assessment of the costs is appropriate. He has a number of choices:

(a) Summary assessment of all the costs

The judge may decide to carry out a summary assessment of all the costs, including any additional liability which he is in a position to assess, then and there.   CPR 44.3A(2)(a)

If he decides that, while summary assessment is appropriate, it is not practicable to carry it out then and there, he should give directions for it to take place before him on a later occasion. He may not delegate a summary assessment to a costs officer.   *CPD 13.8*

(b) Detailed assessment of all the costs

If the judge decides that summary assessment is not appropriate at all, he may order:

- that the costs should be the subject of detailed assessment; and   CPR 44.3A(2)(c)

- that the paying party should make a payment on account – see chapter 16.

(c) Base costs now, additional liability later

In a case where there is an additional liability, and the judge is in principle able to make a summary assessment of it because the case has come to an end, he may nevertheless decide to make a summary   CPR 44.3A(2)(b) assessment only of the base costs, and order detailed assessment of the additional liability.

(d) Where some or all of the additional liability is disallowed between the parties

If you want to claim any shortfall from the receiving party, the court will give directions enabling you to apply for the amount payable by the receiving party to be determined at a later hearing. Such a determination may be made there and then only if both you and the receiving party agree that it should, the receiving party is present and the court is satisfied that the issue can be fairly decided on that occasion.

CPD 20.3

50.11 How should the judge conduct the summary assessment?

(a) The general approach

The *SCCO Guide to the Summary Assessment of Costs* states at paragraph 7 that the 'general approach to summary and detailed assessment should be the same'. It follows that if the summary assessment is to involve more than the judge just thinking of a figure that seems right to him, it ought to be conducted as a detailed assessment in miniature. This means that the oral argument will cover similar ground to that which would be covered in points of dispute and replies.

CD-ROM 03.01

The paying party will be asked whether he agrees that the amounts claimed in the receiving party's schedule are reasonable and, if not, what other sums he proposes. The receiving party should be given an opportunity to reply.

The judge has to assess not just the solicitor's profit costs, but also counsel's fees and any disbursements.

(b) The issues that may arise

As in a detailed assessment, the issues that arise, and which the court must take into consideration, may include:

- the reasonableness of each item claimed;   *CPR 44.5(1)(a)*

- proportionality (if the assessment is being conducted on the standard basis);   *CPR 44.5(1)(a)*

- the conduct of the parties (including conduct before and during the proceedings and the efforts made, if any, before and during the proceedings in order to try to resolve the dispute);   *CPR 44.5(3)(a)*

- the amount or value of any money or property involved;   **CPR 44.5(3)(b)**

- the importance of the matter to all the parties;   **CPR 44.5(3)(c)**

- the particular complexity of the matter or the difficulty or novelty of the questions raised;   **CPR 44.5(3)(d)**

- the skill, effort, specialised knowledge and responsibility involved;   **CPR 44.5(3)(e)**

- the time spent on the case;   **CPR 44.5(3)(e)**

- the place where and the circumstances in which work or any part of it was done; and   **CPR 44.5(3)(f)**

- the level of any additional liability, if the court is assessing the costs at the end of the proceedings.   *CPD 11*

(c) Do lower charging rates apply to summary assessments?

Appendix 2 to the *SCCO Guide to the Summary Assessment of Costs* (entitled 'Guideline Figures for the Summary Assessment of Costs') contains a table of hourly charging rates for four different grades of fee-earner, divided into four geographical bands.   **CD-ROM 03.02**

When the first version of these guideline figures was published in 1999 many of the rates it contained were lower than those routinely allowed in the local courts concerned. This gave the impression that there was a principle that the rates to be allowed on summary assessments would be lower than those allowed in detailed assessments. This was not so, and the false impression has been corrected by:

- the introduction to the 'Guideline Figures' stating that 'The guideline rates for solicitors are broad approximations only. In any particular area the Designated Civil Judge may, after consultation between District Judges and local Law Societies, supply more exact guidelines for rates in that area'; and

- paragraph 7 of the *Guide to the Summary Assessment of Costs* stating that the 'general approach to summary and detailed assessment should be the same'.   **CD-ROM 03.01**

50.12 How should the order be formulated?

(a) Identifying the elements of costs awarded

Although the general idea of summary assessment is that the court awards a lump sum, the order should normally apportion this lump sum between two separate figures: *CPD 13.7*

- one covering the base costs and, if appropriate, the additional liability allowed as solicitor's charges, counsel's fees, other disbursements and any VAT; *CPD 13.7(1)*

- the other being any amount awarded for fast track trial costs under Part 46. *CPD 13.7(2)*

In a case where there is an additional liability and the base costs are summarily assessed, having just one composite figure for the solicitor's charges, counsel's fees, other disbursements and VAT will cause problems if and when the additional liability comes to be assessed at the end of the case because, for example, it will not be possible to say exactly how much of the composite figure related to the solicitor's charges on which a success fee is to be calculated. The costs rules therefore provide that in such a case the order may show separately the base costs as allowed as: *CPD 9.2(1)* *CPR 46* *CPD 14.6(1)*

- solicitors' charges;

- counsel's fees;

- any other disbursements; and

- any VAT.

The statements of costs on which the judge based his summary assessment are to be kept on the court file. *CPD 14.6(2)*

(b) Defining the arrangements for payment

If the assessment is made:

- at any point in a case not affected by an additional liability; or

- at the end of a case where there is an additional liability, and that additional liability has also been assessed

no special provisions are needed for, in such circumstances, unless the court orders otherwise, payment of the costs so assessed will be due within 14 days. *CPR 44.8*

If the assessment is made before the end of a case in which the receiving party may not finally be entitled to recover the costs of the proceedings (see 50.3(b)), the court can avoid potential problems by: *CPD 14.4*

- directing that the costs should be paid into court to await the outcome of the case; or

- directing that the order for costs should not be enforceable until further order; or

• postponing the receiving party's right to receive payment 'in some other way'.

Even where the statement of costs bears the prescribed certificate (see 50.8(c)), if the court is not satisfied that, in respect of the costs claimed, the receiving party is at the time liable to pay to his legal representative an amount equal to or greater than the costs claimed, it will not make an order for payment. Presumably the receiving party's solicitors will have to satisfy the court on this point either at the end of the case or by making an application at some earlier stage.

CPD 14.3

50.13 What if we have agreed terms?

(a) If the substantive order and the costs are agreed

If an application is made, but the parties then agree a consent order on the basis that neither party need attend the hearing, they should either:

• agree the figure for costs to be inserted in the order (which must be stated to be by consent); or

CPD 13.4
CPD 13.13(a)

• agree that there should be no order for costs.

(b) If the substantive order is agreed, but the costs are not

If they cannot agree the costs position, there has to be an attendance, but unless good reason can be shown for failing to deal with the costs as above, the court will not allow any costs for the attendance.

(c) If the substantive order is not made by consent, but the costs are not disputed

If the judge is asked to make an order which is not by consent, but the paying party does not challenge the receiving party's statement of costs, then:

CPD 13.13(b)

• the judge is still responsible for seeing that the final figure is neither disproportionate nor unreasonable;

• he may take the lack of dispute as to the amount of costs as some indication that the amount is proportionate and reasonable; but

• he will intervene if he is satisfied that the costs are so disproportionate that it is right to do so.

50.14 Can we appeal against the assessment?

As the costs rules contain no specific provisions for appeals against summary assessments, any appeal will only be possible under the provisions of CPR 52 – see chapter 38.

50.15 What about misconduct in summary assessments?

The court's powers to punish misconduct – see 35.6 – applies to summary assessments just as it does to detailed assessments.

CPR 44.14(1)(a)

50.16 What should we do after the assessment?

If the costs summarily assessed are to be paid either within the usual 14 days or by some other set date, diarise the date for payment so that follow-up action will be taken if no payment arrives.

CPR 44.8

CHAPTER 51

'Costs only' proceedings

51.1 What is the purpose of them?

As explained at 3.2, you can only begin detailed assessment proceedings if you have a legal 'peg' on which to hang them. The only kinds of peg are orders or events in substantive proceedings.

If a receiving party makes a claim, and that claim is settled without the issue of substantive proceedings on terms that his opponent pays his costs, there will be no such peg on which you can hang detailed assessment proceedings should you be unable to agree the amount of those costs.

The idea of 'costs only' proceedings is to provide a simple and inexpensive way of obtaining an order for detailed assessment, which then acts as the peg on which you hang detailed assessment proceedings.

51.2 When can we use them?

(a) Where no proceedings have been issued

You can issue 'costs only' proceedings where:

• the parties to a dispute have reached an agreement on all the issues (including which party is to pay the costs) and the agreement is made or confirmed in writing;

• they have failed to agree the amount of those costs (note that, although the costs rules do not say so, the court may expect a proper attempt at agreement to have been made); and

• (except in the circumstances mentioned at (b)) no proceedings have been started.

(b) Where proceedings have been issued, but only on behalf of a child or a patient

Where a claim is made on behalf of a receiving party who is:

• a child (which means a person under 18), or   CPR 21.1(2)(a)

• a patient (which means a person who by reason of mental disorder   CPR 21.1(2)(b)
within the meaning of the Mental Health Act 1983 is incapable of

managing and administering his own affairs); then

that claim can only validly be settled with the approval of the court, for which proceedings have to be issued.

CPR 21.10(1)

Although, as part of the process of approving the settlement, the court would normally make an order for the assessment of the receiving party's costs, the costs rules make 'costs only' proceedings available as an alternative. They are an alternative that would only be needed if for some reason no order for assessment had been made by the court when it approved the settlement.

51.3 How can we start the proceedings?

'Costs only' proceedings can be started by either party to the dispute issuing a claim form under Part 8 (which provides an alternative procedure to the usual one under Part 7 and is intended for use in cases which are unlikely to raise substantial disputes of fact).

CPR 8.1

Because Part 8 proceedings will prove a complete waste of time if the defendant contests them or seeks a different remedy, you will minimise the risk of failure if, before issuing proceedings, you obtain the defendant's written agreement to the terms of the order for which you will apply.

51.4 In which court do we issue proceedings?

The normal court in which to issue proceedings will be the court in which substantive proceedings would have been issued.

• Normally this would be your local county court.

• If the dispute to which the agreement relates 'was of such a value or type that, had proceedings been begun, they would have been commenced in the High Court', issue in the appropriate High Court district registry.

CPD 17.1

• If you would have issued substantive proceedings in the High Court in the Royal Courts of Justice, issue in the SCCO.

CPD 17.2

51.5 How do we issue the claim?

(a) The prescribed form

The prescribed Part 8 claim form is form N208, which is reproduced in Appendix III. It is also on the CD-ROM, together with the notes on completing it (form N208A).

Form N208

CD-ROM 05.05

CD-ROM 05.06

(b) The required information

The claim form should:

CPR 8.2

• state that Part 8 applies;

CPR 8.2(a)

• identify the claim or dispute to which the agreement to pay costs relates;

CPR 8.2(b)
CPD 17.3(1)

• state the date and the terms of the agreement on which the claimant relies;

CPR 8.2(b)
CPD 17.3(2)

• set out or have attached to it a draft of the order which the claimant seeks;

CPD 17.3(3)

• state the amount of the costs claimed;

CPD 17.3(4)

• state whether the costs are claimed on the standard or indemnity basis (if no basis is specified the costs will be treated as being claimed on the standard basis);

CPD 17.3(5)

• if the claimant is claiming in a representative capacity, state what that capacity is; and

CPR 8.2(d)

• if the defendant is sued in a representative capacity, state what that capacity is.

CPR 8.2(e)

Follow the guidance given in the notes (form N208A).
   Specimen details of claim for inclusion in the claim form and a draft order are on the CD-ROM.

CD-ROM 05.06
CD-ROM 06.14
CD-ROM 06.15

(c) Supporting evidence

You must file any written evidence on which you intend to rely when you file the claim form.

CPR 8.5(1)

   This evidence must include copies of the documents on which you rely to prove the defendant's agreement to pay costs.

CPD 17.4

(d) The court fee

The fee is currently £30 whether you issue in the High Court (fee number 1.5(b)) or the county court (fee number 1.6(b)).
   The cheque should be made payable to 'H M Paymaster General'.

(e) The fixed costs on issue

The box in which to show the amount of fixed costs on issue should be left blank, as you will probably want the court to make an order that the costs of the application should be in the detailed assessment – see 51.7.

(f) Service of the claim form

You will normally leave the court to serve the claim form.

51.6 What happens next?

(a) If the Defendant does not contest the claim

Although the form of acknowledgement of service has no box for the defendant to tick stating that he does not contest the claim, if this is the response he gives to the court, the order should be issued in the terms requested. This is the quickest and easiest way of obtaining the order.

CPD 17.6

The SCCO's standard form of order granting the application is on the CD-ROM.

CD-ROM 06.16

There is no need to apply for a consent order unless, for example, you ask the court to make an order in terms other than those set out in the claim form. In that case the usual consent order procedure applies – see 25.4.

CPD 17.7
CPR 40.6

(b) If the Defendant fails to respond

If the defendant does not file an acknowledgement of service within 14 days of service on him of the claim form, you can write to the court asking it to make an order in the terms of your claim.

CPD 17.6

(c) If the Defendant opposes the claim

If the defendant files an acknowledgement of service stating that he intends to contest the claim or to seek a different order, the claim will be treated as opposed and the court will immediately make an order dismissing it. Unless that order gives you liberty to apply to set aside or vary it, or to apply for your costs of the application, you will have no opportunity to make representations and you will have lost your court fee. That is why it is important to be sure that the terms of the proposed order are agreed before you issue.

CPD 17.9(1)(a)
CPD 17.9(2)

Such a dismissal does not prevent you from issuing another claim, either under Part 8 or under Part 7, based on the agreement or alleged agreement to which the dismissed claim related.

CPD 17.9(2)

Note that a claim will not be treated as opposed if the defendant files an acknowledgement of service stating that all he disputes is the amount of the claim for costs.

CPD 17.9(1)(b)

The SCCO's standard form of order dismissing an application is on the CD-ROM.

CD-ROM 06.17

51.7 What orders can the court make?

(a) RTA 'fixed recoverable costs cases'

See 52.1 for the definition of this type of case.
The usual order will be one that allows the receiving party the fixed recoverable costs, the disbursements and any success fee provided for by rules 45.9–45.11.

CPR 45.7
CPR 45.9–45.11

However, if the receiving party claims costs greater than these, the court will need to decide whether the claim is appropriate, and the orders made will depend on its decision in this respect – see 52.6.

(b) All other cases

The most for which you can reasonably hope is an order stating:

• that the defendant should pay the claimant's costs of the claim in relation to which terms of settlement were agreed;

• the basis on which those costs are to be assessed; and

• that the costs of the application are to be in the assessment (ie the party in whose favour the court makes an order for costs at the end of the detailed assessment proceedings will be entitled to his costs of this application).

The *SCCO Guide* states (at para 21.3(d)) that 'unless all parties consent the order for costs will not include an order for a payment of costs on account. In 'costs only' proceedings the only issue to be decided by the court when making the order is whether or not there should be a detailed assessment', ie 'costs only' proceedings give you the peg on which to hang the detailed assessment and nothing more.

CPD 17.8(1)

It follows that, even where you had served a full bill on the defendant and he had served points of dispute before it became clear that the costs would not be agreed, there is no point in seeking any directions designed to shorten the process of getting to a detailed assessment hearing. You will have to go through all the necessary stages of the detailed assessment proceedings, starting with the preparation and service of the notice of commencement – see chapters 8–10.

51.8 What are the weaknesses of the system?

(a) The need for consent at every stage

If the defendant contests the terms of the order for which you are applying, your application will fail. As suggested at 51.3, you would be unwise to issue 'costs only' proceedings without having first obtained the defendant's written agreement to the terms of the order sought. If he then reneged on that agreement, you would have ammunition for an application that he should pay the costs of the application, provided the order dismissing it gave you liberty to apply as to costs.

(b) Problems over the basis of assessment

Under the costs rules, the only orders that can be made in 'costs only' proceedings are for assessment on the standard basis, or on the indemnity basis. Few agreements for the settlement of disputes without the issue of proceedings are likely to provide for the prospective defendant to pay the prospective claimant's costs on the indemnity basis. While some will state that the prospective defendant will pay the prospective claimant's costs on the standard basis, many state only that the prospective defendant will pay the prospective claimant's 'reasonable' costs, thus leaving open the exact basis of assessment.

It can be argued that the costs of a claim that is settled without the issue of proceedings are non-contentious in nature, and should therefore be assessed on the basis prescribed for such costs by the Solicitors (Non-Contentious Business) Remuneration Order 1994. While that basis is very close to the indemnity basis, it is not exactly the same. That distinction seems to be recognised by CPR 44.4(6), which provides that costs can be assessed on that basis. **CPR 44.4(6)** **CPD 17.3(5)** **CPD 54.2(1)**

However, because CPD 17.3(5) does not provide for such an order as an option in 'costs only' proceedings, you cannot use such proceedings to obtain one. You therefore have three options:

- to persuade the defendant to agree to an order for assessment on the indemnity basis as the closest thing to assessment on the basis prescribed by the 1994 Order (your leverage being the threat of the additional costs that will be incurred if you have to issue a Part 7 claim to obtain an order for assessment on the 1994 Order basis); **CPR 7**

- to agree to the costs being assessed on the standard basis as the price you pay for the simplicity and economy of Part 8 'costs only' proceedings compared to a claim under Part 7 (but what you gain in this way might be outweighed by what you lose at detailed assessment, **CPR 7** particularly in cases where proportionality is an issue); or

- to issue a Part 7 claim (see 51.9) to obtain an order for assessment on the basis prescribed by the 1994 Order (taking account of the greater cost of these proceedings and the risk that the court might not accept your argument as to the correct basis of assessment). | CPR 7

It is possible that this situation has arisen because elsewhere the costs rules treat the basis prescribed by the 1994 Order as if it were identical to the indemnity basis, eg 'Costs as between a solicitor and client are assessed on the indemnity basis' – CPD 54.2(1). There do not seem to be any reported cases on this point. A skeleton argument is on the CD-ROM in case you want to be a pioneer (at your own risk, of course). | *CPD 54.2(1)* **CD-ROM 12.01**

(c) No shortening of the detailed assessment proceedings

Because you are expected to make some attempt to negotiate the costs before starting 'costs only' proceedings, it is quite possible that a full bill and points of dispute will already have been served. Nevertheless, as they stand, the rules provide no scope for shortening the detailed assessment proceedings.

51.9 What is the alternative?

If for any of the reasons identified above, Part 8 'costs only' proceedings are not able to provide the order for detailed assessment that you want, the alternative is to issue an ordinary claim form under Part 7 of the CPR. The costs rules expressly preserve this right. A detailed explanation of this 'ordinary' procedure is outside the scope of this book, but the following points should be taken into consideration: | CPR 7 *CPD 17.11*

- The claim would be a contractual one, based on the terms of settlement of the substantive claim, one of which required the prospective defendant to pay the prospective claimant's costs.

- If the claim was defended to the extent that the amount claimed by the prospective claimant was disputed, it is likely that at some point judgment would be entered for the costs to be determined by detailed assessment.

- That judgment would be the peg on which detailed assessment proceedings could be hung. Unless the court also gave directions for the conduct of the detailed assessment proceedings, they would have to be started in the usual way, by the service of a notice of commencement.

The main disadvantage of the Part 7 procedure is the level of court fees to be paid, as these would be payable on issue, on allocation and on listing for trial, if the matter went that far. By way of illustration, at current rates, the total court fees payable to reach the point at which you could start the detailed assessment of a £7,000 bill could be over £500.

CHAPTER 52

'Fixed recoverable costs' in minor road traffic accident cases

52.1 To what cases does this regime apply?

Part II of CPR 45, which came into force on 6 October 2003, introduced a fixed costs regime which applies when:

- 'costs only' proceedings have been issued in a case where the substantive dispute was settled without the issue of proceedings; | CPR 45.7(1)

- the substantive dispute arose from a road traffic accident (which means an accident resulting in bodily injury to any person or damage to property caused by, or arising out of, the use of a motor vehicle on a road or other public place in England and Wales – see CPR 45.7(4) for definitions of 'motor vehicle' and 'road'); | CPR 45.7(2)(a) / CPD 25A.1 / CPR 45.7(4)

- the accident which gave rise to the substantive dispute occurred on or after 6 October 2003; | CPD 25A.1

- the agreed damages include damages in respect of personal injury (which includes any disease and any impairment of a person's physical or mental condition), damage to property, or both; | CPR 45.7(2)(b) / CPR 2.3(1)

- the total value of the agreed damages does not exceed £10,000 (see CPD 25A.3 for details of how you work out the amount of the damages); | CPR 45.7(2)(c) / CPD 25A.2 / CPD 25A.3

- the total value of the agreed damages is above the small claims limit (currently £1,000 if there is a claim for personal injuries, or £5,000 if the claim is only for damage to property); | CPR 45.7(2)(d) / CPD 25A.2 / CPR 26.6(1)–(3)

- the Claimant is not a litigant in person; and | CPR 45.7(3)

- the substantive dispute is not one falling within the scope of the Untraced Drivers Agreement dated 14 February 2003 (but substantive disputes falling within the scope of the Uninsured Drivers Agreement dated 13 August 1999 are covered). | CPD 25A.4

52.2 How does the regime work?

The recoverable costs are calculated mainly by reference to the agreed | CPR 45.8

damages payable to the receiving party. The costs rules provide a formula for working out the figure for profit costs. In addition disbursements and a success fee may be recoverable.

The regime (introduced after negotiations at a 'Costs Forum' arranged by the Civil Justice Council) is meant to avoid 'unproductive skirmishing created by problems with costs'. Although the amount of costs recovered in any particular case is unlikely to be the exact amount incurred, the idea is that what you lose on some cases you will gain on others, so that over a spread of cases the overall result should be fair. Time will tell whether this is so, and the regime is due to be reviewed within two years.

52.3 What is the formula for calculating the recoverable profit costs?

(a) The basic calculation

The recoverable profit costs are the total of: | CPR 45.9(1)

• £800; | CPR 45.9(1)(a)

• 20 per cent of the damages agreed up to £5,000; and | CPR 45.9(1)(b)

• 15 per cent of the damages agreed between £5,000 and £10,000. | CPR 45.9(1)(c)

For example, if you settle a case for agreed damages of £7,523.00, you can recover profit costs of £2,178.45, calculated as follows: £800 + (£5,000 x 20%) + (£2,523 x 15%). | *CPD 25A.5*

(b) The London area weighting

An extra 12.5 per cent may be added to the basic profit costs calculated as shown at (a) above where the claimant (i) lives or works and (ii) instructs a firm of solicitors who practise in the county court districts of Barnet, Bow, Brentford, Bromley, Central London, Clerkenwell, Croydon, Dartford, Edmonton, Gravesend, Ilford, Lambeth, Mayors and City of London, Romford, Shoreditch, Uxbridge, Wandsworth, West London, Willesden and Woolwich. | CPR 45.9(2) *CPD 25A.6*

(c) Multiple claimants

Where there is more than one potential claimant in relation to a dispute and two or more of them instruct the same solicitor or firm of solicitors, the regime applies in respect of each claimant. | *CPD 25A.7*

(d) VAT

Where appropriate, VAT may be recoverable in addition to the basic profit costs calculated as shown at (a) and (b) above.

CPR 45.9(3)

52.4 What disbursements are recoverable?

The court may not allow any disbursements other than the following types:

CPR 45.10(1)

(a) Records and reports

The cost of obtaining:

• medical records;

• a medical report;

• a police report;

• an engineer's report;

• a search of the records of the Driver and Vehicle Licensing Agency.

(b) After the event insurance premium

This means 'a sum of money paid or payable for insurance against the risk of incurring a costs liability in the proceedings, taken out after the event that is the subject matter of the claim'.

CPR 45.10(2)(b)
CPR 43.2(1)(m)

(c) Where the claimant is a child or patient

Where they are necessarily incurred by reason of one or more of the claimants being a child or patient:

CPR 45.10(2)(c)
CPR 21

• fees payable for instructing counsel;

• court fees payable on an application to the court.

It seems odd that you are able to issue 'costs only' proceedings in cases where proceedings have already been issued in relation to the substantive claim, even if those proceedings were only issued to obtain the court's approval to the proposed settlement. You would expect an order for detailed assessment to have been applied for in those proceedings.

(d) Other disbursements

You may recover 'any other disbursement that has arisen due to a particular feature of the dispute' provided you can show both an exceptional feature of the dispute and that the disbursement was necessary.

CPR 45.10(2)(d)
CPD 25A.9

The 'Costs Forum' was concerned that the limits on recoverable profit costs should not be circumvented by outsourcing work so that what should really be claimed as profit costs is instead presented as a disbursement. You can therefore expect the court to be alert to any such attempts.

52.5 Are success fees recoverable?

(a) When may one be recovered?

A claimant may recover a success fee if he has entered into a 'funding arrangement,' ie an arrangement where he has entered into a conditional fee agreement or a collective conditional fee agreement which provides for a success fee within the meaning of s58(2) of the Courts and Legal Services Act 1990.

CPR 45.11(1)
CPR 43.2(1)(k)(i)

(b) How is it to be assessed?

As the rules stood at 6 October 2003, if the amount of the success fee is not agreed between the parties the court will assess it.

CPR 45.11(2)

When the regime was being discussed by the 'Costs Forum' it was proposed that the success fee should be fixed at 5 per cent of profit costs. That limit did not appear in the costs rules, so at the time of writing it seems that the amount should be assessed in accordance with the usual principles. However, a further agreement mediated by the Civil Justice Council in October 2003 set the success fee at 12.5 per cent of base costs in cases where no substantive proceedings were issued. There are likely to be further changes to the rules to implement this agreement early in 2004.

CPD 11.8–11.9

52.6 What if we want to claim more than the fixed profit costs?

(a) The need to show exceptional circumstances

The court will entertain a claim for an amount of profit costs greater than the fixed recoverable amount only if it considers that there are exceptional circumstances making it appropriate to do so.

CPR 45.12(1)
CPD 25A.8

(b) If the court finds exceptional circumstances

If the court thinks that such a claim is appropriate, it may:

CPR 45.12(2)

• assess the costs; or

CPR 45.12(2)(a)

• make an order for the costs to be assessed.

CPR 45.12(2)(b)

(c) If the court does not find exceptional circumstances

If it does not think the claim is appropriate, it must make an order for fixed recoverable costs only.

CPR 45.12(3)

(d) The need to achieve at least a 20 per cent increase

If the court finds exceptional circumstances making it appropriate to entertain a claim for more than the fixed profit costs, and it assesses the costs so claimed, then if the amount so assessed is less than 20 per cent more than the amount of the fixed recoverable costs, the court must order the defendant to pay the claimant the lesser of:

CPR 45.13

• the fixed recoverable costs; and

• the assessed costs.

This means that there is a theoretical possibility of recovering less than the fixed recoverable costs.

(e) The costs penalty for failure

If the court does not find exceptional circumstances (see (c) above) or it finds them but the claimant fails to achieve the 20 per cent increase (see (d) above), then it must:

• make no award for the payment of the claimant's costs in bringing the proceedings under rule 44.12A; and

CPR 45.14(i)

• order that the claimant pay the defendant's costs of defending those proceedings.

CPR 45.14(ii)

For this reason you need to be very confident of success before claiming more than the fixed recoverable costs.

52.7 What is the procedure?

The procedure for obtaining fixed recoverable costs is that for 'costs only' proceedings, using a Part 8 claim form – see chapter 51.
 In the claim form you should include details of:

CPD 25A.8

281

- any exceptional circumstances of the kind mentioned at 52.6(a); *CPD 25A.8*

- any disbursements or success fee being claimed; and *CPD 25A.9*

- the exceptional feature of the dispute giving rise to any claim for a disbursement of the kind mentioned at 52.4(d) and why the claimant considers it was necessary. *CPD 25A.9*

52.8 What if the figure for profit costs is agreed?

If you have agreed with the paying party the amount of the fixed recoverable base profit costs and the only dispute is as to the payment of, or amount of, a disbursement or as to the amount of a success fee, then you should issue ordinary 'costs only' proceedings, and not proceedings referring to this regime. *CPD 25A.10*

52.9 Who pays the costs of the 'costs only' proceedings?

Except for the automatic costs penalty referred to at 52.6(e) for receiving parties who fail in their attempts to recover more than the fixed recoverable costs, there are no special rules about who should pay the costs of the 'costs only' proceedings. As you can generally make no progress in 'costs only' proceedings without the consent of the paying party to the terms of the order for assessment (see chapter 51), you will probably have had to propose that the costs of the 'costs only' proceedings should be 'in the assessment'. In the normal course of things, this should result in them being awarded to the receiving party when the court makes the order that the receiving party should be entitled to fixed recoverable costs.

52.10 When are we likely to need to issue 'costs only' proceedings?

(a) In 'ordinary' cases

When the substantive claim is settled, it should be obvious whether or not the fixed recoverable costs regime will apply. If it does, it would be prudent to agree the exact amount payable under the regime as part of the settlement and see that it is paid at the same time as the agreed damages

Even if this is not done, you can reasonably expect the paying party to agree the calculation of the fixed recoverable costs after the settlement and to pay them. However, if you cannot get a response from the paying party or, having agreed the costs, he fails to pay them, you may need to take 'costs only' proceedings even though all you are seeking to recover is the ordinary amount of fixed recoverable costs.

(b) In 'exceptional' cases

If you want more than the ordinary fixed recoverable costs the paying party is unlikely to agree them and in those circumstances you will need to take 'costs only' proceedings if you want more than the fixed recoverable costs, unless you try to avoid the regime altogether – see 52.11.

52.11 Can the regime be avoided?

The provision in the costs rules that expressly preserves your right to issue 'ordinary' Part 7 proceedings instead of Part 8 'costs only' proceedings has not been disapplied to cases where fixed recoverable costs would be expected to apply.

CPD 17.11

This means that you could seek to avoid the risks of taking 'costs only' proceedings in a case where you want to recover more than the fixed costs (see 52.6) by issuing Part 7 proceedings, provided you had not agreed with the paying party that the only costs payable would be the ordinary fixed recoverable ones. This would, however, be expensive in court fees (see 51.9) and, because the costs of the exercise would be in the discretion of the court, you could expect the court to make a costs order unfavourable to you if it felt that you had issued Part 7 proceedings for no other reason than to circumvent the fixed recoverable costs regime.

52.12 What is the effect of the indemnity principle?

(a) As between you and the paying party

The rules fail to disapply the indemnity principle to cases where the costs are subject to this regime. It is therefore open to a paying party to argue that if the fixed recoverable costs exceed the costs which are payable to you by the receiving party, he should not have to pay the excess. A similar problem arises with fast-track fixed trial costs, but there the Chief Costs Judge thought that all would be well provided the receiving party's solicitor accounted to the receiving party for the excess – see *Guidance Given by the Senior Costs Judge to the Designated Civil Judges Conference* on 24 November 2000, which you can find on the SCCO's website (see 2.5).

(b) As between you and the client

If the fixed recoverable costs are more than the amount you are able to charge the client under your retainer, see (a) above for what might be the position. If the fixed recoverable costs are less than the amount you would otherwise have sought to charge the client, you may wish to claim the shortfall from him. Whether you must account to him for any surplus or can charge him for any shortfall will depend upon the terms of your retainer. The drafting of retainers is outside the scope of this book, but see the *Law Society Gazette*, 2 October 2003, page 35 for some suggestions and a warning as to the effect of section 74 of the Solicitors Act 1974.

APPENDIX I

SPECIMEN WORKSHEETS

WORKSHEET No 1

TOTAL COSTS CLAIMED BETWEEN THE PARTIES

1-Mar-04

Solicitors' charges

As claimed in bill:	£8,258.50
VAT thereon @ 17.5%:	£1,445.24
	£9,703.74

Counsel's fees

As claimed in bill:	£350.00	
VAT thereon @ 17.5%:	£61.25	
		£411.25

Disbursements

As claimed in bill:	£827.50	
VAT thereon:	£4.81	
		£832.31
Total costs of substantive proceedings:		**£10,947.30**

Interest on substantive costs to date

Statutory rate:	8.00%	
Date from which entitlement begins:	12-Dec-03	
No of days elapsed:	80	
Interest accrued to date:		£191.95

Total substantive costs and interest:	**£11,139.25**

Daily rate of interest:	**£2.40**

WORKSHEET No 2

IMPLICATIONS OF PRE-EMPTIVE OFFER

1-Mar-04

Solicitors' charges

As claimed in bill:		£8,258.50
Less: discount offered:	**5.00%**	£412.62
Net solicitors' charges:		£7,845.88
VAT thereon @ 17.5%:		£1,373.03
		£9,218.91

Counsel's fees

As claimed in bill:		£350.00
Less: discount offered:	**5.00%**	£17.50
Net counsel's fees:		£332.50
VAT thereon @ 17.5%:		£58.19
		£390.69

Disbursements

As claimed in bill:		£827.50
VAT thereon:		£4.81
		£832.31
Total costs of substantive proceedings:		**£10,441.91**

Interest on substantive costs to date

Statutory rate:	8.00%	
Date from which entitlement begins:	12-Dec-03	
No of days elapsed:	80	
Interest accrued to date:		£183.09

Amount of pre-emptive offer:	**£10,625.00**

WORKSHEET No 3

AMOUNT PAYABLE UNDER DEFAULT COSTS CERTIFICATE

26-Mar-04

Solicitors' charges
As claimed in bill: £8,258.50
VAT thereon @ 17.5%:   £1,445.24
                                                                        £9,703.74

Counsel's fees
As claimed in bill: £350.00
VAT thereon @ 17.5%:   £61.25
                                                                £411.25

Disbursements
As claimed in bill: £827.50
VAT thereon: £4.81
                                                                £832.31
Total costs of substantive proceedings: **£10,947.30**

Interest on substantive costs to date
Statutory rate: 8.00%
Date from which entitlement begins: 12-Dec-03
No of days elapsed: 105
Interest accrued to date: **£251.94**

Sub-total substantive costs and interest: **£11,199.24**

Fixed costs of default costs certificate
Solicitors' charges: £68.09
VAT thereon @ 17.5%:   £11.91
                                                   £80.00
Court fee on N254:   £40.00
                                                                £120.00

Total of all costs and interest to date: **£11,319.24**

Daily rate of interest: **£2.40**

WORKSHEET No 4

IMPLICATIONS OF PAYING PARTY'S OFFER

22-Mar-04

Solicitors' charges
As claimed in bill:		£8,258.50
Less: reduction if offer accepted:	**36.38%**	£3,004.59
Net solicitors' charges:		£5,253.91
VAT thereon @ 17.5%:		£919.44
		£6,173.35

Counsel's fees
As claimed in bill:		£350.00	
Less: reduction offered by counsel's clerk:	**10.00%**	£35.00	
Net counsel's fees:		£315.00	
VAT thereon @ 17.5%:		£55.13	
			£370.13

Disbursements
As claimed in bill:	£827.50	
VAT thereon:	£4.81	
		£832.31
Total costs of substantive proceedings:		**£7,375.78**

Interest on substantive costs to date
Statutory rate:	8.00%
Date from which entitlement begins:	12-Dec-03
No of days elapsed:	101
Interest accrued to date:	£163.28

Sub-total substantive costs and interest:	**£7,539.06**

Costs of detailed assessment to date
No of hours spent:	4.50	
Rate per hour:	£125.00	
Solicitors' charges:	£562.50	
VAT thereon @ 17.5%:	£98.44	
		£660.94

Total offered by Defendant:	**£8,200.00**

WORKSHEET No 5

VALUATION OF PAYING PARTY'S POINTS OF DISPUTE

22-Mar-04

Item No in bill	Party/topic etc	Grade of fee-earner	Work type	Time claimed in bill (hrs)	Bill charging rates	Costs claimed at bill rates	Paying party's charging rates	Costs of time claimed but at paying party's rates	Time objected to by paying party (hrs)	Time accepted by paying party (hrs)	Costs of accepted time at paying party's rates	LSC charging rates	Costs objected to recalculated at LSC rates
6	Hearing	A	Advocacy	0.4	£165.00	£66.00	£160.00	£64.00		0.4	£64.00	£66.00	£0.00
		A	Travelling	0.6	£165.00	£99.00	£160.00	£96.00		0.6	£96.00	£29.20	£0.00
		A	Waiting	0.3	£165.00	£49.50	£160.00	£48.00		0.3	£48.00	£29.20	£0.00
14	Claimant	A	Attendances	1.1	£165.00	£181.50	£160.00	£176.00		1.1	£176.00	£66.00	£0.00
		B	Attendances	3.7	£150.00	£555.00	£145.00	£536.50	0.8	2.9	£420.50	£66.00	£52.80
		B	Letters out	2.5	£150.00	£375.00	£145.00	£362.50	0.5	2.0	£290.00	£66.00	£33.00
		B	Telephones	1.9	£150.00	£285.00	£145.00	£275.50	0.3	1.6	£232.00	£36.50	£10.95
		D	Telephones	0.9	£100.00	£90.00	£80.00	£72.00	0.5	0.4	£32.00	£36.50	£18.25
15	Defendant	B	Letters out	2.4	£150.00	£360.00	£145.00	£348.00		2.4	£348.00	£66.00	£0.00
		B	Telephones	1.1	£150.00	£165.00	£145.00	£159.50		1.1	£159.50	£36.50	£0.00
		D	Telephones	0.3	£100.00	£30.00	£80.00	£24.00		0.3	£24.00	£36.50	£0.00
16	Med records	B	Letters out	0.6	£150.00	£90.00	£145.00	£87.00		0.6	£87.00	£66.00	£0.00
		D	Telephones	0.1	£100.00	£10.00	£80.00	£8.00	0.1	0.0	£0.00	£36.50	£3.65
19	Med expert	B	Attendances	1.4	£150.00	£210.00	£145.00	£203.00		1.4	£203.00	£66.00	£0.00
		B	Letters out	0.6	£150.00	£90.00	£145.00	£87.00		0.6	£87.00	£36.50	£0.00
		D	Telephones	0.8	£100.00	£80.00	£80.00	£64.00	0.4	0.4	£32.00	£36.50	£14.60
21	Calculations	A	Preparation	1.2	£165.00	£198.00	£160.00	£192.00	0.7	0.5	£80.00	£66.00	£46.20
		B	Preparation	5.8	£150.00	£870.00	£145.00	£841.00	2.8	3.0	£435.00	£66.00	£184.80
22	The LSC	B	Letters out	0.3	£150.00	£45.00	£145.00	£43.50	0.3	0.0	£0.00	£66.00	£19.80
		B	Telephones	0.5	£150.00	£75.00	£145.00	£72.50	0.5	0.0	£0.00	£36.50	£18.25
23	Court office	B	Letters out	0.5	£150.00	£75.00	£145.00	£72.50		0.5	£72.50	£66.00	£0.00
		B	Telephones	0.3	£150.00	£45.00	£145.00	£43.50		0.3	£43.50	£36.50	£0.00
24	Counsel's clerk	B	Letters out	0.5	£150.00	£75.00	£145.00	£72.50	0.2	0.3	£43.50	£66.00	£13.20
		B	Telephones	0.6	£150.00	£90.00	£145.00	£87.00	0.4	0.2	£29.00	£36.50	£14.60
25	Documents	A	Preparation	2.3	£165.00	£379.50	£160.00	£368.00	1.3	1.0	£160.00	£66.00	£85.80
		B	Preparation	16.9	£150.00	£2,535.00	£145.00	£2,450.50	4.9	12.0	£1,740.00	£66.00	£323.40
		D	Preparation	3.6	£100.00	£360.00	£80.00	£288.00	2.6	1.0	£80.00	£66.00	£171.60
26	Preparing bill	C	Preparation	5.0	£125.00	£625.00	£80.00	£400.00	0.5	4.5	£360.00	£66.00	£33.00
27	Checking bill	B	Preparation	1.0	£150.00	£150.00	£145.00	£145.00	0.5	0.5	£72.50	£66.00	£33.00
	Totals:			57.2		£8,258.50		£7,687.00	17.3	39.9	£5,415.00		£1,076.90

Total of all disallowances / reductions sought by paying party: £2,843.50

WORKSHEET No 6

IMPLICATIONS OF VARYING DEGREES OF SUCCESS BY PAYING PARTY

22-Mar-04

Solicitors' charges

As claimed in bill:		£8,258.50
Reductions/disallowances sought:	£2,843.50	
Percentage of objections that succeed:	**50.00%**	£1,421.75
Net solicitors' charges:		£6,836.75
VAT thereon @ 17.5%:		£1,196.43
		£8,033.18

Counsel's fees

As claimed in bill:		£350.00
Reductions/disallowances sought:	£100.00	
Percentage of objections that succeed:	**50.00%**	£50.00
Net counsel's fees:		£300.00
VAT thereon @ 17.5%:		£52.50
		£352.50

Disbursements

As claimed in bill:		£827.50
Reductions/disallowances sought:	£150.00	
Percentage of objections that succeed:	**50.00%**	£75.00
Net disbursements:		£752.50

VAT on disbursements

As claimed in bill:		£4.81
Reductions/disallowances sought:	£0.00	
Percentage of objections that succeed:	**0.00%**	£0.00
Net VAT on disbursements:		£4.81

Total costs of substantive proceedings: £9,142.99

Interest on substantive costs to date

Statutory rate:	8.00%
Date from which entitlement begins:	12-Dec-03
No of days elapsed:	101
Interest accrued to date:	£202.40

Total substantive costs and interest: £9,345.39

WORKSHEET No 7

IMPLICATIONS OF COMPLETE SUCCESS BY PAYING PARTY

22-Mar-04

Solicitors' charges

As claimed in bill:		£8,258.50
Reductions/disallowances sought:	£2,843.50	
Percentage of objections that succeed:	**100.00%**	£2,843.50
Net solicitors' charges:		£5,415.00
VAT thereon @ 17.5%:		£947.63
		£6,362.63

Counsel's fees

As claimed in bill:		£350.00
Reductions/disallowances sought:	£100.00	
Percentage of objections that succeed:	**100.00%**	£100.00
Net counsel's fees:		£250.00
VAT thereon @ 17.5%:		£43.75
		£293.75

Disbursements

As claimed in bill:		£827.50
Reductions/disallowances sought:	£150.00	
Percentage of objections that succeed:	**100.00%**	£150.00
Net disbursements:		£677.50

VAT on disbursements

As claimed in bill:		£4.81
Reductions/disallowances sought:	£0.00	
Percentage of objections that succeed:	**0.00%**	£0.00
Net VAT on disbursements:		£4.81

Total costs of substantive proceedings:	**£7,338.69**

Interest on substantive costs to date

Statutory rate:	8.00%
Date from which entitlement begins:	12-Dec-03
No of days elapsed:	101
Interest accrued to date:	£162.46

Total substantive costs and interest:	**£7,501.14**

WORKSHEET No 8

IMPLICATIONS OF RECEIVING PARTY'S COUNTER-OFFER

30-Mar-04

Solicitors' charges
As claimed in bill:		£8,258.50
Less: discount offered:	19.87%	£1,641.25
Net solicitors' charges:		£6,617.25
VAT thereon @ 17.5%:		£1,158.02
		£7,775.27

Counsel's fees
As claimed in bill:		£350.00	
Less: discount offered:	10.00%	£35.00	
Net counsel's fees:		£315.00	
VAT thereon @ 17.5%:		£55.13	
			£370.13

Disbursements
As claimed in bill:	£827.50	
VAT thereon:	£4.81	
		£832.31
Total costs of substantive proceedings:		**£8,977.71**

Interest on substantive costs to date
Statutory rate:	8.00%	
Date from which entitlement begins:	12-Dec-03	
No of days elapsed:	109	
Interest accrued to date:		£214.48

Sub-total substantive costs and interest:	**£9,192.19**

Costs of detailed assessment to date
No of hours spent:	5.50	
Rate per hour:	£125.00	
Solicitors' charges:	£687.50	
VAT thereon @ 17.5%:	£120.31	
		£807.81

Amount of counter-offer:	**£10,000.00**

WORKSHEET No 9

UPDATED TOTAL CLAIMED FOR INTERIM COSTS CERTIFICATE

15-Apr-04

Solicitors' charges
As claimed in bill:		£8,258.50
VAT thereon @ 17.5%:		£1,445.24
		£9,703.74

Counsel's fees
As claimed in bill:	£350.00	
VAT thereon @ 17.5%:	£61.25	
		£411.25

Disbursements
As claimed in bill:	£827.50	
VAT thereon:	£4.81	
		£832.31
Total costs of substantive proceedings:		**£10,947.30**

Interest on substantive costs to date
Statutory rate:	8.00%	
Date from which entitlement begins:	12-Dec-03	
No of days elapsed:	125	
Interest accrued to date:		£299.93

Total substantive costs and interest:	**£11,247.22**

WORKSHEET No 10

POSSIBLE TRANSFERS TO CLAIM AGAINST CLS FUND

29-Apr-04

Item No in bill	Party/topic etc	Grade of fee-earner	Work type	Time claimed in bill (hrs)	Time objected to by paying party (hrs)	LSC charging rates	Costs objected to recal-culated at LSC rates
14	Claimant	B	Attendances	3.7	0.8	£66.00	£52.80
		B	Letters out	2.5	0.5	£66.00	£33.00
		B	Telephones	1.9	0.3	£36.50	£10.95
		D	Telephones	0.9	0.5	£36.50	£18.25
16	Med records	D	Telephones	0.1	0.1	£36.50	£3.65
19	Med expert	D	Telephones	0.8	0.4	£36.50	£14.60
21	Calculations	A	Preparation	1.2	0.7	£66.00	£46.20
		B	Preparation	5.8	2.8	£66.00	£184.80
22	The LSC	B	Letters out	0.3	0.3	£66.00	£19.80
		B	Telephones	0.5	0.5	£36.50	£18.25
24	Counsel's clerk	B	Letters out	0.5	0.2	£66.00	£13.20
		B	Telephones	0.6	0.4	£36.50	£14.60
25	Documents	A	Preparation	2.3	1.3	£66.00	£85.80
		B	Preparation	16.9	4.9	£66.00	£323.40
		D	Preparation	3.6	2.6	£66.00	£171.60
26	Preparing bill	C	Preparation	5.0	0.5	£66.00	£33.00
27	Checking bill	B	Preparation	1.0	0.5	£66.00	£33.00
	Totals:			**47.6**	**17.3**		**£1,076.90**

WORKSHEET No 11

RESULT OF FINAL SETTLEMENT

29-Apr-04

Solicitors' charges

As claimed in bill:		£8,258.50
Less: discount given to achieve settlement:	**23.67%**	£1,954.55
Net solicitors' charges:		£6,303.95
VAT thereon @ 17.5%:		£1,103.19
		£7,407.14

Counsel's fees

As claimed in bill:		£350.00
Less: discount given to achieve settlement:	**10.00%**	£35.00
Net counsel's fees:		£315.00
VAT thereon @ 17.5%:		£55.13
		£370.13

Disbursements

As claimed in bill:		£827.50
VAT thereon:		£4.81
		£832.31
Total costs of substantive proceedings:		**£8,609.58**

Interest on substantive costs to date

Statutory rate:		8.00%
Date from which entitlement begins:		12-Dec-03
No of days elapsed:		139
Interest accrued to date:		£262.30

Sub-total substantive costs and interest:		**£8,871.88**

Costs of detailed assessment to date

No of hours spent:	7.00	
Rate per hour:	£125.00	
Solicitors' charges:		£875.00
VAT thereon @ 17.5%:		£153.13
		£1,028.13

Costs agreed between the parties:		**£9,900.00**

Daily rate of interest:	**£1.89**	

WORKSHEET No 12

COSTS OF DETAILED ASSESSMENT PROCEEDINGS INCURRED SINCE COMMENCEMENT OF THEM ON 3 MARCH 2004

As at: 13-May-04

Date	Details of work done	Actual time spent	Claimed against Defend-ant	Claimed against LSC	Non-charge-able
23-Mar-04	Considering Defendant's offer and preparing calculation showing implications of accepting it (1 page)	0.3	0.3		
23-Mar-04	Perusing Defendant's points of dispute (6 pages), annotating bill to identify items disputed and locating and flagging relevant documents and notes in files	1.8	1.5		0.3
23-Mar-04	Preparing replies to points of dispute (5 pages); updating calculation of interest claimed to date; preparing covering letter (1 page) serving replies	2.0	1.7		0.3
23-Mar-04	Preparing calculation of costs of detailed assessment to date	0.3	0.2		0.1
23-Mar-04	Preparing valuation of Defendant's points of dispute (1 page) and calculation showing implications of varying degrees of success (1 page)	0.9	0.8		0.1
24-Mar-04	Working out time estimate for detailed assessment hearing; preparing letter to Defendant seeking agreement to it (1 page)	0.3	0.2		0.1
24-Mar-04	Preparing application in form CLAIM 4 for payment on account of court fee for detailed assessment hearing	0.2		0.2	
24-Mar-04	Preparing explanatory letter to LSC-funded Claimant (6 pages) and response form (1 page)	0.7		0.7	
30-Mar-04	Updating calculation of interest and costs of detailed assessment; formulating counter-offer; discussing offer and counter-offer with counsel's clerk	0.8	0.8		
15-Apr-04	Preparing request for detailed assessment hearing (form N258), checking and collating enclosures and preparing covering letter to court (2 pages)	0.6	0.4	0.1	0.1
15-Apr-04	Updating calculation of interest and costs of detailed assessment claimed to date; preparing application notice for interim costs certificate (2 pages), draft order (1 page), draft certificate (1 page) and covering letter to court	0.9	0.7		0.2
29-Apr-04	Preparing for negotiations, including updating calculation of interest and costs of detailed assessment	0.4	0.2		0.2
29-Apr-04	Negotiating with Defendant's costs draftsman; preparing fax recording terms of agreement (1 page) and preparing letter to Claimant reporting settlement (2 pages)	0.5	0.4	0.1	
29-Apr-04	Preparing fax to court notifying settlement of costs claimed between the parties and requesting 'LSC only' assessment of remaining costs at a later date (1 page)	0.2	0.1	0.1	
29-Apr-04	Identifying items objected to by Defendant for transfer to claim against CLS Fund	0.2		0.2	
	Totals:	**9.8**	**7.0**	**1.4**	**1.4**

APPENDIX II
COSTS PRECEDENTS

SCHEDULE OF COSTS PRECEDENTS
PRECEDENT E

Legal Aid/LSC Schedule of Costs

IN THE HIGH COURT OF JUSTICE   1999 - B - 9999

QUEEN'S BENCH DIVISION

BRIGHTON DISTRICT REGISTRY

BETWEEN

AB	Claimant
~ and ~	
CD	Defendant

CLAIMANT'S BILL OF COSTS: LEGAL AID/LSC SCHEDULE

Item No.	Description of work done	V.A.T.	Disbursements	Profit Costs
6	Issue fee	—	£ 400.00	
7	Allocation fee	—	£ 80.00	
8	Solicitor's fee for hearing Engaged 0.75 hours £55.50 Enhancement thereon at 50% £27.75 Travel and waiting 2.00 hours £65.40 Total solicitor's fee for attending			£ 148.65
9	Fee on listing	—	£ 400.00	
10	Solicitor's fee for hearing Engaged 1.5 hours £111.00 Enhancement thereon at 50% £55.50 Travel and waiting 2.00 hours £65.40 Total solicitor's fee for attending			£ 231.90
11	Counsel's fee	£ 105.00	£ 600.00	
12	Solicitor's fee for trial Engaged in court 5.00 hours £182.00 Engaged in conference 0.75 hours £27.30 Enhancement thereon at 50% £104.65 Travel and waiting 1.50 hours £49.05 Total solicitor's fee for attending			£ 363.00
13	Counsel's brief fee for trial	£ 350.00	£2,000.00	
14	Expert's fee for trial	—	£ 850.00	
15	Witnesses' expenses	—	£ 84.00	
	To summary	£ 455.00	£4,414.00	£ 743.55

Item No.	Description of work done	V.A.T.	Disburse-ments	Profit Costs
16	Solicitor's fee for trial (second day) Engaged in court 3.00 hours £109.20 Engaged in conference 1.50 hours £54.60 Enhancement thereon at 50% £81.90 Travel and waiting 1.50 hours £49.05 Total solicitor's fee for attending			£ 294.75
17	Counsel's fee for second day of trial	£ 113.75	£ 650.00	
18	Timed attendances on Claimant (1) 7.5 hours £555.00 Enhancement thereon at 50% £277.50			£ 832.50
19	Routine communications with Claimant (1) Letters out - 14 £103.60 Telephone calls - 12 £49.20			£ 152.80
22	Timed attendances on and communications with witnesses of fact 5.2 hours £384.80 Enhancement thereon at 50% £192.40			£ 577.20
23	Routine communications with witnesses of fact Letters out - 4 £29.60 Telephone calls - 2 £8.20			£ 37.80
24	Paid travelling	4.02	22.96	
25	Timed attendance on medical expert 0.33 hours £24.42 Enhancement thereon at 50% £12.21			£ 36.63
26	Timed communications with medical expert 0.25 hours £18.50 Enhancement thereon at 50% £9.25			£ 27.75
27	Timed communications with medical expert 0.2 hours £14.80 Enhancement thereon at 50% £7.40			£ 22.20
28	Routine communications with medical expert Letters out - 6 £44.40 Telephone calls - 4 £16.40			£ 60.80
29	Expert's fee for report	—	£ 350.00	
30	Timed communications with solicitors for Defendant 0.25 hours £18.50 Enhancement thereon at 50% £9.25			£ 27.75
31	Routine communications with solicitors for Defendant Letters out - 18 £133.20 Telephone calls - 6 £24.60			£ 157.80
32	Routine communications with the court Letters out - 8 £59.20 Telephone calls - 1 £4.10			£ 63.30
	To summary	£ 117.77	£1,022.96	£2,291.28

Item No.	Description of work done	V.A.T.	Disbursements	Profit Costs
33	Routine communications with Counsel Letters out - 11 £81.40 Telephone calls - 8 £32.80			£ 114.20
36	Work done on documents 57.25 hours £4,236.50 Enhancement thereon at 50% £2,118.25			£6,354.75
37	Work done on negotiations Engaged - 1.5 hours £111.00 Enhancement thereon at 50% £55.50 Travel and waiting - 1.25 hours £40.88			£ 207.38
38	Other work done (1) Preparing and checking bill			£ 370.00
40	VAT on total profit costs set out above (17.5% of £10,216.86)	£1,787.95		
	To summary	£1,787.95	£ —	£7,046.33

	SUMMARY			
	Page 1	£ 455.00	£4,414.00	£ 743.55
	Page 2	£ 117.77	£1,022.96	£2,291.28
	Page 3	£1,787.95	£ —	£7,046.33
	Totals:	£2,360.72	£5,436.96	£10,081.16
	Grand total:			£17,878.84

SCHEDULE OF COSTS PRECEDENTS
PRECEDENT F

Certificates for inclusion in bill of costs

• Appropriate certificates under headings (1) and (2) are required in all cases. The appropriate certificate under (3) is required in all cases in which the receiving party is an assisted person or a LSC funded client. Certificates (4), (5) and (6) are optional. Certificate (6) may be included in the bill, or, if the dispute as to VAT recoverability arises after service of the bill, may be filed and served as a supplementary document amending the bill under paragraph 39.10 of this Practice Direction.

• All certificates must be signed by the receiving party or by his solicitor. Where the bill claims costs in respect of work done by more than one firm of solicitors, certificate (1), appropriately completed, should be signed on behalf of each firm.

(1) CERTIFICATE AS TO ACCURACY

I certify that this bill is both accurate and complete [and]

☐ *(where the receiving party was funded by legal aid/LSC)*
[in respect of Part(s) ..... of the bill] all the work claimed was done pursuant to a certificate issued by the Legal Aid Board/ Legal Services Commission granted to [the assisted person] [the LSC funded client].

☐ *(where costs are claimed for work done by an employed solicitor)*
[in respect of Part(s) .... of the bill] the case was conducted by a solicitor who is an employee of the receiving party.

☐ *(other cases where costs are claimed for work done by a solicitor)*
[in respect of Part(s) ..... of the bill] the costs claimed herein do not exceed the costs which the receiving party is required to pay me/my firm.

(2) CERTIFICATE AS TO INTEREST AND PAYMENTS

I certify that:

☐ No rulings have been made in this case which affects my/the receiving party's entitlement (if any) to interest on costs.

or

☐ The only rulings made in this case as to interest are as follows:
[give brief details as to the date of each ruling, the name of the Judge who made it and the text of the ruling]

and

☐ No payments have been made by any paying party on account of costs included in this bill of costs.

or

☐ The following payments have been made on account of costs included in this bill of costs:
[give brief details of the amounts, the dates of payment and the name of the person by or on whose behalf they were paid]

(3) CERTIFICATE AS TO INTEREST OF ASSISTED PERSON/ LSC FUNDED CLIENT PURSUANT TO REGULATION 119 OF THE CIVIL LEGAL AID (GENERAL) REGULATIONS 1989

I certify that the assisted person/ LSC funded client has no financial interest in the detailed assessment.

or

I certify that a copy of this bill has been sent to the assisted person/ LSC funded client pursuant to Regulation 119 of the Civil Legal Aid General Regulations 1989 with an explanation of his/her interest in the detailed assessment and the steps which can be taken to safeguard that interest in the assessment. He/she has/has not requested that the costs officer be informed of his/her interest and has/has not requested that notice of the detailed assessment hearing be sent to him/her.

(4) CONSENT TO THE SIGNING OF THE CERTIFICATE WITHIN 21 DAYS OF DE-TAILED ASSESSMENT PURSUANT TO REGULATION 112 AND 121 OF THE CIVIL LEGAL AID (GENERAL) REGULATIONS 1989

I certify that notice of the fees reduced or disallowed on detailed assessment has been given in writing to counsel on [date].

or

I certify that: there having been no reduction or disallowance of counsel's fees it is not necessary to give notice to counsel.

I/we consent to the final costs certificate being issued immediately.

(5) CERTIFICATE IN RESPECT OF DISBURSEMENTS NOT EXCEEDING £500

I hereby certify that all disbursements listed in this bill which individually do not exceed £500 (other than those relating to counsel's fees) have been duly discharged.

(6) CERTIFICATE AS TO RECOVERY OF VAT

With reference to the pending assessment of the [claimant's/defendant's] costs and disbursements herein which are payable by the [claimant/defendant] we the undersigned [solicitors to] [auditors of] the [claimant/defendant] hereby certify that the [claimant/defendant] on the basis of its last completed VAT return [would/would not be entitled to recover would/be entitled to recover only percent of the] Value Added Tax on such costs and disbursements, as input tax pursuant to Section 14 of the Value Added Tax Act 1983.

SCHEDULE OF COSTS PRECEDENTS
PRECEDENT G

IN THE HIGH COURT OF JUSTICE   2000 B 9999

QUEEN'S BENCH DIVISION

BRIGHTON DISTRICT REGISTRY

B E T W E E N

AB

Claimant

- and -

CD

Defendant

POINTS OF DISPUTE SERVED BY THE DEFENDANT

Item	Dispute	Claimant's Comments
General point	Base rates claimed for the assistant solicitor and other fee earners are excessive. Reduce to £100 and £70 respectively plus VAT. Each item in which these rates are claimed should be recalculated at the reduced rates.	
(1)	The premium claimed is excessive. Reduce to £95.	

Item	Dispute	Claimant's Comments
(14)	The claim for timed attendances on claimant (schedule 1) is excessive. Reduce to 4 hours ie. £400 at reduced rates.	
(29)	The total claim for work done on documents by the assistant solicitor is excessive. A reasonable allowance in respect of documents concerning court and counsel is 8 hours, for documents concerning witnesses and the expert witness, 6.5 hours, for work done on arithmetic, 2.25 hours and for other documents, 5.5 hours. Reduce to 22.25 hours ie. £2,225 at reduced rates (£3,380 in total).	
(31)	The time claimed is excessive. Reduce solicitors time to 0.5 hours ie. to £50 at reduced rates and reduce the costs draftsman's time to three hours ie. £210 (£260 in total).	
(32)	The success fee claimed is excessive. Reduce to 25% ie. £100 plus VAT of £17.50.	
(33)	The total base fees when recalculated on the basis of the above points amount to £7,788, upon which VAT is £1,362.90.	
(34)	The success fee claimed is excessive. Reduce to 25% of £7,788 ie £1,947.50 plus VAT of £340.73.	
(36)	The success fee claimed is excessive.Reduce to 50% ie £1,625 plus VAT of £284.38.	

Served on .... [date] by .... [name] [solicitors for] the Defendant.

APPENDIX III
PRESCRIBED FORMS

Notice of commencement of assessment of bill of costs

In the	
Claim No.	
Claimant (Include Ref.)	
Defendant (Include Ref.)	

To the claimant(defendant)

Following an . . . . (*insert name of document eg. order, judgment*) dated . . . .
(copy attached) I have prepared my Bill of Costs for assessment. The Bill totals *£ . . . . If you choose to
dispute this bill and your objections are not upheld at the assessment hearing, the full amount payable (including the
assessment fee) will be £ . . . . (together with interest (*see note below*)). I shall also seek the costs of the
assessment hearing

Your points of dispute must include

- details of the items in the bill of costs which are disputed

- concise details of the nature and grounds of the dispute for each item and, if you seek a reduction in
  those items, suggest, where practicable, a reduced figure

You must serve your points of dispute by . . . . (*insert date 21 days from the date of service
of this notice*) on me at:- (*give full name and address for service including any DX number or reference*)

You must also serve copies of your points of dispute on all other parties to the assessment identified below (*you do not
need to serve your points of dispute on the court*).

I certify that I have also served the following person(s) with a copy of this notice and my Bill of Costs:- (*give details of
persons served*)

If I have not received your points of dispute by the above date, I will ask the court to issue a default costs certificate
for the full amount of my bill (*see above**) plus fixed costs and court fee in the total amount of £ . . . .

Signed . . . . Date . . . .
(Claimant)(Defendant)('s solicitor)

Note: Interest may be added to all High Court judgments and certain county court judgments of £5,000 or more under the
Judgments Act 1838 and the County Courts Act 1984.

The court office at

is open between 10 am and 4 pm Monday to Friday. When corresponding with the court, please address forms or letters to the Court Manager and quote the claim number.

N252 Notice of commencement of assessment of bill of costs (12.99)

The Court Service Publications Unit

Notice of Amount Allowed on Provisional Assessment

In the	
Claim No.	
Claimant (including Ref.)	
Defendant (including Ref.)	
Date	

To [Claimant][Defendant]['s Solicitor]

Take notice that the [claimant's][defendant's][receiver's] bill of costs has been provisionally assessed and is returned with this notice

If you wish to be heard on the assessment, you must, within 14 days of the receipt of this notice inform the court in writing and return the bill of costs to the court. A date for assessment will then be fixed.

If you accept the provisional assessment as final, please complete and return the bill together with the balance of the assessment fee.

Note: In Legal aid only/LSC only cases

1) Within 7 days of receipt of the notice the solicitor must notify counsel in writing where the fees claimed on counsel's behalf have been provisionally reduced or disallowed.

2) The solicitor should not accept the provisional assessment as final without first enquiring whether any counsel whose fees have been provisionally reduced or disallowed has also accepted it.

3) Attention is drawn to the need to endorse on the bill a certificate in the form of precedent F(4) before returning the bill to the court.

The court office at

is open between 10 am and 4 pm Monday to Friday. Address all communications to the Court Manager quoting the claim number
N253 Notice of amount allowed on provisional assessment (7.00)

311

Request for a Default Costs Certificate

In the	
Claim No.	
Claimant (include Ref.)	
Defendant (include Ref.)	

I certify that (1) notice of commencement (2) the bill of costs and (3) a copy of the document giving the right to detailed assessment, were served on the paying party . . . .

(and give details of any other party served with the notice)

on . . . . *(insert date)*

Copies of (1) and (3) are attached.

I also certify that I have not received any points of dispute and that the time for receiving them has now elapsed.

I now request the court to issue a certificate for the amount of the bill of costs plus such fixed costs and court fees as are appropriate in this case.

Signed . . . . **Date** . . . .
(Claimant)(Defendant)('s Solicitor)

The court office at

is open between 10 am and 4 pm Monday to Friday. When corresponding with the court, please address forms or letters to the Court Manager and quote the claim number.

N254 Request for a Default Costs Certificate (07.02)   *The Court Service Publications Branch*

312

Default Costs Certificate

In the	
	County Court
Claim No.	
Claimant (including Ref.)	
Defendant (including Ref.)	
Date	

To [Claimant][Defendant][*s Solicitor]

As you have not raised any points of dispute on the [defendant's][claimant's] bill of costs, the costs of the claim have been allowed and the total sum of £   is now payable.

You must pay this amount to the [defendant][claimant] [within 14 days from the date of this order] [on or before [   ]]

The date from which any entitlement to interest under this certificate commences is [   ]

─────── **Take Notice** ───────

To the defendant (claimant)

If you do not pay in accordance with this order your goods may be removed and sold or other enforcement proceedings may be taken against you. If your circumstances change and you cannot pay, ask at the court office about what you can do

Further interest may be added if judgment has been given for £5,000 or more or is in respect of a debt which attracts contractual or statutory interest for late payment.

If you do not pay as ordered, this judgment may be registered on the Register of County Court Judgments. This may make it difficult for you to get credit. **If you then pay in full within one month** you can ask the court to cancel the entry on the Register. You will need to give proof of payment. You can (for a fee) also obtain a Certificate of Cancellation from the court. If you pay the debt in full after one month you can ask the court to mark the entry on the Register as satisfied and (for a fee) obtain a Certificate of Satisfaction to prove that the debt has been paid.

─────── **Address for Payment** ───────

─────── **How to Pay** ───────

- PAYMENT(S) MUST BE MADE to the person named at the address for payment quoting their reference and the court case number.
- DO NOT bring or send payments to the court. THEY WILL NOT BE ACCEPTED.
- You should allow at least 4 days for your payment to reach the claimant (defendant) or his representative.
- Make sure that you keep records and can account for all payments made. Proof may be required if there is any disagreement. It is not safe to send cash unless you use registered post.
- A leaflet giving further advice about payment can be obtained from the court.
- If you need more information you should contact the claimant (defendant) or his representative.

The court office at

is open between 10 am and 4 pm Monday to Friday. Address all communications to the Court Manager quoting the claim number

N255 Default costs certificate

Final Costs Certificate

In the
County Court

Claim No.	
Claimant (including ref)	

To [Claimant][Defendant][’s Solicitor]

Defendant (including ref)	

Date	

In accordance with [identify the document giving the right to detailed assessment]

District Judge [   ] has assessed the total costs as £   [including £   for the costs of the detailed assessment]

[And £   already having been paid under the interim costs certificate issued on [   ]]

You must pay [the balance of]£   to the [claimant][defendant] [within 14 days from the date of this order] [on or before[   ]]

The date from which any entitlement to interest under this certificate commences is [   ]

─────── **Take Notice** ───────

To the defendant (claimant)

If you do not pay in accordance with this order your goods may be removed and sold or other enforcement proceedings may be taken against you. If your circumstances change and you cannot pay, ask at the court office about what you can do

Further interest may be added if judgment has been given for £5,000 or more or is in respect of a debt which attracts contractual or statutory interest for late payment.

─────── **Address for Payment** ───────

If you do not pay as ordered, this judgment may be registered on the Register of County Court Judgments. This may make it difficult for you to get credit. **If you then pay in full within one month** you can ask the court to cancel the entry on the Register. You will need to give proof of payment. You can (for a fee) also obtain a Certificate of Cancellation from the court. If you pay the debt in full after one month you can ask the court to mark the entry on the Register as satisfied and (for a fee) obtain a Certificate of Satisfaction to prove that the debt has been paid.

─────── **How to Pay** ───────

- PAYMENT(S) MUST BE MADE to the person named at the address for payment quoting their reference and the court case number.
- DO NOT bring or send payments to the court. THEY WILL NOT BE ACCEPTED.
- You should allow at least 4 days for your payment to reach the claimant (defendant) or his representative.
- Make sure that you keep records and can account for all payments made. Proof may be required if there is any disagreement. It is not safe to send cash unless you use registered post.
- A leaflet giving further advice about payment can be obtained from the court.
- If you need more information you should contact the claimant (defendant) or his representative.

The court office at

is open between 10 am and 4 pm Monday to Friday. Address all communications to the Court Manager quoting the claim number
N256 Final cost certificate (7.00)

Final Costs Certificate

In the High Court of Justice	
Division District Registry	
Claim No.	
Claimant (including Ref.)	
Defendant (including Ref.)	
Date	

To [Claimant][Defendant]['s Solicitor]

In accordance with [identify the document giving the right to detailed assessment]

Master/District Judge [   ] has assessed the total costs as £   [including £   for the costs of the detailed assessment]

[And £   already having been paid under the interim costs certificate issued on [   ]]

You must pay [the balance of]£   to the [claimant][defendant] [within 14 days from the date of this order] [on or before [   ]]

The date from which any entitlement to interest under this certificate commences is [   ]

—— **Take Notice** ——

To the defendant (claimant)

If you do not pay in accordance with this order your goods may be removed and sold or other enforcement proceedings may be taken against you. If your circumstances change and you cannot pay, ask at the court office about what you can do

—— **Address for Payment** ——

—— **How to Pay** ——

- PAYMENT(S) MUST BE MADE to the person named at the address for payment quoting their reference and the court case number.
- DO NOT bring or send payments to the court. THEY WILL NOT BE ACCEPTED.
- You should allow at least 4 days for your payment to reach the claimant (defendant) or his representative.
- Make sure that you keep records and can account for all payments made. Proof may be required if there is any disagreement. It is not safe to send cash unless you use registered post.
- A leaflet giving further advice about payment can be obtained from the court.
- If you need more information you should contact the claimant (defendant) or his representative.

The court office at

is open between 10 am and 4 pm Monday to Friday. Address all communications to the Court Manager quoting the claim number

N256 (HC) Final cost certificate (7.00)

Interim costs certificate

In the	
Claim No.	
Claimant (including ref)	
Defendant (including ref)	
Date	

To [Claimant][Defendant]['s Solicitor]

Upon application by the [claimant][defendant] for [a detailed assessment hearing] [the issue of an interim costs certificate by agreement].

[Master][District Judge][   ] has ordered that you must pay £   to the [claimant][defendant] [within 14 days from the date of this order][on or before [   ]] [into court to await the issue of a final costs certificate].

─────── **Take Notice** ───────

To the defendant (claimant)

If you do not pay in accordance with this order your goods may be removed and sold or other enforcement proceedings may be taken against you. If your circumstances change and you cannot pay, ask at the court office about what you can do

─────── **Address for Payment** ───────

─────── **How to Pay** ───────

- PAYMENT(S) MUST BE MADE to the person named at the address for payment quoting their reference and the court case number.
- DO NOT bring or send payments to the court. THEY WILL NOT BE ACCEPTED.
- You should allow at least 4 days for your payment to reach the claimant (defendant) or his representative.
- Make sure that you keep records and can account for all payments made. Proof may be required if there is any disagreement. It is not safe to send cash unless you use registered post.
- A leaflet giving further advice about payment can be obtained from the court.
- If you need more information you should contact the claimant (defendant) or his representative.

The court office at

is open between 10 am and 4 pm Monday to Friday. Address all communications to the Court Manager quoting the claim number

N257 Interim cost certificate

Request for detailed assessment hearing
(general form)

In the	
Claim No.	
Claimant (include Ref.)	
Defendant (include Ref.)	

I certify that the Notice of Commencement was served on the paying party ....

(and give details of any other party served with the notice)

on .... *(insert date)*

I now ask the court to arrange an assessment hearing.

I enclose copies of *(tick as appropriate)*

☐ the document giving the right to detailed assessment;

☐ a copy of the Notice of Commencement;

☐ the bill of costs;

☐ the paying party's points of dispute, annotated as necessary in order to show (1) which items have been agreed and their value and (2) which items remain in dispute and their value;

☐ points in reply (if any);

☐ a statement giving the names, addresses for service and references of all persons to whom the court should give notice of the hearing;

☐ the relevant details of any additional liability claimed;

☐ a copy of all the orders made by the court relating to the costs of the proceedings which are to be assessed;

☐ any fee notes of counsel and receipts or accounts for other disbursements relating to items in dispute;

☐ [where solicitors' costs are disputed] the client care letter delivered to the receiving party or the solicitor's retainer.

I believe the hearing will take .... *(give estimate of time court should allow)*.

I enclose my fee of £ ....

Signed .... **Date** ....
(Claimant)(Defendant)('s solicitor)

The court office at

is open between 10 am and 4 pm Monday to Friday. When corresponding with the court, please address forms or letters to the Court Manager and quote the claim number.
N258 Request for detailed assessment hearing (general form) (7.00) *The Court Service Publications Unit*

317

Request for detailed assessment
(Legal aid/ Legal Services Commission only)

In the	
Claim No.	
Claimant (include Ref.)	
Defendant (include Ref.)	

I now ask the court to provisionally assess the bill (arrange an assessment hearing as the assisted person/LSC funded client wishes to be heard)

I enclose copies of (*tick as appropriate*)

☐ The document giving the right to detailed assessment;

☐ the bill of costs;

☐ a statement giving the names, addresses for service and references of all persons to whom the court should give notice of the hearing;

☐ a copy of all the orders made by the court relating to the costs of the proceedings which are to be assessed;

☐ any fee notes of counsel and receipts or accounts for other disbursements relating to items claimed;

☐ all civil legal aid certificates and LSC certificates and amendments to them; notice of discharge or revocation and specific legal aid authorities;

☐ the relevant papers in support of the bill (Supreme Court Costs Office/ PRFD assessments only)

*I certify that the assisted person/LSC funded client wishes to attend the assessment hearing and I believe the hearing will take . . . . (*give estimate of time court should allow*).

I enclose my fee of £ . . . .

(delete if not applicable)

Signed .... Date ....
(Claimant)(Defendant)('s solicitor)

The court office at

is open between 10 am and 4 pm Monday to Friday. When corresponding with the court, please address forms or letters to the Court Manager and quote the claim number.
N258A Request for detailed assessment (legal aid/LSC only) (7.00)   *The Court Service Publications Unit*

318

Request for detailed assessment
(Costs payable out of a fund other than the Community Legal Service Fund)

In the	
Claim No.	
Claimant (Include Ref.)	
Defendant (Include Ref.)	

I now ask the court to provisionally assess the bill or arrange an assessment hearing.

I enclose copies of (*tick as appropriate*)

☐ The document giving the right to detailed assessement;

☐ the bill of costs;

☐ a statement giving the name and address for service of any person having a financial interest in the outcome of the assessment;

☐ a copy of all the orders made by the court relating to the costs of the proceedings which are to be assessed;

☐ any fee notes of counsel and receipts or accounts for other disbursements relating to items claimed;

☐ the relevant details of any additional liability claimed;

☐ the relevant papers in support of the bill (Supreme Court Costs Office/ PRFD assessments only)

I enclose my fee of £ . . . .

Signed .... **Date** ....
(Claimant)(Defendant)(Receiver)('s solicitor)

The court office at

is open between 10 am and 4 pm Monday to Friday. When corresponding with the court, please address forms or letters to the Court Manager and quote the claim number.
N258B Request for detailed assessment (cost payable out of a fund other than the Community Legal Service Fund) (7.00)   *The Court Service Publications Unit*

319

Legal aid/ Legal Services Commission assessment certificate

Claimant/Petitioner

In the	
Claim/Case No.	
Certificate No.	
Solicitors Ref.	

Defendant/Respondent

The costs in this matter have been assessed as set out in boxes A, B and C below and are claimed from the Community Legal Service Fund.

SEAL

The costs are those of the
(please tick)

☐ Claimant   ☐ Petitioner

☐ Defendant   ☐ Respondent   ☐ Other

They were assessed in the   ☐ High Court   ☐ County Court

Total pre-certificate costs, which are not being claimed, were   £
(including disbursements, profit costs and VAT)

Dated _____ Signed _____

(Solicitor)

A. Costs payable by another party as allowed or as in legal aid/LSC schedule if appropriate
(Do not include any pre-certificate costs, or the costs of assessment).

Profit costs	
VAT	
Counsel's Fees	
VAT	
Disbursements	
VAT (where appropriate)	
Total	£

B. Legal aid only/LSC only costs
(Do not include the costs of assessment)

Profit costs	
VAT	
Counsel's Fees	
VAT	
Disbursements	
VAT (where appropriate)	
Total	£

C. Costs of Assessment
(Allowed in respect of A and B above)

For Part A	
VAT	
Court fee (where appropriate)	
For Part B	
VAT	
Court fee (where appropriate)	
Total	£

D. Total Claimed
(Add totals A, B and C)

Total part A	
Total part B	
Total part C	
Total	£

Sealed by the court on _____

EX80A Legal Aid /LSC Assessment Certificate (7.00)

Produced on behalf of The Court Service

Index

References are to paragraph numbers in the text.